Praise for
Refugia Faith

"Debra Rienstra has hit on a truly powerful new metaphor for helping us feel our way through an almost impossible moment in our career as a species. Her idea of 'refugia' offers some combination of solace, realistic hope, and inspiration; one prays that, in particular, people of faith will use this as a goad and a help to take the actions we all know we must. This book is a small classic."
—Bill McKibben, author of *The Flag, the Cross, and the Station Wagon: A Graying American Looks Back on His Suburban Boyhood and Wonders What the Hell Happened*

"At a time when we are too often consumed with talk of scarcity, devastation, deconstruction, polarization, and alienation, *Refugia Faith* offers more than a breath of fresh air. It presents us with a glimmer of genuine hope, a hope that resides in the small places. Filled with beauty, wisdom, and a vision for how things might be, this book itself serves as a refuge for the weary, discouraged, and disheartened. Imaginatively conceived and gorgeously written, it is a work of profound insight and deep goodness."
—Kristin Kobes Du Mez, *New York Times* best-selling author of *Jesus and John Wayne: How White Evangelicals Corrupted a Faith and Fractured a Nation*

"For most of us, a crisis like climate change is cause for panic and withdrawal. Rienstra beautifully, winsomely invites us to flip this script. Rather than viewing it as an insurmountable challenge, she argues that the climate crisis is an opportunity for transformation—if only we have the courage, imagination, and resiliency to seize it."
—Kyle Meyaard-Schaap, vice president, Evangelical Environmental Network; named to Midwest Energy Group's 40 Under 40 and American Conservation Coalition's 30 Under 30 for his work on climate change education and advocacy; Yale Public Voices on the Climate Crisis Fellow for 2020; featured in news outlets such as PBS, NPR, CNN, NBC News, *New York Times*, Reuters, and *U.S. News and World Report*

"Now more than ever I believe we need refugia in our country, communities, and churches. Debra Rienstra's *Refugia Faith* is a reminder and challenge to seek a new way amid the climate crisis—to deconstruct our current way of life and create a new order that rightfully places God at the center. Only then will we be in right relationship with creation. I highly recommend this book for people of faith as we live in the tension between our current climate-related suffering and the hope for what is possible for our planet."

—Karyn Bigelow, co-executive director at Creation Justice Ministries

"When you talk with Debra Rienstra, it doesn't take long to realize she has a deep consciousness of what is happening in our world on the ecological front, the dire consequences we all face, and the faith to which she anchors her understanding. Fortunately for us, her reality-based knowledge and her amazing hope for the future are available in *Refugia Faith: Seeking Hidden Shelters, Ordinary Wonders, and the Healing of the Earth.* She offers actionable hope for those who have become discouraged or even fatalistic about our ecological future. Get ready to rediscover your sense of wonderment!"

—Randy Woodley, author/activist and co-sustainer, Eloheh Indigenous Center for Earth Justice and Eloheh Farm & Seeds, Yamhill, Oregon

"I didn't know what *refugia* meant until I read this book, I can't tell one plant or tree from another, and I likely suffer from what is popularly known as 'nature deficit disorder.' In short, I am not Debra Rienstra's target reader. But that's why I loved this smart, funny, passionate book. It has connected the dots for me, beautifully and cogently, and shown me what's at stake environmentally and theologically when I fail to care."

—Jana Riess, senior columnist for Religion News Service and author of *Flunking Sainthood*

"*Refugia Faith* provides a lyrical and personal reflection on the critical need for Christians to respond to the environmental crises that surround and threaten the earth. Rienstra is a steady guide in helping readers navigate the vast terrain of ecotheology, offering insightful and inspirational commentary. Readers will benefit from the thoughtful portraits and deliberate insistence that we reexamine our relationship to God's good creation."

—Paul Galbreath, professor of theology, Union Presbyterian Seminary,
Charlotte, North Carolina

"What would happen if Christians determined to become known as 'the people of refugia'? That question, posed by Debra Rienstra on her blog site in 2019, sparked her podcast series that led to this book. And what a masterful book it is! Blending beautiful and prophetic prose, Rienstra tells the stories of individuals and faith communities who are striving to be the people of refugia, nurturing ecological communities and their souls in the face of frightful challenges. Read this to be encouraged and to find hope for the future."

—David S. Koetje, professor of biology, Calvin University,
Grand Rapids, Michigan

"*Refugia Faith* is one of the best books in print on how people of faith can summon the hope and the courage needed to heal and restore our home planet. Employing an astonishingly wide range of sources—from Paul Santmire on the Christian tradition to E. O. Wilson on biophilia, from Dante's beatific vision to Robert Bullard's take on environmental racism, from David Ackerly on bioclimates to John Calvin on creation as a theatre of divine glory—Rienstra weaves a brilliant web in beautiful prose to make her case for the importance of refugia: small, humble, safe places where ecological restoration can take root. The web also includes rich readings of biblical texts and insightful theological reflections, as well as personal vignettes of people and places that illustrate different kinds of refugia. And perhaps most notable is her unflinching honesty about the obstacles ahead, combined with her clear-eyed hope about living in a world facing climate crisis. Take up and read."

—Steven Bouma-Prediger, Leonard and Marjorie Maas Professor
of Reformed Theology, Hope College, Holland, Michigan, and
author of *For the Beauty of the Earth: A Christian Vision for Creation Care*
and *Earthkeeping and Character: Exploring a Christian Ecological Virtue Ethics*

"*Refugia Faith* is a very personal journey combining Debra Rienstra's faith, family history, and tender sense of place in west Michigan. Her destination offers a badly needed return to a countercultural Christianity, to refugia in the face of looming climate catastrophe. It's a vision for a faith that is more communal, more local, more just, and more loving—especially to our more than human kin. One can almost miss how her scholarship is wonderfully interdisciplinary, weaving together climate science, theology, ecology, history, and literature, rendered as it is with grace and bracing clarity. But more importantly, it's beautiful."

—Tim Van Deelen, professor of wildlife ecology, University of Wisconsin–Madison; interested in population biology and conservation and the ecology of the Great Lakes region; graduate of Calvin University with graduate degrees from the University of Montana and Michigan State University

REFUGIA FAITH

REFUGIA
FAITH

Seeking Hidden Shelters,
Ordinary Wonders,
and the Healing of the Earth

DEBRA RIENSTRA

Fortress Press
Minneapolis

To Mia, Josh, Jacob, Philip, Heidi, and all young people
who long for refugia and worry about the future

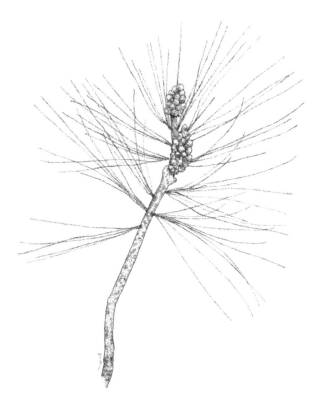

EASTERN WHITE PINE
PINUS STROBUS

Contents

October—*Douglas, Michigan* 1

INTRODUCTION: THE GREAT WORK AND THE LITTLE WORK . . . 3

January—Douglas, Michigan 19

CHAPTER 1: FROM DESPAIR TO PREPARATION 23

February—Grand Rapids, Michigan 49

CHAPTER 2: FROM ALIENATION TO KINSHIP 53

April—Douglas, Michigan
Summers, 1970s—Holland and Grand Haven, Michigan 81

CHAPTER 3: FROM CONSUMING TO HEALING 85

August—Sleeping Bear Point, Michigan 115

CHAPTER 4: FROM AVOIDING TO LAMENTING 119

February—Grand Haven, Michigan 147

CHAPTER 5: FROM RESIGNATION TO GRATITUDE 151

July—Douglas, Michigan 179

CHAPTER 6: FROM PASSIVITY TO CITIZENSHIP 183

September—Douglas, Michigan 213

CHAPTER 7: FROM INDIFFERENCE TO ATTENTION 217

Acknowledgments 237
Notes 243
Suggested Resources 265

AMERICAN BEACH GRASS
AMMOPHILA BREVILIGULATA

October
Douglas, Michigan

It's been raining and raining and raining, and now the wind comes, taking long, hard breaths across the water. I love this weather out at the lake—as long as I'm sitting cozy under a blanket, inside the warm cottage.

I imagine being out on the dunes today. With the right gear, it could be exciting for a while. Wellies, a warm sweater, a good rain jacket with sturdy hood cinched around my face. The lake churning indifferently. The wind, though! The great lake is ever-changing, implacable, profoundly wild. Even on days when the water is gentle and the breeze warm, you still feel as if you are somehow caught in the pocket of wild forces, the mildness only a momentary reprieve. The lake says, Delicate beauties are brief. What lasts is tough and unglamorous—tenacious, companioned to the wind.

I walked north on the beach the other day and then turned back into the southwesterly wind. My eyes watered and smarted, and I had to keep one eye closed and push on, half blind. The sun was searing white but offered little warmth, slipping at intervals behind steely clouds. The trees trembled, the lake tossed, its choppy surface metallic. By six thirty, darkness swallowed all but the roar of the waves, and I was safe in the quiet stronghold of our little family cottage.

I have been thirsty for silence, glad for this place to be alone. Here inside in the silence, on the edge of wildness, I wonder what my work might be now, in my older years, in these crisis times. What might God say to me if I can be quiet enough to listen? What did God mean a few months ago when I heard in the Scriptures, in my prayers, "I am making all things new"?[1] How shall I look for new life when everything seems chaotic, churning with sorrows both ancient and fresh?

Most of us long for steadiness, but instead we must adapt constantly. We live in an age of upheaval. We must be tenacious and tough.

I'm watching a cottonwood dance in the wind. It's a tall, slim thing, like a fringed flagpole, but pliant as rubber. It bends and dips in the gusts. If it snapped at the waist, I wouldn't be surprised. But its roots are strong, its sap full of dreams.

Introduction

The Great Work
and the Little Work

I am like a desert owl, like an owl among the ruins.
—PSALM 102:6 NIV

When Mount Saint Helens erupted in May of 1980, it lost 1,300 feet of elevation and gained a new mile-and-a-half-wide crater. The debris and ashfall from the volcanic blast devastated the mountain and its surroundings for miles, crushing, burning, killing, and coating everything in hot ash. Everyone assumed life could return to this apocalyptic death zone only very slowly, maybe over several human lifetimes.

Instead, forty years later, the mountainsides are covered with lush grasses, prairie lupines, alders. Critters scamper, streams flow. It will take a few hundred more years for the vegetation to return to something like old-growth forest. But still. Why did life come back with such vigor, and so quickly? As Kathleen Dean Moore explains in her book *Great Tide Rising*, "What the scientists know now, but didn't understand then, is that when the mountain blasted ash and rock across the landscape, the devastation passed over some small places hidden in the lee of rocks and trees. Here, a bed of moss and deer fern under a rotting log. There, under a boulder, a patch of pearly everlasting and the tunnel to a vole's musty nest." These little pockets of safety are called *refugia*. They are tiny coverts where plants and creatures hide from destruction, hidden shelters where life persists and out of which new life emerges.[1]

We are living in a time of crisis eruption. Our failures of vision and restraint have propelled us into ecological danger on a scale never before seen in human history. The future is uncertain; it always is. We do not know exactly what's coming. But the earth teaches that extreme disturbance can be survived and can even bring renewal—and one way this happens is through refugia.

This book asks the question, How can people of faith become people of refugia? How can we find and create refugia, not only in the biomes of the earth, but simultaneously in our human cultural systems and in our spirits? We will need a tough, new kind of resilience and a greater capacity for cooperation. Is it possible to work together, applying all our love and creativity to this task as never before?

As a person of faith, I believe in the divine mystery, a loving God who is always calling us through the wonders and suffering of this world to transform our ways, a God who draws us relentlessly toward the divine purpose of flourishing for the whole earth and all its creatures. At least I try to believe that. In recent years, it has been difficult to keep a steady grip on this vision. The worldwide disruption we experienced during the Covid-19 pandemic made our vulnerability obvious and urgent, exacerbating our already inflamed anxiety. On any given day during those long months, I would ricochet from anxiety about the virus, to anger about the president's latest insulting tweet, to an aching sorrow over abusive church leaders or racist judicial systems or tar sands extraction—whatever nightmare heaved to the surface of the day's news. In the next minute, I might rejoice in a downy woodpecker at the bird feeder.

Even now that it seems we have found our way through the worst of those awful days, the churning feelings linger. We still live precariously on fault lines. They send fissures through our neighborhoods, our churches and religious organizations, our national and local politics, our families. The anxieties may have subsided, but only from acute to chronic. In the United States, we still navigate seemingly separate realities constructed from our information sources, convictions, and identities and bundled together by our fears. All of this detracts from our ability to work on our generation's greatest challenge: the climate crisis. In fact, our world seems to be in crisis convergence, and it all feels overwhelmingly tangled and impossible. Even when millions set their shoulders to the task of healing, the powers of destruction and evil loom large.

Where is God? I've wondered that more than ever in these past few years. All those promises in the Scriptures about God bringing justice and renewing the earth: Why do they remain unfulfilled? Centuries ago, the prophet Isaiah cried out to God, "Tear open the heavens and come down!" (Isa 64:1), and these words echo in our minds. As for my fellow Christians: how often they disappoint. We are distracted or indifferent. We drag our feet and justify our complicities in evils small and great. We are swayed by lies and seduced by power. We are supposed to be people of hope, people who witness to God's good purposes. But are we? As I have struggled in these past few years to process growing alarm about the climate crisis as well as eruptions of ugliness in American politics and the American church, I look to those threads of Scripture where the people of God cry out, "How long, O Lord?" (Ps 13:1; 79:5; etc.). And I wonder why, after all these millennia, we're still pleading.

Yet I know from the broad sweep of Scriptures, from history, and from my own experience that God is always at work somehow and that God loves to work in small, humble, hidden places. The more I think about it, the more I realize that God loves refugia. The refugia model calls us to look for the seed of life where we are, concentrate on protecting and nurturing a few good things, let what is good and beautiful grow and connect and spread. Trust God's work. As the etymology of the term implies, refugia are places of refuge. They are places to find shelter—but only for a time. More importantly, refugia are places to begin, places where the tender and harrowing work of reconstruction and renewal takes root. In human terms, refugia operate as microcountercultures where we endure, yes, but also where we prepare for new ways of living and growing. They are places of trust, because in biological as well as cultural refugia, we have to surrender our illusions of full control. In fact, sometimes what seems impossible is exactly the place to begin, because divine powers are at work far beyond our ability to perceive.

Refugia, then, are neither bunkers nor beachheads. In times of crisis, religious people are sometimes tempted to remove ourselves from "society" out of fear and disgust, hoping to wall off a space safe from pollutants where we can protect some fantasia of holiness and purity.[2] The opposite temptation is a kind of triumphalism, in which we seek strategic dominance, infiltrating and controlling every aspect of society for God, as if God needs our human systems of dominance to squash out the competition. People have always mustered persuasive arguments for these impulses—to hide or to conquer. But as I hope to demonstrate in the pages that follow, God's preferred way seems less like walls or combat boots and more like a tray of seedlings. God seems to appreciate the humble, permeable, surprising potentials of refugia. I think of refugia faith, then, as a sort of alternative posture, a posture not of retreat or conquest but of humble discernment and nurture. Refugia faith continually asks, Where are refugia happening, and how can we help? Where do refugia need to happen, and how can we create them?

World religions scholar Mary Evelyn Tucker observes that, since the last decades of the twentieth century, the world's great religions have been entering their "ecological phase."[3] The question, she writes, is whether religious people and organizations will entrench in old ways or, alternatively, dig deep into their traditions, cherish the treasures awaiting there, and transform those resources for survival in a new era. Many wise and prophetic people have begun this work of digging, cherishing, and transforming. Thanks to their example, I've come to believe that, in these times of crisis convergence, the Christian faith offers treasures both ancient and new, yet we have only begun to draw on those treasures.

Christianity is not the only source of wisdom for these times, of course. Pope Francis himself makes this point in his 2015 encyclical, *Laudato si'*: "If we are truly concerned to develop an ecology capable of remedying the damage we have done, no branch of the sciences and no form of wisdom can be left out, and that includes religion and the language particular to it."[4] We will need to draw on every stream of wisdom available. For this reason, it's been heartening to see increased interfaith dialogue as well as greater attention to marginalized voices, such as those of Indigenous peoples. While I attend admiringly to these developments and continue to learn from them, Christianity is the stream of wisdom I know best. So as I seek my own role in responding to our crisis convergence, I begin in the only place I can: with my own faith tradition.

As I have rummaged through the Christian tradition, wondering how its richness might help me manage in these confusing days, I have felt missing pieces falling into place. Even after a lifetime of Christian practice, graduate-level biblical and theological study, connection to numerous Christian institutions, and decades of writing about faith, I now realize that until recently I had not thought very deeply about moths or thunderstorms or prairie wildflowers or the crucial role of fungi in a forest ecosystem. For too long, "nature" was something I sang about in church for a verse or two or mined for a handy poetic metaphor. "Creation theology" seemed simple and obvious and not nearly as interesting as, say, theological aesthetics. However, now that our planet is crying out—groaning in loud and obvious ways—I realize that every aspect of theological reflection and faith practice is incomplete if it remains up in the head, bereft of deep engagement with our material life on this earth. I have felt driven to a reassessment of my own faith, sometimes by recovering old treasures, sometimes by devising or seeking new ones. Without this process, I realize, my faith will be left insufficient for the day.

In these pages, then, I try to discern what this time requires and demonstrate what it feels like to wake up to an urgent call. I reflect on my own process of reeducation, my efforts to seek the wisdom of theologians and philosophers, farmers and nature writers, scientists and activists, and especially people leading from the margins, all toward answering this question: How must we adapt Christian spirituality and practice in order to become healers of this damaged earth? How can I join with like-minded people in this work? The urgency of the climate crisis offers us this gift: the opportunity to reassess. In these pages I describe my tentative, initial attempts to adopt a refugia faith.

I offer no one-size-fits-all program for refugia faith, only an invitation to use our shared creativity and common longing to discover what refugia faith might mean. The chapter titles suggest that refugia faith may entail fundamental and perhaps uncomfortable shifts, from consuming to healing, for example. These are, of course, attempts to name matters on the way to understanding them. My hope is that others might find here inspiration, questions to ponder, consolation and challenge.

Survival

Many of us who have been cocooned in privilege now have survival on our minds in ways we never previously imagined. In October of 2018, the Intergovernmental Panel on Climate Change (IPCC), a body commissioned by the United Nations, released a special report. Its conclusions, based on thousands of studies compiled by a huge international team of scientists, urged government and industry leaders of the world to take every step to limit global average temperature rise to 1.5 degrees Celsius above preindustrial levels. This would require, the report states, "rapid and far-reaching" transitions in our entire global infrastructure—energy, agriculture, transportation, manufacturing, trade—our global way of life. While the 2015 Paris Agreement sets a goal of 2 degrees Celsius at most, the IPCC report warns that even allowing temperature rise to reach 2 degrees would multiply the devastating effects of climate change—flooding, storm activity, fires, ocean rise, ocean acidification, drought, disease, forced migrations, and economic and political disruption.[5]

Then in May of 2019, the United Nations released a global assessment report that the *New York Times* describes as "the most exhaustive look yet at the decline in biodiversity across the globe and the dangers that creates for human civilization."[6] This report, authored by another international team of scientists called the Intergovernmental Science-Policy Platform on Biodiversity and Ecosystem Services (IPBES), accounts for terrifying levels of biodiversity loss. Biologists have estimated that species extinction is occurring at something like one thousand times the "background rate," but the IPBES report affirms that the pace is accelerating. This trend is not just about waving a regretful goodbye to a few decoratively rare species of owls or butterflies. This is about ecosystem collapse.

Moreover, time is running out. Reflecting this urgency, in late 2019, a group of scientists published an article in the journal *BioScience* declaring that scientists must communicate "clearly and unequivocally that planet Earth is facing a climate emergency."[7] Over eleven thousand scientists from 153 countries signed on to this declaration. In 2021, the IPCC released another major report, *Climate Change 2021: The Physical Science Basis*, affirming and further clarifying the urgency of climate action. Based on even more extensive and conclusive data than the 2018 report delivers, the 2021 report spells out what is at stake for every region on the globe. The report offers five modeling scenarios, ranging from best to worst. In the best-case scenario, we pull ourselves together and reach net-zero carbon emissions by 2050. Even in that best-case scenario, however, the effects of climate change we are already witnessing in every region of the globe will continue to worsen, and we will reach

1.5 degrees Celsius by 2050. After that, if all goes well, temperatures will begin to stabilize. That is the best-case scenario. I don't want to think about the other possibilities, though they are duly charted and graphed in the report. Meanwhile, what we have done to the ocean—caused warming, glacial melt, sea level rise, and ocean acidification—cannot be undone now, not for centuries.[8]

We live at an inflection point; we live on a knife's edge. In the United States, the general public is gradually starting to catch on to the urgency, with several recent polls indicating increasing awareness of and concern about climate change.[9] President Biden has attempted to elevate the climate crisis as a top priority, proposing clean energy infrastructure initiatives and conservation initiatives and appointing high-level cabinet and staff members tasked specifically with climate action. Reports now appear regularly declaring that major investment firms consider the fossil fuel industry on the decline.[10] Car manufacturers are now racing to produce all-electric vehicles.[11] But with a task this huge before us, how can we make up for the wasted time, especially those crucial years during the previous administration, when the US president and his enablers in Congress were beholden to the fossil fuel industry's entrenched power, insisting on climate crisis denial and resistance to any action, even a cynical reempowering of the industry?

"Have things always been this insane?" my twenty-year-old son asked me one day in early 2020.

"No," I replied. "No, this is a new thing."

And that was before the pandemic hit.

I've lived long enough to see plenty of distressing historical moments. I remember Watergate, Vietnam, the oil crisis, Cold War tensions, 9/11, and any number of shadowy scandals and crises in the United States and abroad. Many Americans would correct my perception that our present insanities are anything new, explaining that they and their ancestors have lived with slavery, Jim Crow, police brutality, land theft, genocide, and other nightmares. Still, the years following 2016 were characterized by especially blatant and unapologetic corruption in the United States that was not only tolerated but defended and championed. We learned phrases like "outrage fatigue," and more of us sat daily with anger as an ever-present companion. After the 2020 election, the constant, high-alert outrage has subsided for many of us but not gone away. Our intractable divisions remain, thwarting rapid, large-scale action on the climate crisis. The damage from those years of delay, disinformation, and destruction cannot be entirely undone.

And where have people of faith been in all this? In the United States, many American Christians have been seduced by Christian nationalism, militarism, and wealth. They have succumbed to what we might call the "church of empire."[12] They imagine that their faith compels them to establish a theocracy at any cost, apparently immune to suggestions that the impulse to dominate may not be the way of Jesus. While it's true that many people, everywhere and across all the world's faith traditions, offer creative resistance to everything that diminishes and destroys, it's also undeniable that White American evangelicalism has been deeply corrupted. What is this darkness that has come over this part of the Christian family? Those of us who love the church have grieved over the state of Christian witness as never before.

I work with young people every day, students at a Christian university. The students I know are not impressed with what their elders have done in this world. They can easily sink into bewilderment and fear, dragging around under the weight of leaden anxiety. What will their future be? Less inured to adult compromises and self-deceptions than we oldsters, they recognize injustice and hypocrisy when they see it. The failures of the church are particularly obvious to them. Most of my students have been raised in the Christian faith, most in some form of Protestantism, and many of them feel confused or even betrayed when they see what their parents and elders claim on the one hand and tolerate on the other. While their churches tear themselves apart over same-sex marriage, the young people I know worry about racism, wealth inequality, and the climate crisis. How can their elders claim to live by grace and follow Jesus—gentle healer of the poor and outcast—and then create churches that seem populated by flag-waving defenders of free markets and White supremacy, eager to reject anyone who doesn't conform? In addressing the great injustices of the day, most of all the peril of the planet, young people often see the church as largely ineffectual or indifferent—unfaithful to its principles and distracted by matters perceived by the young as secondary or preposterous. No wonder young people are leaving the church.

One of my former students, Caitlin Gent, wrote an open letter to the evangelical church of her youth, a letter full of both fury and prophetic love: "While I am often grateful for my baptism and for the friendships you offered to me," she writes, "I don't always sing your praises because, frankly, you have done some evil shit. You have lent your aid countless times to the oppressor: to white supremacy, to homophobia, to misogyny, to trickle-down economics, to laissez-faire gun regulations, to the prosperity gospel."[13] So many of the young people I know long for God, but they no longer expect to find God in church. They find God elsewhere, if they find God at all. Some describe this as a process of deconstruction and reconstruction. They undergo a painful process in which they pull apart the ideas and practices of their childhood faith, examine them, and sometimes reject them. Then slowly and by grace, these young people build faith again from renewed convictions—sometimes quite the opposite of what they were taught—and they find alternative faith contexts. Along the way, they notice that the so-called secularists they were warned to avoid are often the ones most deeply and bravely engaged in the work of justice and restoration. Later in Caitlin's essay, she writes to her church, "Thanks be to God—I know some people, Christian and otherwise, who resemble Christ more fully than you."[14]

Young people are clear-eyed about adult failures, and they feel the weight of the world pressing on them. Youth initiatives in the climate movement and in the gun law reform movement provide ample evidence of their desperation. They wonder, How can we possibly fix all this? Do we even have a future? Should I even plan to have children someday?[15] The weight of change will fall hard on them. They watch the adults blather and self-justify, they watch the days tick by, days of potential repair lost to our collective "derangement," as Amitav Ghosh calls it.[16] It is so tempting to go numb.

I am right there with them. I tend to be an anxious person. I have lain awake at night worrying about many things in my life, but never before have I wondered this: Am I living at the end of days, the end of the human experiment? Or at least at one of those collapse points in history where humanity regresses and resets? In my darkest moments, I find myself grateful that I will probably die by 2055, Lord willing, before it all spins into darkness.

Maybe I'm being overly dramatic, but maybe not. The effects of climate change are not mere projections; they are terrifyingly measurable right now. We have already raised the average global temperature by 1.1 degrees Celsius over preindustrial levels. We have surpassed the safe level of 350 parts per million (ppm) of CO_2—we are now at 419 ppm, higher than at any point in human history.[17] We are witnessing more frequent and stronger storms, larger and more frequent wildfires, increased flooding, and more.[18] Meanwhile, it is well established that the people who have contributed the least to the climate crisis—the poorest and most vulnerable of the world—will continue to suffer the most devastating effects with the least support for their survival.[19]

What will happen if the world fails? What happens if we end up not with the best-case scenario but with one of those worse ones? Quietly, guiltily, I do the calculations: I and mine will probably survive longer than most. We live on high ground near fresh water in a temperate climate. Here in Michigan, we will have more frequent heavy-rain events and flooding. Species extinction will continue, disease-carrying insects will proliferate, trees will die. Food will get more expensive. We will make do with less. Pandemics like Covid-19 will disrupt daily life and the global economy more frequently. And we will watch as heat kills millions, drought starves millions, floods on every coast force mass migrations, and fire ravages the American West and every other tindery place. The world's population could diminish by a third or more. Equatorial regions will become uninhabitable. The remains of civilization in those places will be left to bake in the pitiless sun. Perhaps I have read too many dystopian novels.

In the midst of these apocalyptic worry spirals, my heart aches for my own three children, now all in their twenties. Honestly, I'm not sure I want grandchildren born into the end of days. I am sorry, my precious children, if your father and I brought you into the end of the world. We didn't know. We didn't know.

Is this the end of the world?

In my more stable moments, I recall my study of history and recognize that every age and generation has had reason to believe they were living in the end times—and here we still are, as terrible and magnificent as ever. I remember, too, that life is resilient, that people are resilient, and that many bright and courageous souls, young and old, are hard at work, facing our challenges with ingenuity and determination. In fact, as I will try to demonstrate in the following chapters, philosophers and sages perceive not only a crisis convergence but a convergence of human wisdom too, a new consciousness of our responsibility to each other and to the earth.

So I look to this faith I have cherished and wrestled with all my life, this faith that has entangled me. I wonder if my faith equips me—in my privileged, comfortable little cocoon—to live in these times. Maybe my understanding and practice need a serious training regimen. Everyone seems to agree that what we face is not only a technological, economic, and political crisis but also a spiritual one. Yet in my own religious circles, climate action still seems a niche concern. The leadership of some mainline churches has issued official statements and appointed people to provide education. Activist groups arise among Christians as among people of other faiths. At my university, dozens of my colleagues are deeply involved, and in my church we have a little "Creation Care Team," collaborating with numerous activist groups, religious and nonreligious. I have recently immersed myself in the thriving, relatively young field of ecotheology, which has Jewish and Islamic as well as Christian expressions.

Nevertheless, I had to look for all this, seek it out. We have a long way to go before we have achieved a thorough awakening and adjustment. Meanwhile, I know I'm not the only one seeking to reorient my faith and practice, wondering how to bring the rich resources of faith to bear on all this fear, frustration, anger, and longing. I know I'm not the only one needing new ways to nurture my now-bewildered hope.

The Little Work Begins

I have learned in my reading that environmental writers and ecophilosophers love to quote Catholic theologian Thomas Berry's 1999 book *The Great Work*. Berry, who called himself a "geologian," perceived with many others that we have reached a hinge point in history. We have reached the end of the "lyrical" age, he writes—the age that began sixty-five million years ago and created ideal conditions for all the gorgeous life on this earth, including the rise of human civilization. That age is now ending. This means that those of us living today, like it or not, have a "special role that history has imposed upon" us. Berry writes, "Our own special role, which we will hand on to our children, is that of managing the arduous transition from the terminal Cenozoic to the emerging Ecozoic Era, the period when humans will be present to the planet as participating members of the comprehensive Earth community. This is our Great Work and the work of our children."[20] We humans have become so powerful that what happens next depends on our actions, and our actions in turn depend on our consciousness. Our "Great Work" is to understand and behave as if we are members of a community of beings who all depend on each other. Nothing can thrive unless we all thrive, so it's time for humans to think of more than just ourselves. Buddhist philosopher and activist Joanna Macy calls this moment, similarly, the "Great Turning."[21]

Both Macy and Berry are among those who believe that the human race can indeed rise to the occasion and make this shift. Berry believed we can bring about the "Emerging Ecozoic Era" if we humans abandon our destructive ways and live in intelligent cooperation with earth's natural systems. Moreover, Berry writes, "No one is exempt." All of us have to participate. Our "personal work needs to be aligned with the Great Work," he says.[22] So I suppose that means that each of us has a "little work," and we must each discover what that might be.

Even before reading Thomas Berry, I have felt drawn in recent years toward an emerging sense of my "little work" for reasons I haven't been able to explain. I am an unlikely candidate for any sort of ecological awakening. I do not belong to the societies of campers, kayakers, climbers, fishers, hunters, birders, boaters, wilderness back-packers, gardeners, farmers, biologists, or ecologists. I love gazing out windows, but I'm rather an indoor cat, happiest at my desk, reading. Thanks to the accident of being born in the 1960s as a White person in America, I am, in many ways, the ultimate product of thousands of years of human struggle to conquer nature: an ordinary person of no special status who has never known hunger or lacked shelter, a person made continuously comfortable by the achievements of the industrial age, a first-world consumer coddled by late-stage capitalism. The machinations of history have tossed every comfort onto my little life's shore. When it comes to Maslow's hierarchy of needs, I have on most days of my life enjoyed abundance at every level, including all that self-actualization and fulfillment business at the pointy top. I'm a perfect example of "ecological amnesia,"[23] that phenomenon in which we forget our fundamental dependence on the earth because we are largely shielded from the arduous tasks of deriving our living from it. Indeed, I am minimally intimate with the dirt, plants, animals, wilderness, or oceans that nature writers are always rhapsodizing about.

Perhaps this is precisely what makes me a good test case. Another Berry—the poet, essayist, farmer, and philosopher Wendell Berry—recommended that we begin with affection.[24] So I can begin my ecological awakening there. I have always loved my home region, the lakeshore and inland woods of western lower Michigan. Like many people of this region, I love our dunes, our scruffy eastern white pines, our moody skies almost always crafting some enigmatic message in a medium of clouds. My heart lifts at the sight of a weedy, open field. I enjoy hiking—day hiking, mind you, with a hot shower waiting for me in the evening. And over the years, I've dabbled in the most basic gardening. So for my little work, I will start very small indeed. Thomas Berry traces his own lifelong concern with ecology to a modest, epiphanic moment as a child while literally considering the lilies in a North Carolina meadow.[25] Well, if he can start with that, I can start with my love for the silken horizon of Lake Michigan. I can explore what it takes to sink more deeply into a place, learn more about it, dwell in it, become a better citizen.

In the chapters that follow, I report on discovering my little work through a range of modest adventures. Some are adventures in reading, where I explore a variety of ecological writers and dive into the Christian theological tradition of reflection about the relationships among God, humans, and the rest of creation. Through my reading, I have tried to figure out how ecotheology and literary nature writing can make a difference in our thinking and daily lives. Some of my adventures involve learning directly from wiser people. I've been hanging out with colleagues in the fields of geology, environmental studies, and biology, visiting their field sites and classrooms, pestering them with questions. Some of my adventures involve learning the history of my own home region, attending to it more keenly, getting involved with land conservancy groups. I write about Michigan not because it is more special or important than anywhere else but simply to model what it looks like to root more consciously into one's home region. Also, I want to give some writerly love to our freshwater dunes. Plenty of people write about oceans, deserts, mountains, rivers, prairies, and forests—our dunes deserve some attention too. Finally, I've begun making practical changes in my own life. Ideas are crucial, but so are feelings and practices. I've tried to write about all of it at once, because that's how we live it: all at once.

This is not a book intended to persuade that climate change is real and human caused. I'm assuming readers are already convinced of that. The science is, as the 2021 IPCC report asserts, "unequivocal."[26] Nor is this a how-to book about recycling or eating less meat or political activism. Many other sources offer practical advice and compelling arguments for altering our lifestyles and getting involved. (See the suggested resources section for places to begin.) In any case, although individual changes are vital, they are hardly sufficient. The Covid-19 pandemic underscored how intricately interconnected and dependent on complex global systems we are and how full of vulnerabilities and inequalities those systems are. The pandemic only confirmed what climate models have been telling us already: the human family must make sweeping changes across the globe—infrastructure overhauls, international law reforms—changes that will stretch our meager capacities for working together and laying down our many greeds. Our soul sicknesses and our earth sicknesses, after all, are deeply interrelated.

While we must all, as Thomas Berry says, participate in and promote that Great Work on a large scale, we must also do our little work, nurturing life right where we are, becoming healers right on the soil where we stand. At the end of Milton's *Paradise Lost*, Adam receives an education from the angel Michael, and sums up all he has learned, declaring that his role is "by small / Accomplishing great things, by things deem'd weak / Subverting worldly strong." Michael approves of Adam's summary, responding that Adam must "only add / Deeds to thy knowledge answerable."[27] If we reorient our purpose away from building empires and protecting the power of our particular groups or institutions and instead commit to finding, creating, and nurturing life-giving shelters for the whole household of life, matter and spirit—well, we might be surprised. No one knows how effectively we can reverse course on ecosystem destruction if we try. Much is lost forever, that is certain, and we must somehow reckon with that loss. The moral thing to do, as Kathleen Dean Moore writes, is to work for restoration and protection anyway, though success is hardly guaranteed. Even if mitigation is all we can hope for, that's what we should do.[28] Humans don't always destroy things. We can redeem and restore things too. We might be surprised how vigorously life wants to rebuild, given the chance. That's the promise of a refugia faith.

Christians believe that God came to this world in a hidden refuge, the child Jesus conceived in what Luke 2 describes as his mother's *koilia*—the Greek word for "cavity." Out of that tiny shelter, against all reasonable odds, we believe the Holy Spirit's power overwhelmed the destructive course of human sin with newness of life. The resurrected Jesus, having entered into death and come out the other side, breathed that same Spirit upon the disciples when they huddled, terrified, in the upper room. And that same Spirit still hovers over the face of the deep, still overshadows us. Can we receive it, yield to it?

The ethicist Larry Rasmussen observes, "Ours are hard times for many. They are not for the faint of heart. They will get worse. But they are also times of exhilarating song on the part of a species that was born singing and has never ceased."[29] May we find the courage to let the Spirit's power overwhelm us too, so that even in these crisis days we might sing a new and exhilarating song.

COMMON BUCKTHORN
RHAMNUS CATHARTICA

January
Douglas, Michigan

Everything changed late last night. The wind came up from the north-west, rolling the lake into motion, pushing long ridges of churning foam into shore. Quick and steady, quick, quick, the big lake pulsing its tireless rhythm through the night.

This morning, the sky rumples with cotton-batten clouds, bright against the sharp line of the water's horizon. The wind has settled some, the waves relaxed. All this year we've watched the lake rise, battering away at the dune. Now levels are almost as high as they have ever been since people have been measuring.[1] Looking out the window, we no longer see beach spreading away from the dune. Our century-old cottage seems to float on the lake, an ark with a weathered deck for a prow.

I bundle up against the cold and head out with our yellow Lab mix, Maizey, to see if there's room to walk along the lake's edge.

The foredune is gone. The steps to the beach end a few feet from the scarp, carved out neatly by the lake like the last square of cake left in the pan. It's an eight-foot drop to the beach below—what's left of the beach. Just enough to walk on, if we can dodge the waves. But how to get down there?

Maizey and I slip around our stair railing and tramp up the steep, leaf-littered dune, through old oaks and wiry saplings, to a spot high on the stairway next door. The steps lead to the tiny county beach—closed now for public safety reasons. Where the stairway makes a turn, we find a foot-wide gap in the wooden railing. A makeshift wire fence covers the gap, but the wire is loose. I push it aside so that Maizey and I can squeeze through. We clatter down the public beach steps.

The bottom few steps are covered with wet sand. They were battered by waves overnight. Maizey hesitates, refusing to acrobat her old bones over a missing step near the bottom. I have to lift her over. But when her paws hit the beach, her Lab face lights up. Too good to be true! The smells! The freedom! Let's go!

We walk north. No one else is around. The cottages up and down the lakeshore are silent and cold, asleep on the edge of the wild lake.

The lake has done its winter work. The cottages starting with ours are protected by a steel seawall put in over thirty years ago, during the last period of extremely high lake levels. The wall is holding back the dune behind it, barely. A three-foot-thick layer of sand and marram grass frosts the top of the wall, neatly cross-sectioned out by waves and wind. Tangles of twining roots—scouring rush, this plant is called—bulge over the wall in other places, the roots dangling with cloudy blobs of ice, like jewels on a chain.

Six cottages down, past the seawall: devastation. Every ten feet I can't help myself: "Holy shit!" Decks slump precariously down the eroded dune slope, the foredune carved right out from under them. Steps are reduced to wreckage. Trees thirty feet tall dip their tops in the water, the dune washed away from under their roots. One family built a prop out of two-by-fours for the front end of their deck; all the original footings are exposed and dangling in midair, as if the deck were caught with its pants down. Another family strapped their deck to trees higher on the dune. It will have to be rebuilt, but at least they have all the pieces.

Maizey and I walk on. The beach opens up. Cottages are much higher on the dune here, plenty of slope between them and the scarp. I can see that the lake has retreated from recent stormy aggressions. The foredune scarp is fronted by another little drop, a ledge of more soily sand. Tracings of debris—algae mats, driftwood, pieces of deck from who knows where—lay where the waves sculpted them into scalloped curves and then pulled back. An offering? Or a statement of power. This is what I can do, says the lake. Remember that.

Great Lakes levels rise and fall in cycles. We know this because people have been keeping records of lake levels since 1860. Current high lake levels are not connected to ocean level rise, because the Lake Michigan–Huron basin is about six hundred feet above sea level, and its waters come down from the higher Lake Superior as well as from thousands of rivers around the basin and, of course, from rainfall. Lake levels, therefore, result from an interplay of precipitation and evaporation. More precipitation raises levels, obviously, but warmer winters mean decreased ice cover, which increases evaporation. Hotter temperatures in spring, summer, and especially the fall can increase evaporation, though higher humidity diminishes that effect. Although our record keeping and understanding of lake hydrology continue to gain in precision over the decades, it's still difficult to predict lake levels, especially as climate patterns continue to shift. Some scientists are predicting that the lake's natural rise and fall will be exacerbated by increasing chaos in global weather patterns. Higher highs, lower lows. No one knows for sure.[2]

My friend Deanna van Dijk, a coastal geographer, has been studying a certain foredune near Muskegon, Michigan, for over twenty years. Every fall she and her student assistants lug heavy equipment along the beach and up the foredune, where she plants anemometers and sand traps in strategic spots. The gadgets measure wind speed and direction, temperature, and sand deposition, recording reams of data during the autumn storm season. Deanna has been trying to understand exactly by what mechanisms the lake giveth and the lake taketh away. This year, the foredune she's been tracking for twenty years is just gone. Swallowed by the lake, dissipated by wind. At least she has her data.

So much changes, so quickly. Last time I was out here, I came as always to see the horizon, to find perspective. That time, the wind was still, the lake calm except for a subtle, rippling perturbance on the surface. The trees, nothing but sticks, leaned outward toward the water, yearning. A damp cold chilled to the bone, a mist in the air so fine all I could see was a wash of dove gray as if the whole world misted into oblivion twenty yards ahead.

I had come to look at water and sky, but I could see neither. Only the faintest horizon, somewhere in that wash of gray nothingness.

Chapter 1

From Despair to Preparation

Then shall all the trees of the forest sing for joy.
—PSALM 96:12

'm in my car, of course, because 28th Street is no place to be on foot. I'm on my way to Meijer, the original one-stop-shopping megastore. Long before Walmart, the Meijer chain (pronounced "Meyer") began with a little grocery business opened in 1934 by Fred Meijer right here in Grand Rapids. In fact, the Meijer location I usually patronize was built on the site of that original store. Today there are more than 250 megastore locations throughout Michigan, Ohio, Illinois, Indiana, Kentucky, and Wisconsin. You can get all your groceries at Meijer, plus baby booties, air filters, lawn chairs, goldfish (the living kind as well as the little crackers), video games, earbuds, gardening gloves, hammers, work boots, panty hose, greeting cards, live orchids, booze of all sorts, lottery tickets, laundry baskets, and lamps. Your prescription drugs too. There's a pharmacy, a bank branch, and a nail salon. "If Meijer doesn't have it, you don't need it." That's what we say in West Michigan.

We have Costco too, and I like shopping there. I appreciate buying in bulk. It's convenient and efficient. If I have to go to Costco *and* Meijer, then I'll head east out 28th Street and go to the big Cascade Meijer across from the Costco. It's right by Target and Dick's Sporting Goods, past the Home Depot. On my way out there, I'll pass car dealerships, dozens of restaurants, gas stations and oil-change joints, two big malls, a couple strip malls, a Bed Bath & Beyond. Our house is located in a pleasant residential neighborhood only a couple miles from 28th Street, and thus we enjoy easy access to any shopping we need. From my yard, I can hear the traffic noise from 28th Street, but it's fine. I'm used to it.

I'm also used to the ugliness of 28th Street. I don't even think about it. Two lanes of traffic each way plus the middle "suicide lane" for left turns, utility poles lining each side, a jungle of power cables strung across and along the road, traffic lights about every quarter mile, a riot of signs filling my view for miles ahead. Apart from the sad excuse for grass struggling to grow in the curb strips, everything is paved as far as I can see. There's a sidewalk carved out between the big-box-store parking lots and the roaring streams of traffic. One feels sorry for people who need to walk down it. Here and there, trees that look like lone survivors of an asphalt invasion breathe acrid exhaust from cars and trucks. Some businesses attempt to cultivate a few flower planters near their doors or some hardy daylilies at the bases of their thirty-foot signs. Otherwise, it's asphalt, concrete, metal, and electric light everywhere you look.

Behold the pinnacle of postindustrial consumer capitalism, at least the end-user part of it. It doesn't exactly feed the soul, but as I say, it's convenient. I rarely think about the land beneath the asphalt or what's been destroyed or what's missing. Woods? Was this place covered with eastern white pine before White people settled here? Maybe it was one of Michigan's famous oak openings? Were there wetlands with herons and frogs and fish? Did Ottawa clans establish seasonal camps here? I have no idea. Does it matter now? As far as I remember, it's always been 28th Street.

The standard North American middle-class lifestyle—affluent, comfortable, even fun—is the simultaneously wondrous and absurd culmination of human struggle over millennia. Who can condemn our deep-seated drive to relieve suffering and live better? No one wants to starve or freeze or die of disease. We have found ways over centuries, via a vast web of human ingenuity, to give us (in the United States and other highly developed countries anyway) ridiculously abundant food, convenient roads and transportation, widespread literacy, astounding building technologies, tailored consumer goods for every need and comfort, and choice, choice, choice. That's the dream.

At least it was. Today more of us are coming to understand that our glittering panoramas of prosperity are built on ugly scaffoldings of environmental devastation and injustice. This way of life is unsustainable for the planet and unfair for the people whose lives and landscapes are sacrificed to provide it. But what now? What do we do? In nature, a state of imbalance usually prompts some kind of disturbance, and out of that disturbance the system trends toward some new and maybe different equilibrium. Perhaps we can begin, then, by inviting a disturbance of thought and conviction in this moment. We can ask what assumptions and habits we ought to deconstruct and what new commitments we might make. This is what happens in refugia during a severe disturbance: much is dying, but much is also being renewed. Refugia, therefore, are painful but also brave spaces.

The Great Acceleration

My parents came of age during World War II and were married in 1948. They began their adult lives precisely on the cusp of America's postwar boom. My mother's parents were immigrants from the Netherlands and my father's mother from Hungary. Their families were poor during the Great Depression, so after the war, Mom and Dad fully embraced the American dream of upward mobility and prosperity. They had suffered their share of poverty and insecurity, they figured, and now they wanted a beautiful home, nice things, and money in the bank. They wanted the college educations for their children that were never possible for them. And that's exactly what they got. Postwar America delivered.

Bill Bryson, in his wry and irreverent memoir, calls the 1950s "The Age of Excitement," and I know what he means based on Mom and Dad's attitudes.[1] In their minds, everything was just great in America. We were building the economy, making big cars and major appliances. We were the most powerful, amazing nation in the world. Technology, given a little time, was going to solve every problem. One of Mom's favorite sayings, in the context of any complex problem—from communicable disease to rocket propulsion—was "They'll think of something." Who "they" were was never entirely clear, but . . . someone? Some expert somewhere?

She was expressing her trust in the myth of progress. In ancient times, people looked back to a golden age, a time of perfection that could never be recovered, only longingly mythologized. They imagined history on a slow, downward slope. From the beginnings of the modern era, though, people began to shift their gaze forward toward a golden future. Renaissance-era Europeans imagined a fresh start in the "New World," and later, with the Industrial Revolution, people in the West believed a new age of prosperity would arrive thanks to technology and the indomitable human spirit.[2] White America in the 1950s exemplified that future-oriented optimism, and Mom and Dad were swept up in it.

They were also devout Christians. I don't mean to belittle their faith in God by describing their simultaneous faith in American ingenuity and prosperity. My mother, especially, lived her Christian faith sincerely and well. But they were people of their time and place, as are we all. And thus it's unsurprising that they, like many other ordinary adults in the 1950s and '60s, did not much worry about brewing ecological crisis. The compulsion to be hopeful and positive was too strong, the cornucopian promises of consumer advertising too alluring. Mom and Dad concerned themselves with their children, friends, church, and weekly bargains at the grocery store and the shopping mall. Beneath this enthusiasm, it's true, lurked shadows of childhood scarcity they could never entirely relinquish. My dad fretted over every small extravagance because it might land them "back in the poor house." Nevertheless, nestled in prosperous, Midwestern, White America, they took for granted technological progress and economic growth. Sure, there were troubles, but overall, the world was getting better and better.

They both died in 2015, having lived through what now looks to be a sweet spot of human optimism. In their later years, they had enough to deal with just managing the typical hardships and griefs of old age, so we didn't talk much about world events. I wonder what it would be like to try to explain the climate crisis to them now. "Well, you see," I would have to say, "all that fantastic prosperity was created without paying sufficient attention to nature's limits. Humans just took and took and took, ignoring the fact that we were destroying at a pace much faster than nature could replenish. And then there's the human cost: slavery, exploitation, land theft, wars over resources. Can we talk about White supremacy?" I don't think they would be dismissive, but still, this would be an earful for people whose lives were based on a promise of limitless prosperity that seemed to be true.

Now we know. We can't avoid the truth. We can't use the earth as both "supply-house and sewer" indefinitely.[3] Nature has its limits. There's only so much it can supply and only so quickly it can repair itself. All life systems are interrelated too, so it's virtually impossible to avoid cascading effects. Cut down a rain forest, and you doom wildlife to death by habitat destruction, reduce the carbon absorption the trees provided, release more carbon into the atmosphere by burning, and invite soil erosion and desertification. Destroy or alter enough of the earth and burn enough fossil fuels, and you literally alter global weather patterns, acidify the oceans, and turn earth into—as Bill McKibben puts it—a "tough new planet."[4] In our determination to make human life more secure and more pleasant for some, the powerful have ignored all this, sometimes stupidly, sometimes knowingly. In fact, we sometimes cultivate ignorance to cover our malevolence and greed. As Thomas Berry observed in the 1990s, "Because of our need to fuel the industrial world, we have created a technosphere incompatible with the biosphere."[5] One group estimates that if everyone on earth, all 7.8 billion people, were to live like average Americans, we would require the resources of four earths to support that way of life. Americans aren't even the most extravagant. We're ranked fifth in resource use, behind Kuwait, Australia, United Arab Emirates, and Qatar.[6]

The most commonly cited metric for the trouble we're in is, of course, atmospheric carbon dioxide concentration. Beginning around 1750 at the dawn of the Industrial Revolution, the amount of carbon dioxide in the atmosphere began to rise, and the pace of increase accelerated steadily until around 1950. At that point, the carbon load shot upward, so the graph tracing this increase looks, famously, like a hockey stick. But the problem is not just CO_2. Other graphs look like hockey sticks too as they trace increases in population, of course, as well as water use, fertilizer consumption, and international travel. Right along with steep increases in carbon dioxide levels came similarly shocking rates of increase in methane production, average surface temperature, flooding, deforestation, and species extinction.[7] This period is sometimes called the Great Acceleration.[8]

This incredible transformation of the planet was made possible by the amazing power of fossil fuels—coal, natural gas, and oil—which increase the energy at human disposal by many powers of ten. Ethicist Larry Rasmussen notes, "While in the early years of the industrial era, 94 percent of the world's energy was supplied by human labor and animals, and fossil fuels and water only 6 percent, by the time of the dramatic upswing of the 1950s, 93 percent of all energy was supplied by oil, coal, and natural gas."[9] In fact, he writes, "In the prodigious half-century from 1950 to 2000, the global consumer economy produced, transported, and consumed as many goods and services as *throughout the entirety of prior history*."[10] We humans have been extracting and then wielding fantastic power.

Unfortunately, as Bill McKibben wrote prophetically back in 1989, fossil fuel also allowed us to bring about the "end of nature."[11] He meant, at the time, that there is now no place on the planet that does not feel the influence of human activity. Even the remotest Antarctic ice sheet is affected by temperature rise resulting from fossil fuel emissions. Even the loneliest stretch of ocean is affected by acidification as the ocean attempts to absorb the huge load of carbon dioxide in the atmosphere. Nature has its ways of restoring balance, but humans are now too powerful. Nature can't keep up.[12] Since 1989, the acceleration has gotten much worse. We are on the steep upward slopes of a lot of hockey sticks. Even if we were to stop carbon emissions tomorrow, the carbon already in the atmosphere will continue to affect the earth's systems for centuries.[13] The most recent Intergovernmental Panel on Climate Change report offers particular models of how much, where, and when. The effects of our human carbon dump, for example, will mean continued sea level rise "for centuries to millennia."[14]

As frightening as it is to look at all those graphs and read the grim predictions about feedback loops and tipping points, we might be tempted to say, with my mom, "They'll think of something." Can't we just fix this with technological advances? After all, "they" are already thinking of—and implementing—solar panels, permaculture farming, electric cars, and a thousand other genius ideas. Didn't I hear that carbon sequestration is coming right along? A lot of us are changing our lifestyles now. A little.

It won't be enough. We can spur each other on to personal piety all we want, and it won't be enough. It's true that individual actions are important. They help shift our own hearts and nudge us all toward a new normal. Still, we are caught up in global systems here, powers and principalities that our personal nibbles of virtue aren't going to alter by themselves. Environmental writer Mary Annaïse Heglar, in a 2019 article, describes how people she meets feel the need to apologize to her for all their personal environmental sins. She really does not care about people's personal sins or pieties, she writes, because there are much bigger things at stake: "While we're busy testing each other's purity, we let the government and industries—the authors of said devastation—off the hook completely. This overemphasis on individual action shames people for their everyday activities, things they can barely avoid doing because of the fossil fuel-dependent system they were born into."[15] In other words, we cannot possibly muster enough personal consumer virtue to alter the fundamental systems in which we live. This is both a practical and spiritual fact.

We will need every technological tool we can summon, along with a daunting amount of unified political will, to bring about rapid shifts in our entire energy infrastructure, transportation systems, agricultural practices—everything, really. It's the Great Work, as Thomas Berry put it, not the Easy Work. Wise and inspired people of all backgrounds are trying to lead the way, but it's difficult to move entrenched power even one inch. And we're all implicated, all embedded in these ways of life. Nothing we do is entirely innocent.

Even so, I'm trying. I ride down 28th Street in my electric car, and I try to avoid buying things at Costco or Meijer wrapped in ridiculous amounts of excess packaging. I buy eggs and some pasture-raised meat from a local farmer. We recycle, of course, and never buy bottled water. We even put solar panels on our roof—which earns us a *lot* of virtue points along with a tax credit. Still, I feel vaguely guilty about every bag of trash I put on the curb, every gallon of gas I burn in our second car, every plastic shampoo bottle full of palm oil. I can't do enough. Or maybe I don't want to. There's always some other "sin" I haven't repented of. I don't even know how to live a completely virtuous life, earthwise. That's not how I was raised.

I was raised in the Christian faith, though, and now I wonder: What does my faith offer to help me make sense of this moment in history?

Clash of Kingdoms

While the Christian church in the West—as many have observed—has largely cooperated or at least coexisted with the myth of progress and the promise of affluence, Christian tradition also offers resources to critique and challenge that myth. During the four weeks leading up to Christmas, for example, many branches of the Christian church observe the season of Advent, which means "coming." In the lead-up to Christmas, we are invited to anticipate not only the coming of the infant in the manger but also the return of Christ in judgment at the end of history. That double anticipation makes for an uncomfortable juxtaposition, a startling concoction of sweet coziness and mortal terror. It's tempting to turn Advent into merely a lovely time of evergreen swags and glowing candles, beloved hymns about angels, joyful anticipation of warm feelings about a nice baby. But that's not what Advent is supposed to be. Advent is about a clash of kingdoms.

The whole reason for that baby to arrive is to overturn the powers of this world in all their corruption and cruelty. That baby is supposed to become the Prince of Peace, ushering in the grace, justice, and beauty the Scriptures claim God intends for the world. To prepare for this, we're invited to dwell in that painful tension between what's actually happening and what God promises. We're supposed to look around and feel the aching sorrow of the world, because even though the baby entered history way back when, the redemption work he came to proclaim is hardly finished. The fact is, things are still pretty bad. Hence that dual focus on the unveiling of God in the manger and the unveiling of God's full glory in some future manifestation.

Apocalypse just means "revealing," and Advent is the church's most apocalyptic season. We sink into the truth about our world's deep sicknesses in order to awaken our full Advent longing. After all, we hardly need a savior if we're comfortable with the way things are. So the first week of Advent always features the story of John the Baptist—that camel-hair-wearing, locust-eating weirdo—crying out in the wilderness. He harks back to the bracing words of the Hebrew prophets before him: "Repent! Get your priorities straight! Turn your desires toward a new thing! Get ready, because the ax is at the foot of the tree!" The prophet reminds us that some things will have to be destroyed to make way for the new. That's just how the world works.

We can see this pattern of preparatory destruction in biological contexts as well. Nature renews itself through disturbance, even violent disturbance. Refugia are those places where things start again, and they are not typically safe, cozy, Edenic grottos. Refugia persist amid surrounding crisis, even disaster, and it may be that they are fairly frightening places. I don't know whether patches of pearly everlasting or musty voles felt terror amid the devastation of Mount Saint Helens's eruption. I don't know whether lodgepole pines that survive a pine bark beetle infestation feel bewilderment, or whether koalas that survive a bushfire imagine how to heal their habitat and long for that renewal. Perhaps they do, in their own way. In any case, biological refugia are places of difficult perseverance and regrowth. Some refugia are what biologists call "in situ" refugia: the creatures can shelter in place, lucky to find shelters in their accustomed habitat, however stressed that habitat might be. In other situations, creatures must leave their accustomed habitat and seek shelter elsewhere. They must find "ex situ" refugia. Either way, even amid destruction, the forces of life yearn for renewal. A refugia faith, similarly, regards our dire conditions honestly but immerses fear and despair in longing for God's promised new life. That longing gives us the courage to face the difficult preparations necessary for a renewed world, however painful and disorienting they may be. Sometimes those preparations require us—even if we physically stay put where we are—to change our thinking and habits in ways that feel disruptive.

That characteristic Advent tension—between the "world in sin and error pining"[16] and the flourishing and just community of life we long for—I've never felt that tension so keenly as in the past few years. The climate crisis is forcing more of us privileged North Americans to peel back the layers and look, soberly and urgently, at our fundamental soul sicknesses. It turns out that the crises we face right now—climate, politics, racial injustice, even the pandemic[17]—are all of a piece. At root, what has brought us to this point is what Lutheran theologian H. Paul Santmire calls "the spirit of domination." Santmire is naming that fundamental human drive to dominate and exploit, to indulge greed and cultivate denial. This drive is ancient, primal. It takes the remarkable gift of human adaptability and distorts it toward violence and disregard for the value of other living things, including other humans, so that one can garner more and more power to oneself and perhaps one's own clan. The spirit of domination, unsurprisingly, creates structures of domination.[18] Those structures take any number of forms, from military juntas to race-based slavery to extraction economies.

That spirit of domination has transmuted the myth of progress into a kind of religion. If a religion is where we truly place our ultimate value—as revealed not by what we claim but by how we arrange our habits of life—then it's not hard to see how a growth economy can be a kind of god. We offer our daily sacrifices to this god, worry about its wrath being visited upon us, long for its favor. People of all religious faiths and no faith are tempted to worship this idol. Jesus said we cannot serve both God and Mammon, but we sure do try. During the Covid-19 pandemic, people argued about the relative importance of reopening the economy versus risking more lives lost. It became clear that we didn't quite have the tools to make a moral calculation about this, because the economy has become more than just a way to meet people's practical needs. It's an entity we worship and serve. We are willing to sacrifice people to it.

Increased human flourishing is a good thing, of course, but every idol is a distortion of something good, the bloating of a reasonable value into an ultimate value. The drive toward flourishing easily curdles into domination, and thus the glories and achievements of civilization have never been evenly distributed. Colonialism has enslaved and destroyed peoples and lands so that others might prosper, with wreckage that persists all over the world. Even now, the millions of people in China and India and other countries just showing up to the affluence party—well, sorry, but the party is almost over. It has long been destroying the premises, especially the premises of people who weren't even invited. This is because we lucky ones have far overshot our goal, so that none of us can live in consumerist luxury anymore, at least not for long. Idolatries inevitably become cruelties.

It's so hard to admit our idolatries and cruelties, so easy to turn away. But when we face, square on, the patterns of war and exploitation, habitat destruction, soil degradation, fishery depletion, and flagrant pollution beneath the extraction-consumer economic system; when we witness the callousness and cynicism of powerful people; when we watch governments and religious groups enable and defend injustice; when we witness the spirit of domination in its sickening, even ludicrous forms in American politics and in corporate greed—the pain of all this can and should tempt us to despair. But pain should also, simultaneously, awaken our longing for God's intended flourishing. This clash of kingdoms can thrust us into a place of bewilderment as we wonder when God will *do something* about all this.

I've leaned hard into the prophet-in-the-wilderness aspect of Advent in recent years. I've appreciated that the church is honest—can be, anyway—about how much of the life of faith is spent waiting for what seems like an absent God, taking sweet divine time to show up and fix things. *Deus absconditus.* The God who is hidden. This sense of darkness I have felt is evidently nothing new, seeing as there's a Latin phrase for it. I notice that the characters in the Advent stories—the old and disgraced Elizabeth, the young and ignored Mary, the faithful elders Simeon and Anna, the whole nation of Israel under Roman occupation—they're all waiting for the mighty deeds of God, the kinds of miraculous interventions that rescued their ancestors from slavery and then from exile. Ages seem to pass. It's not as if their people's fortunes are much improving. And still they wait. Despair must have lurked for them as it does for us. Despair is never far away.

Then John the Baptist appears on the cusp of some imperceptible moment, crying out in the wilderness. Come *into* this wilderness, he says. Come into a place of honest encounter with the pain. Here we can dwell in that tension between what is and what could be. Here we can feel our own complicity and helplessness, the ways in which we bow down to idols, the frustrating impotence of even our best efforts to steer this world toward what is righteous. Here we can dismantle what is corrupt in us. Here we can prepare for what's coming.

In light of these Advent patterns, deep in the church's traditions, I've been wondering. If this is the time of the Great Work, the time of a Great Transition, then are we in some kind of Advent moment? Maybe if facing the truth about what humans have done to our planet drives us into what feels like a wilderness, a bewilderment, then that's exactly where we should go: an ex situ refugium. Wilderness sojourns have a long and distinguished history among the Abrahamic faiths. God seems to make a habit of offering fierce revelation in the wilderness, where comforts and distractions are stripped away. Perhaps today's crisis convergence is not only an ending but—like all wilderness sojourns in the biblical stories—a severe and merciful reorientation.

Cutover Dreams

"Wilderness" is a complicated concept and a controversial one these days. An understanding of wilderness the way John Muir and Henry David Thoreau thought of it—as a means of encountering the sublime, as a tonic for the city weary, as the "preservation of the world"[19]—is a fairly recent phenomenon. For most of history, wilderness has represented threatening powers indifferent to human survival. You either avoid it or find some way to conquer it. That's what the hero-king Gilgamesh and his friend Enkidu do in the most ancient story we have—together they conquer the nature god Humbaba. They hem and haw about it—whether they should, whether they can—but in the end, they kill Humbaba and cut down a sacred cedar tree. It's an archetypal representation of the human drive to conquer and absorb the "wild"— that which is uncontrollable and threatening—in order to survive. This pattern encapsulates much of human history.

Today, ecophilosophers point out that heading out into the wilderness to experience sublime beauty and have an adventure constitutes a kind of privilege. They also suggest that, when humans impose our conceptualizations on landscapes, we practice a kind of epistemological colonialism. They challenge, Why do humans get to define what a landscape *is* and what its boundaries and purpose are?[20] Such thinkers are right in pointing out that our ideas about what a landscape is powerfully determine how we interact with it—for good or ill. In my own state's history, for example, we find a case study of human ambivalence about wilderness. Early White settlers in Michigan inherited from the Romantic period the idea that our forests and grasslands represented a wild beauty worth reveling in. They also inherited the idea that land and waters are merely resources intended for human use, to be transformed from "waste" into human prosperity. Both attitudes, of course, place human desire at the center—the earth is *for us*, for our aesthetic as well as our practical needs. Unsurprisingly, the spirit of domination tends to win out over our reverence for beauty. Thus Michigan's history illustrates a pattern of justified domination repeated all over this country and indeed the world.

Last summer I visited the Au Sable Institute in the woods near Mancelona, in the northwestern region of Michigan's mitten. Some of my colleagues and friends teach summer conservation courses there for undergraduates. I tagged along one day as my friend Tim Van Deelen, a wildlife biologist, brought his class to the Hartwick Pines State Park. Of the park's 9,700 acres, 49 acres are protected as one of the only old-growth forest remnants in Michigan. We stood beneath a canopy of white pine, beech, hemlock, and maple, noting how beech bark disease crinkled and blistered the beeches and how the overabundant deer in this area were nibbling away all the seedlings except for the maples, which reproduce so prolifically they keep ahead even of voracious deer.

Then we walked on to the park's lumbering museum, a well-curated replica of a nineteenth-century Michigan lumber camp. There, in one of the buildings, we beheld a room full of massive logging gear that strongly reminded one of a torture chamber. I suppose from the trees' point of view, it was. Two hundred years ago, Michigan had barely been settled by White people, and about 73 percent of the land across the two peninsulas was covered by conifer or hardwood forests and another 21 percent by wooded swamp areas. In 1820, Lewis Cass, the governor of Michigan Territory, led an expedition of forty people across the region. The plan was to help promote White settlement, spy on British traders, and implement Indian policy.[21] By 1836, to make way for imminent waves of White settlers, the Treaty of Washington effectively ousted the Ottawa peoples from two-thirds of their land north of the Grand River, not long after the Potawatomi had ceded their land south of the river in 1821.

White settlers started coming, and so did eager industrialists. Copper, iron, lumber—soon Michigan's natural riches were being loaded onto ships and railcars for profit. Starting in 1840, almost all of Michigan's old-growth forests were cut down—a period now called "the cutover." Trees between 250 and 300 years old and up to 150 feet tall were felled by the thousands. By the 1870s, 1,600 sawmills were operating in Michigan, processing a billion board feet per year.[22] According to Michigan historian Camden Burd, "From 1869–1909, 16.8 billion board feet of lumber were removed from Michigan and shipped to larger cities."[23] By the 1890s, loggers had clear-cut so much of Michigan's native white pine that they were moving on to the hardwoods. Michigan led the growing nation's hardwood production from 1900 to 1910. By 1929, 92 percent of Michigan's original forest was cut or burned.[24] That small area in Hartwick Pines was missed in the cutover, most likely because the logging company paused their operations in 1893 due to an economic recession known as "the panic of '93." By the time they started cutting again in 1896, they had built a new logging camp and narrow-gauge railway in order to log a more valuable nearby acreage, and they never went back to log the previously missed acres.[25]

The mass cutting of Michigan's trees was only one piece of the nineteenth-century deforestation frenzy, all in the name of building a nation. Before White settlement, half the total land area of what is now the United States was covered with forests, some one billion acres. By 1907, one-third of it was gone.[26] Today, although conservation efforts and reforestation efforts have renewed some US forests, less than 1 percent of old-growth forest remains intact.

Literary scholar John Knott, surveying the literature of the cutover period, finds in novels and poems of this period a clear expression of that central paradox about wilderness. On the one hand, White settlers were awed by the beauty of this land. They had been schooled in "the myth of a pristine world with inexhaustible natural resources," for example, by the writings of Henry Wadsworth Longfellow and Henry Rowe Schoolcraft, and settlers' writings demonstrate they were not insensitive to the beauty of the woods, the wildflowers, the shining inland lakes.[27] On the other hand, White settlers regarded the wilderness as a challenge to their human ingenuity and determination. Their task was to "battle" the land and subdue it to the cause of civilization.

In 1831, Alexis de Tocqueville, that perceptive French observer of American life, visited the dense pine forests near what is now Pontiac, Michigan. He expected to find, in this untamed wilderness, a sense of the sublime and evidence of an orderly God. Instead, he was dismayed and afraid. Knott writes, "The frightening aspects of the forest were magnified by what [de Tocqueville] perceived as a chaos of undergrowth and broken and uprooted trees in various stages of decay, radically different from the managed European forests to which he was accustomed."[28] The clouds of mosquitoes didn't help either. Eventually, the expedition group arrived back at some cabins on a river, and de Tocqueville felt better. He reminded himself happily that this land was on the verge of "civilization and industry."[29]

In literature of the cutover period, Knott observes, aesthetic appreciation of the landscape tends to get overwhelmed by the thrill of its conquest. Exciting accounts of the loggers' lives describe danger faced with the manliest of manly skills, felling gigantic trees with hand tools, dragging them with oxen to the riverways that would float the logs on spring floods to the holding booms at river mouths. The ever-dramatic logjams made many a great story climax, with lumberjacks jumping atop logs and skillfully maneuvering them into motion—or strategically dynamiting them loose. Readers all over the country loved these tales of the heroic loggers, doing the dangerous and skilled labor necessary to build a nation. This is what people do: they come up with ingenious skills to fight back the threatening wilderness and make way for farms, towns, and easier lives.

Some of the literature also details the less heroic side of the cutover period: corrupt land speculators and scamming wildcat banks, for example.

The lumber work itself was extremely dangerous. The lumber museum at Hartwick Pines features a replica bunkhouse, which helpfully explains how men from a variety of backgrounds came to these camps for the winter, enduring physical injury, cold, loneliness, terrible food, bedbugs, and lice, all for meager pay. Lumberjack songs of the period, recorded by the great folk song scholar Alan Lomax, celebrate the comradery and skill of the loggers but also bewail the various miseries. In one song, a logger laments his troubles and hopes to God there is "no greater hell than Michigan-I-O."[30]

One scene in a 1909 novel by Stewart Edward White encapsulates well the paradox of this period in Michigan's history. The protagonist, an enterprising and noble logger named Orde, converses with his lady love, Carroll, after a walk from the beach through the woods. Carroll represents in the novel a sensitivity to the beauties of place, an empathetic sadness over what is being lost. As the couple survey a recently cut area of the woods, now nothing but burned stumps, Carroll calls her fiancé to account: "You do this," she accuses. In response, he turns her around to gaze instead at a pleasant, farmed valley and replies, "And this." He then explains, "That valley was once nothing but a pine forest—and so was all the southern part of the State, the peach belt and the farms. And for that matter Indiana too, and all the other forest states right out to the prairies. Where would we be now if we *hadn't* done that?"[31] Orde expresses here the fundamental principles White settlers largely agreed on, at least at first: the land was a collection of resources intended for their use. It was "nothing but a pine forest" till he and his ilk came along and made something of it. The burned stumps were therefore "a stage on the way to settled and agriculturally productive land."[32]

Orde was mistaken, it turned out. Over the next decades, in the late nineteenth and early twentieth centuries, Michigan residents began to realize that the lumber barons' philosophy—"cut out and get out"—left Michigan stripped of its forests and saddled with the costs of clean up and restoration. Cutover land typically reverted to government ownership when lumber companies refused to pay taxes and abandoned the land, moving ever west for fresh timber. The government then made the land available for aspiring farmer-settlers, but sandy forest soil turns out to be ill-suited for farming, as several decades of disappointed settlers and failed land claims proved. By the early twentieth century, many Michigan residents joined in the fledgling conservation and managed-forestry movements, striving to understand how to restore some form of what had been so quickly and ruthlessly destroyed.

Nevertheless, Orde's basic rationalization still sums up the deal we make with the planet and each other, doesn't it? Deforestation is only one example of how greedily we can destroy in the name of survival. We have to live, so we have to cut down trees. It's too bad, but there it is. Where would we be if we didn't? This is a powerful rationalization, because it's based on truth: all living beings alter their surroundings to survive. In those moments when we feel guilty about destructive human behavior, we have devised numerous effective ways to contain that guilt. We create noble-sounding nostalgia over what is lost, romanticizing the "vanishing Indian," for example, as Longfellow did in his enormously popular 1855 poem *The Song of Hiawatha*. Or we write fiction in which a female character ruefully points to a clear-cut wood, so her virile fiancé can justify his vocation and she can melt into his arms and become his wifely helpmeet, affirming the inescapable truth of human privilege to use nature as needed—not to mention White privilege to displace Indigenous people. We can always figure out a way to retell the story, to create mythologies that hide the violence and make it all sound noble. Manifest Destiny. The Doctrine of Discovery. Jobs. Technological progress. Economic growth.

Grief, Deconstruction, Preparation

As much as I lament the cutover now, I can hardly change the past. Instead, I have to admit: that whole period of history made my comfortable lifestyle possible today, here in this city where I live. I recently discovered the Michigan Natural Features Inventory website, featuring a series of maps that show what Michigan vegetation looked like circa 1800. So I have now figured out that 28th Street, before White settlement, was covered with beech-sugar maple and oak-hickory forest. My whole corner of the city was forested.[33] In only a few generations, progress swept through, leaving today only a pocket of trees here and there amid fine neighborhoods and one of the state's busiest commercial strips. We got here through a combination of well-meaning ingenuity and greedy rapaciousness rooted deep in White settler history, deep in the philosophies and practices of our economy, deep in the structures of the global economy inherited from past and current colonialisms.

The settling of the American continent and, more recently, the Great Acceleration hardly constitute an entirely new approach to the planet. These developments arise from the most ancient impulses. This is why the Great Work we face now is so hard.

In any time of vast cultural upheaval, people respond along a spectrum. Some people, usually a minority, readily transition toward new ideas. Most people try to stay put, adhering more or less to conventional wisdom. Others reach back, desperately clinging to what felt like a more secure past. When these different response styles crisscross, in ourselves and our communities, we feel inevitable cultural conflict and discomfort.[34] This seems to describe fairly well where we are today with regard to the climate crisis. Some people are truly "alarmed" about the climate crisis.[35] They're the scientists, cultural elders, activists, and leaders who are trying to persuade everyone else to adopt new ways of life on the planet. While we all live, inevitably, under the influence of dominant values and ideas, those of us in this emergent category are nevertheless trying to imagine what a "sustainable future" can mean—and if it's possible.

Other people fall in that middle group, largely operating with dominant values and practices. They're worried but unsure what to do or what to believe, so they go about their familiar ways. And then there are the resisters, dismissers, and deniers. As much as that resistance infuriates me, I do understand. Change is always hard, and there will be losses. No one enjoys a paradigm shift. This particular hinge point in history is especially terrifying because stakes are high across the globe. As Franciscan priest Richard Rohr observes, "*We all come to wisdom at the major price of both our innocence and our control.* Which means that few go there willingly. Disorder must normally be thrust upon us. Why would anyone choose it? I wouldn't."[36] Disorder has now been thrust upon us. As many people understood more viscerally during the Covid-19 pandemic, disorder brings fear of the uncertain future, as well as a recognition of our complicity in huge systems beyond our conception, beyond our control, beyond our ability to influence all that much. Worse, these are systems we are tempted to idolize.

If we imagine this uncomfortable between-time as a kind of Advent moment, then biblical stories and church traditions surrounding Advent might suggest some ways to live into this moment rather than deny or resist the truths it offers. An Advent moment is a place of disorder and bewilderment where apocalyptic unveiling has dissolved our illusions of innocence and control. As we've noticed, biblical stories tend to drive bewilderment into wilderness, not as a place to be conquered or merely contemplated, but as a picture of the work that gets done in refugia. Wilderness places become refugia—places where the work of grief, deconstruction, and preparation begins. Some things will need to be released, even destroyed, before something new gets built. The challenge in cultural and spiritual refugia is to discern what to destroy, what to rebuild.

At the risk of metaphorizing a landscape—at least for a moment—we can go back to our Advent prophet, John the Baptist, luring us into the desert wilderness. In the Bible, desert wilderness is where you go for a bracing lesson in how humans are *not* in charge. Actually, that's not a bad definition of wilderness in any time and place. As Barbara Brown Taylor says, "It's not wilderness unless there's something that can kill you."[37] Spiritually speaking, wilderness is where we empty ourselves in order to reckon honestly with God. John the Baptist knew that for the people of Israel, the desert lands had deep resonance as places of transition: leaving behind the old, preparing for the new. As a man zealous for God, fulfilling his role in the Gospel narrative, John depended on a long tradition of Israelite prophets, and of course on that defining wilderness experience of Israel's identity: the exodus out of slavery in Egypt.

It's always striking to me, reading the exodus story, how badly the Israelites behave in their desert wanderings. Pharaoh's dead army is still rotting on the Red Sea shore, the Israelites have barely put away the tambourines after singing triumph songs, and already they're complaining. Not even a chapter break separates the songs and the complaints. From then on, the wandering tribes complain so frequently it's almost comical. Who can blame them, though? Granted, the Lord brought them out of Egyptian slavery with a mighty hand and an outstretched arm, but now it's sand and heat and meager provisions as far as they can see. They're thrilled to be free, but then they start to grapple with loss. No wonder they tell Moses, over and over, they would rather go back to Egypt, where at least there was meat in the stew and they knew where the fresh water was.[38] No wonder they accuse God, more than once, of dragging them into the desert to die.

The fact is, God *did* bring them into the desert to die. They had to die to their slavish ways in order to be completely reconstructed into a free people. They had to give up idolatries and learn a whole new set of laws, a whole new way to encounter a mysterious God. They had to practice and learn from trial and much error. It took a long time, a whole generation. The elders who entered the desert did not come out. Only the young people made it, eventually, to the other side—because old ways are hard to give up, and trust is so hard to learn. Theologian Belden Lane remarks, "The God of Sinai is one who thrives on fierce landscapes, seemingly forcing God's people into wild and wretched climes where trust must be absolute."[39]

Deconstruction and reconstruction are never easy. God knows that wilderness is the place to do them, though, because there, you can no longer cling to your comforting illusions. It's the threat, the fear, that brings us to that necessary reckoning with the true God who burns away our idols. In the exodus story, we see the fear and grief in the Israelites' complaints. When it gets hard, they want to go back to what they know, even if it means going back to slavery. We might feel that too. Why not live the way we've always lived? Maybe we're slaves to the fossil fuel industry or something, but who cares? We've already destroyed the world. Let's just live it up until doomsday comes! This attitude is surprisingly common, and it's rooted in fear and grief.[40] We do not want to face what we are losing, and we cannot manage the fear, so we try to run back to Egypt. As Chuck DeGroat writes, "As much as we believe that God can redeem our journey through the wilderness, we should never underestimate its destructive force."[41] Wilderness *will* bring loss.

The loss and deprivations are difficult enough, but the uncertainty is almost worse. The Israelites flee into the desert mostly unprepared. Sure, ten plagues of warning lead up to the exodus, but when the time finally comes, they get one night to prepare a lamb, paint blood on their doorposts, and chow down their unleavened bread with their cloaks tucked into their belts, their sandals on, and their walking sticks in hand. They do not have time for seminars in desert survival techniques. And once they get to the desert, they face numerous changes of direction and weeks of waiting while Moses confers with God on the top of a mountain. They have only uncertain notions of where they are headed or how long it will take to get there or what enemies they might face on the way. They are expected to trust God's guidance and provision on a need-to-know basis—a pillar of fire, a pillar of cloud, such infuriating mystery. It's no surprise that during Moses's second, lengthy mountaintop campout with this inexplicable

God, the people down below beg for something tangible, a god they can see, maybe a nice golden calf. A fertility god—now *that* is a familiar way to cope. *That* they understand.

Similarly, right now in our own wilderness between-time, we might feel as if we are floundering, unprepared and full of uncertainty. Deconstruction is a painful mess. Sure, we've heard warnings for decades about climate change and unsustainable growth and pollution, but most of us haven't been paying much attention. Now we're rushing into the wilderness barely prepared and with none of the right skills. We affluent Westerners don't know how to wait or suffer or trust day to day. Our life skills are adapted to a global consumer economy. We can use an ATM and buy life insurance, but growing our own food or sharing with neighbors—those are more of a challenge. God, meanwhile, seems more mysterious than ever. Doesn't God bless us with prosperity if we are virtuous? Isn't the growth economy God's latest, greatest intention for humankind? I thought God promised never to destroy the earth again after the whole Noah episode. Or maybe God has given up on humans altogether, disgusted with us after all we've done. How long will we be in this scary place? Will we ever get out?

Throughout the wilderness wanderings, the Israelites are not sure they will survive. Many of them do not. On the way, though, they find that the desert has become a refugium. This is where the life of their people will endure in this time of crisis and transition. This is how they, as a people, will get through to the other side. God provides water from a rock, quail, manna. At first their desert sojourn seems like a temporary subsistence lifestyle, but eventually the people figure out there's more going on. This is where they will build new capacities to prepare for their life beyond the refugium.

The blueprint for these new capacities comes in the law given at Sinai. In the law, God outlines for them how to live in a more just and peaceful community, in a relationship of love and trust with God. Eventually, God gives further instructions on how to build a tabernacle, a place for God's presence. God wishes to dwell among them in a combination of the tangible and the ineffable so that these people might grasp God's nearness as well as God's otherness. The tabernacle's design beautifully recapitulates the story of creation, with each of its areas signifying one of the days of creation. As the high priest moves from the outer court to the holy of holies at the tabernacle's heart and then back out to the people, he traces a pattern through those successive days of creation. His journey thus represents the unmaking and remaking of creation: deconstruction and reconstruction, the pattern of renewal always at the heart of God's redemptive purposes.[42] The tabernacle becomes an embodiment of another lesson God wants to teach: I am not like other gods; *I* am your refugium.

Biologists might compare the desert wanderings to an *ex situ* refugium. The people of Israel seek a new place to start anew. In human terms, I would call this a pilgrimage refugium. The destination is important, but so is the process of moving toward it, the transformation that happens along the way. In those desert wanderings, we might say that God is leading the Israelites through a process of grief, deconstruction, and preparation. God is reshaping this "stiff-necked" cluster of tribes into a people of refugia. Not only are they learning to depend on God's merciful shelter amid crisis, but they are themselves becoming a refugium through which the world can be blessed and renewed. They become a microcounterculture that will carry the ways of justice and mercy to the world: *tikkun olam*, as the Jews say. Christians believe Israel became the beloved root, the stump of Jesse from which the Redeemer comes. The whole arc of the exodus narrative reminds us that refugia in the wilderness are places of painful deconstruction but also of preparation for what God is making new.

The exodus stories lie in the background of John the Baptist's calls to repentance and preparation in that first week of Advent. After that first week, the church's tradition draws us back into John's origin story, to remind us that if we want to see God showing up at hinge points in history, we should look to the margins. Just as with the enslaved Israelites, God opposes empire with the small, the hidden, the seemingly powerless. In the gospel stories, God comes to a young girl and an old woman, members of a colonized people in some Judean backwater. The power of God enables both Mary and Elizabeth to conceive. To underline God's upside-down ways, God silences even the good-hearted priest Zechariah, so the two women can speak out for a while. According to the Gospel of Luke, Mary understands completely what God is up to. She perceives—because she knows the history of Israel—that God works with the small and hidden to overturn the great kingdoms of the earth. In her feisty, political exaltation, she sings:

He has brought down the powerful from their thrones,
  and lifted up the lowly;
he has filled the hungry with good things,
  and sent the rich away empty. (Luke 1:52–53)

God maneuvers around the powerful and nurtures refugia where no one is looking. The Advent stories layer concentric circles of refugia: the people of Israel amid the Roman Empire, ordinary women in the rural countryside, the babies hidden in the women's bodies.

Advent emphasizes the sharp distinctions between the dominant powers and what God is bringing about. One ancient tradition of Advent prayer, the O Antiphons, invites the people of God to anticipate the coming of Christ—both at Christmas and at the end of history—by praying with seven scriptural names for Christ, all from the prophet Isaiah: Wisdom, Lord, Root of Jesse, Key of David, Radiant Dawn, King, Emmanuel. On each of the seven days leading up to Christmas, the faithful pray a prayer based on one of the names. By prompting the faithful to name these names, this prayer tradition shapes our grief and instructs our longing. The prayer for the first day names Christ as Sapientia, Wisdom, drawing on the Hebrew wisdom traditions:

O Wisdom,
You come forth from the mouth of the Most High.
You hold all things in the universe together with strength and
  sweetness.
O come to teach us the way of prudence.[43]

This prayer trains us to expect a God who orders this world with strength and sweetness, like a skilled and gracious householder. Anyone who has run a household understands that doing so well requires strength and discipline but also graciousness and beauty: spaces arranged for comfort, maybe the smell of baking bread, soaps in the soap dish for guests, neatly made beds. The prayer reminds us that the world is not a wilderness to conquer with the spirit of domination but a household of life, a household that divine Wisdom cares for with strength and sweetness.

Our time of bewilderment can become a pilgrimage refugium, even if we are not literally migrating. God is drawing us into the wilderness as a pilgrimage, to become people of refugia. This journey is uncomfortable and even terrifying, but it's also a time when we can be honest about what we grieve, what we long for. We can confront the question of whether we will allow our lust for dominance and empire to be deconstructed. Can we relinquish our idols and prepare for a world ordered by strength and sweetness?

Nor Thorns Infest the Ground

When my family moved into our current home in 2010, we were thrilled: with two teens, a preteen, and a dog, we were tired of the cramped quarters in our former home, and this new place felt like a palace. The house sits on a roughly triangular one-third-acre lot, wide along the street and backing into a tiny wooded area. I mean tiny: maybe fourteen yards by thirty yards. When we arrived, along the entire perimeter of the side- and backyards ran a dense hedge of dark, leafy shrubbery maybe 15 feet high—about 160 linear feet of it. "Nice privacy," people would remark. Sure, but we felt like the princess in the fairy tale, our castle encased in briars.

We quickly realized that managing this hedge was beyond our skills. We tried sheering it back, but that only encouraged it. It had already completely entangled three gnarly old hawthorn trees and was threatening to swallow four spruces too. It leaned ominously over the slim side lawn and fully shaded the little terraced plantings in the back.

Eventually, I invited over one of the landscaping guys from my university. Henry advised us on how to renovate the neglected plantings around the base of the house, and he also gave us the bad news about that hedge: it was buckthorn. Common buckthorn (*Rhamnus cathartica*) is a non-native invasive species. People planted it in their yards around here in the 1980s to create privacy screens. It worked great: it sets leaves early in the spring, drops leaves late in the fall, grows fifteen feet or more tall, and spreads like mad. It outcompetes everything else for sun and soil nutrients. In fact, some theorize that it's an allelopathic species, which is to say, it adjusts soil pH in order to make the soil unfriendly to any other plants. It's a bully, in other words, and like all bullies, it's a pain to get rid of. It drops a zillion shiny, black berries in the fall, which can lie happily in the soil for years. You can kill every stem you've got, and a whole new crop will shoot up the next spring from seeds held in the ground over the winter.

"Get rid of it," Henry advised. "And keep at it. It will take a few years." Hoo boy. Now we had a deconstruction project. I started sitting on the little balcony deck off the three-season room in the back, surveying my domain, eyeing the buckthorn with a steely gaze and daydreaming about chain saws. How could I uproot this enemy surrounding me? All we had was an old lawn mower and some dull loppers, and these buckthorn stems were everywhere, ranging from little patches of sprouts to stems eight inches in diameter, trying to pose as innocent trees.

I called in reinforcements. Henry had suggested that one of our restoration ecology experts at the university, Michael, could give good advice and maybe even provide some student labor through the university's Plaster Creek Stewards program. Michael came over and agreed with Henry completely: get rid of it. Our neighborhood was situated in the Plaster Creek watershed, and buckthorn was one of the many problems the Stewards project had been working on for years in their effort to restore healthy native plant diversity suited to this region. I was a little surprised Michael would be so vehement about killing the stuff. Weren't ecology people supposed to cherish every living thing? Apparently not. Michael and I had a hilarious conversation one afternoon about how, theologically speaking, buckthorn was totally depraved. He had no problem chopping it down and spraying it with an herbicide. Don't worry, he assured me, they mixed the herbicide themselves to break down quickly, so it wouldn't linger in the soil.

Thus began Operation Buckthorn-B-Gone, our own private cutover. I was learning my first big lesson in ecological paradox and ambiguity: heedless resource extraction involves destruction, but so does ecosystem restoration. The difference between the bad kind of destruction and the good kind is a complex alchemy of knowledge, intention, and scale. So we launched headlong into several sessions of chainsawing and ax chopping and one extremely long, hot day of feeding gigantic stems into an oily, chugging old wood chipper. I have to say, shoving stems into that chipper was oddly satisfying, if obnoxiously loud. It felt good to start conquering my wilderness; in fact, I rather relished putting my ax to the roots of these trees.

I can't even remember now how many hours this initial demolition process took—or how many dollars to pay student helpers and rent the chipper. I do remember that on one of the early days of chopping, we had a few high school–age helpers through the Plaster Creek Steward's internship program. They were hacking away with axes along the property line, and out comes my elderly neighbor from the other side of the hedge. I had never met him before. I didn't even know what existed on the other side of that hedge. Well, he was not happy. I could tell it didn't help that the high school kids wielding axes had brown skin. He started questioning them aggressively, as if they were delinquents invading the neighborhood just to chop down people's trees. I hustled over to intervene, sweaty and dirt smudged, trying to explain what was happening. My neighbor was only barely placated, never mind that this hedge was on my side of the property line. I apologized for the surprise and tried to explain about non-native invasives. He eyed the youths suspiciously.

After that, I sent letters around to all the neighbors explaining what I was doing and why, and what I planned to do once the buckthorn was gone: beautiful new plantings, I promised. Nevertheless, my elderly neighbor never forgave me for *not asking him first*. I've found out in a few subsequent encounters that he's a bitter person who can't be pleased or satisfied, certainly not by an uppity lady neighbor.

I don't know his story or why he was so angry about an altered view from his yard, which he never used and only minimally cared for. I suspect he just didn't like not being in control. I do understand that part: change is uncomfortable. We experienced that too. Once we had cleared all the big stuff, the whole yard felt bare and exposed. I could see right through to all my backyard neighbors' yards. I wasn't sure at first whether I liked it. Did we make a mistake? Well, we couldn't go back now. We had paid the cost and let go of something we knew was destructive. Now it was time to work toward something new.

Eastern Cottonwood
Populus Deltoides

February
Grand Rapids, Michigan

Morning, West Window

The sky feels oddly bright, considering the snow falling in dense, clustered flakes. The wind gusts at intervals, whirling flakes into powder, snowglobing our backyard vista. For a moment, a cloud of white obscures the trees, the neighbors' backyards, the whole world. Then the wind settles, the world returns. Hide-and-seek.

I am warm and dry, still in my pajamas, instructed by traffic managers to stay home. Most of us are hunkering today, cozy in our elaborate shelters, padding about our houses in delight or dismay. Our deadlines and obligations succumb to windchills and snowdrifts. We are forced to stay still.

Meanwhile, the wind frolics. "What a fine blizzard we have going here!" it says. The birds play along. Our resident sparrows, fluffed into silly sparrow puffs, flit from their beloved brush pile to the neighbor's coldly empty feeders. Three hefty crows take turns at a surveillance post on the topmost curve of a shepherd hook, flapping to the ground as needed to contend with the chirrupy sparrows.

The poor Juneberry tree, creaking with age, has lost some height this week. A daredevil squirrel likes to leap from the roof onto its delicate upper branches, rudely snapping them. The branch ends dangle.

Afternoon, North Window

I should be at my desk, Getting Things Done, but the blizzard mesmerizes me, drawing me to the window again. The river birches are up to their knees in drifts, frosted up one side of their crumpled-paper trunks. The viburnum shrubs, stripped bare for winter, look like sprays of toothpicks stuck in frosting. Hairlike tufts of dried switchgrass poke above the snow, trembling.

The Norway spruces, meanwhile, lumped with heavy slabs of snow frosting, bend their bushy arms, yielding graciously to the weight. In

49

the gray light, their needles look black—no, blue—no, green. Darkest green. Darkest green-blue-black.

I slept well last night, and my desk work summons. But never mind. The trees beckon me to yield, wait, rest. I feel myself sinking into a nap.

Sunset, East Window

Frost feathers the lower windowpanes. Just outside the window, the dogwood's generous branches arc downward, then turn up at the ends, as if the tree is holding out open hands, fingertipped with incipient buds. Each branch is laden with loaves of snow, each twig-hand holds a crystalled marshmallow.

The snow continues to fall, glittery crystals filling the air. Driveways and walks have disappeared under a smooth, radiant layer. Gray sky, gray-white snow, umber tree silhouettes, the glittering world sinks into blue.

Evening, East Window

Now the neighbors' porch lights glow gold. Gray-blues deepen into violets. Wind ruffles the dogwood branches, but the twig-hands cling to their crusted puffs.

I turn to desk work under a lamp in a darkened room, keeping half an eye on the violet sky receding to blackness. Later, when our windows mostly reflect our lamps, we head downstairs and turn on the TV. We let the dog out one more time. She doesn't go far, stepping through drifts to find the nearest accommodating spot. She slips eagerly back inside, a blast of frigid air sweeping in behind her.

We ourselves have not set even one foot outside since last evening. We are safe and snug with our central heat, our insulating windows, our weather-stripped doors. We are grateful. We crawl under the covers to sleep.

Dawn, Southeast Window

The sky glows with palest blue, the first hint of storm clearing in days. A neighbor comes out, bundled head to toe, to start his truck. He sets it running, then dashes back inside, emerging a few minutes later with a travel mug and bag, off to work.

Now a faint pink radiance silhouettes the rooftops. Now pale peach. The sky rejoices! I look away for a few minutes, and when I look back, a bright orb pierces the spruce stand: light!

The air glitters with a last shimmer of snowfall, but the day stirs new and bright. Never mind the still-frigid air: our confinement is over! Neighbors appear with shovels, plotting their escape from snowbound homes.

Morning

The sun blazes, rousing the world to color, shadow, sparkle. Light pours through all the windows. Tasks set aside seem urgent again. Work thoughts come streaming back, days grind back into motion. We have paused, as bidden. Now we move again.

We pack on the layers and burst outside, determined. Gather those shovels, lean your weight on the handle, shove, lift, pile. The end of the driveway is a Hadrian's Wall of hard-packed snow, thanks to the city's perfunctory overnight snowplow pass. We excavate. We dig out the mailbox. We persist in the work.

It takes an hour. When we come back in the house, stamping and huffing, unwinding scarves and shedding snow-crusted layers, we are exuberant.

Chapter 2

From Alienation to Kinship

Day after day they pour forth speech;
night after night they reveal knowledge.
—PSALM 19:2 NIV

One winter evening, sitting in the corner chair in my bedroom, I was startled out of a quiet moment of meditation when an owl started hooting outside the window. It was obviously an owl, but I didn't know what kind. "Hoot-hoot-hoo-hoooo," he said. Or she. How would I know? I scrambled for my phone and looked up owls likely to be lurking in Michigan, and after listening to an assortment of unearthly screeches, I came upon the lovely barred owl. Birders have decided that the barred owl's call sounds like this: "Who cooks for you? Who cooks for you-allllllllll?" Sure enough.

After that, I started musing on raptors. In my imagination, owls and hawks perched on my shoulders—gently, of course, as they have knife-like talons—and ruffled their wings and bobbed along as I hiked across open meadows in my mind. I don't know why. Apparently, some folk traditions associate owl sightings with imminent death. But my imaginary shoulder riders seemed companionable enough.

Months passed, and that spring, I started doing something I had never really done before: listening to birds. (This was before the Covid-19 pandemic inspired widespread interest in birding.) With the windows open to the warm, sweet spring air, I couldn't concentrate, because birds chittered and chirruped and whistled and whooped in the little wooded area behind my house. Suddenly, I needed to know who these creatures were and what they were saying. Were they louder this spring? I had never found birds so distracting. They were driving me crazy.

That was when I finally realized how ignorant I am. I've lived in this climate and latitude most of my life, surrounded by these fellow creatures going about their quick, fluttery lives, and I know almost nothing about them, not even how to recognize their voices. I could identify a crow's obnoxious caw. I knew the blue jay's squawk and the mourning dove's moan. I could even identify a male pheasant's show-offy declaration: *roik! roik! fludda fludda fludda*. But other ordinary citizens of my neighborhood—the robins, cardinals, sparrows, chickadees, goldfinches—I saw any number of them on any given day and had never listened carefully enough to learn their avian grammar. I had no idea who was saying something, let alone what they were saying. "Stay away"? "Mate with me"? "I'm a happy birdy"? Beyond appreciating the cheerful sounds of birdies-in-general, I had spent most of my life considering their layer of reality unimportant to me. We don't bother to understand what we don't deem important.

That was a few years ago. Since then, I've been introducing myself to my avian neighbors. I have feeders now and identification apps on my phone. I've learned a lot in a short time, but wow—it's hard. For instance, early on I managed to identify a tufted titmouse. It took me a long time to recognize its jaunty whistle: *peter peter peter peter*. Bird books and apps typically help you identify a bird by what it looks like. Well, what if I can't see it? What if I can only hear it? You can't easily search the internet for a whistle. So to identify my *peter*ing neighbor, I searched for birds I thought might be hanging around in my backyard, listened to their various calls on YouTube, and finally found a birdsong that was sort of like what I was hearing, though the song was a slightly different pitch and a different number of *peters*. My bird actually sounded to me more like *heebie heebie heebie jeebie*. Still a tufted titmouse? Well, it turns out each species has several calls and songs, they even have regional dialects, and each bird is an individual. This is complicated, and I'm like a two-year-old learning ABCs. I suppose bird knowledge comes only with patient experience and personal teachers. If there's wisdom to be found among the birds, it's slow wisdom, the kind that takes years of humble apprenticeship to develop.

Why did I suddenly care? I've thought about that question a lot. I wonder if the owls and hawks and cardinals and sparrows seem to beckon me these days to hear their languages because I'm exhausted by human words. Words are the water I swim all year. I read them by the bushel and beguile students into reading them. I write words and wrestle with words and prod students to compose words, and then I evaluate their words. I sing words and listen to them and pray them at church. Our political life is a roaring waterfall of words, much of it stinking and toxic.

Maybe the birds are calling me out of the human-words echo chamber entirely. This comes as a relief, because whatever those birds are saying, cynical skepticism is not required to listen to it. No moral discernment needed, no political judgment. The birds do not lie; neither are they corrupt. Their conversations are refreshingly edifying. The birds are just being birds.

So with an owl on one shoulder and a hawk on the other, in my imagination anyway, I've made a little start. I suppose I'm following where Jesus's finger pointed when he advised that we consider the lilies and look to the birds of the air (Matt 6:26–28). Or maybe I'm with essayist Amy Leach, whose sly little reverie titled "God" observes that hoopoes and bats and ferrets never say that divine name, though people say it incessantly, perhaps too often. People's words are like stones, writes Leach, but creatures are God's words, and sometimes, when we wish to hear God speak, we need to "escape out the back door."[1]

Nature-Deficit Disorder

My ignorance of birdsong is hardly unusual. It's only one symptom of a larger problem: disconnection from the living systems in which we humans are embedded. This disconnection is the result of human ingenuity and affluence, of course. We've figured out how to protect ourselves from many natural threats in order to survive and thrive. We can afford to be ignorant, even alienated from the more-than-human world, or at least we imagine we can. However, our ignorance and alienation have now become dangerous. To become people of refugia, one of our first tasks is to repair this alienation.

Biologists define refugia as "habitats that components of biodiversity retreat to, persist in and can potentially expand from under changing environmental conditions."[2] Refugia, as we have seen, presuppose some sort of crisis. They presume what biologists call "disturbance" and thus the need for adaptations in order to survive that disturbance. If we take biological refugia as our model for persisting in this era of crisis and upheaval, then we have to consider the adaptations we must make—in our actions, yes, but more foundationally in our deepest assumptions, even our unconscious mythologies. For people of faith, repairing our alienation from the more-than-human creation takes on theological significance. Some theological concepts we may have assumed were settled and obvious have actually contributed to this alienation. So we have some difficult work to do, reexamining these theological distortions and striving to correct them as part of our refugia adaptation.

In 1998, two botanist-educators introduced to the botanical science community the term *plant blindness*. The botanists, James Wandersee and Elizabeth Schussler, wanted to call attention to the lack of plant learning in North American schools and homes.[3] Then in 2005, journalist Richard Louv published a book that popularized the term *nature-deficit disorder*.[4] He observed that children are spending less time outside than in previous generations, and he associated this shift with a number of ills, such as the rise in ADHD. Both terms have since come under some criticism. *Blindness* has an ableist tinge, for example, while using the term *disorder* suggests a medical diagnosis, which isn't the intention. Nevertheless, these provocative terms have caught on, probably because, for both children and adults, they describe an alienation from "nature" that a lot of us feel. We can easily ignore trees, plants, birds, fields, rivers, and lakes, considering them nothing more than a background to our existence. We don't necessarily need to pay much attention day to day. A lot of us can't tell a hickory from a beech, and why should we? Why would it matter? Urban life, an industrial foodshed, and a consumer lifestyle insulate us from the need to know much about birds or plants or geographic formations.

More pernicious are the systems that deny some people contact with nature and instead force them to bear the costs of our pollution and waste. People who live in more stressed urban areas may have regular contact with only a few street trees, window boxes of flowers, and maybe a small city park.[5] Or worse, they're living in areas directly adjacent to the industrial waste, runoff, or air pollution the rest of us have the power to avoid.[6] The field of environmental justice, rooted in the civil rights movement and Black liberation theology, has now convincingly documented that people of color are disproportionately more likely to live near heavy manufacturing facilities, oil refineries, chemical plants, and waste dumps.[7] They are "frontline communities"—on the front lines of impacts from the poisons that make our whole planet sick. Reasons for environmental racism are rooted deep in American history, in racist zoning practices such as redlining for example, and the legacy of this injustice persists. People who do not have the means to live in healthier, wealthier neighborhoods instead suffer from increased rates of cancers and respiratory illnesses. Toxic industries have found ways to avoid the responsibility of cleaning up what they do to the air, land, and water by making sure their neighbors do not have the cultural power and financial means to fight them. This is called "toxic colonialism" (probably a redundant term), and it plagues urban as well as rural areas around the world. Powerful corporations intimidate and harass those who resist, while engaging in "economic blackmail"—threatening to take away jobs unless people keep quiet about the ruination of the land and water around the operation. This is an especially pernicious form of purposeful, systematic alienation from nature.[8]

Privileged or not, few of us in an affluent society survive by nature-related knowledge or skills. Only a small number of us depend on our own farming or hunting or animal raising for a living or even for supplemental sustenance. Hardly any of us *need* to know how our food gets from soil to table. That's all conveniently hidden. We don't *need* to know the right way to chop and stack wood in order to survive the winter. That's what forced-air central heat is for, and thank goodness. So alienation leads to ignorance, which creates more alienation and more ignorance.

Even so, people commonly feel a longing to connect with natural things. We feel the alienation, in fact, *because* we also feel that longing to connect. If we have the means, we might practice gardening, birding, hunting, fishing, and hobby farming, perhaps for fun or family tradition, perhaps to supplement our way of life and soothe our modern aches. We enjoy a stroll outside, a jog through the park, some camping or hiking, maybe a vacation trip to a national park. During the Covid-19 pandemic, many people found themselves suddenly drawn to outdoor pursuits, out of cabin fever and the despondence brought about by quarantining. Some of us have tried all along to cultivate a little knowledge about geography or creatures we care about. For the most part, though, we're freed by an industrial and consumer system—or captured by it—into a protective distance from the rest of the living world.

Unfortunately, common ignorance about earth systems and other creatures has made it that much easier to overtax and endanger the physical basis of our existence—to threaten our biosphere with our technosphere, as Thomas Berry put it. Our citizen ignorance turns out to be a high-stakes problem, because we care about only what we perceive, and we perceive only what we have been taught to perceive. Or maybe the problem lies in what we have been taught to unperceive. After all, little children are typically fascinated by other creatures. Even something as humble as a caterpillar shimmying across a sidewalk can thrill a three-year-old. To little kids, pets are people too, the oak tree in the yard gets its own name, and the demise of a houseplant is met with genuine sorrow. Small children often attend respectfully to the *being*ness of other creatures. They demonstrate what naturalist and writer Edward O. Wilson calls *biophilia*—"the innate tendency to focus on life and lifelike processes." We long from childhood to "explore and affiliate with life."[9] Wilson is among many who have surmised that this biophilia is an innate human quality. Somewhere along the way, though, we moderns learn to leave that connection behind. It serves the interests of a consumer economy if we don't pay much attention, if we are more interested, say, in the new movie theater than in the wetland destroyed to build it.

In this time of transition, one of the things that needs to die is our alienation from the more-than-human world. I wonder if relinquishing our alienation requires not only adult savvy and reeducation but also a return to that childlike spirit, where everything in the universe is imbued with wonder.

What Is Nature?

What is "nature," anyway? I've been using the term sloppily, falling into a presumed, working definition of "whatever isn't human or human built." That's a false definition, since humans are inarguably part of "nature." We speak of ourselves in a category apart from all other entities on the planet, because we are indeed different in important ways and because the categories are convenient for the sake of discussion. But imagining ourselves as entirely distinctive and superior is the old and dangerous slippage at the root of our current crises. We could call this assumption "hierarchical anthropocentrism" if we don't mind spending some syllables. Hierarchical anthropocentrism is the idea that humans are at the center of all things and more important than anything else. Questioning hierarchical anthropocentrism requires some uncomfortable humility and some rethinking of common terms. When we speak of *nature*, we could say instead *nonhuman world* or even *other-than-human world*. But those terms still imply that humans are the norm against which everything else is the "non" or "other." So we fumble with ungainly terms like *more-than-human world*, which is designed precisely to counter hierarchical anthropocentrism. *More-than-human world* has the sly advantage of implying, just for a moment, that there's something "more" than us in the world. This is all part of a struggle to rethink "nature" and our proper relationship with it, whatever "it" is. This rethinking is happening across a range of contexts, but those of us in the Christian tradition must reckon with the accusation that Christianity has been a chief contributor to our human arrogance problem.

Since the 1970s, any theological reflection on the more-than-human world must include grappling with the challenge posed by historian Lynn White Jr. His 1967 essay "The Historical Roots of Our Ecological Crisis" places the blame for our then-current, now-much-worse ecological woes squarely on bad theology.[10] The essay sketches out a brief history of Christian ideas in the West, especially ideas about humans being made in the image of God and about our "dominion" over the earth. White observes how those ideas got simplified and then combined with the rise of science and industrial technology, and he concludes that a few fundamental theological ideas about the relationships among God, humans, and nature have been used to bolster attitudes of domination and exploitation that have, in turn, led to our global crisis. In other words, Christian ideas enabled a distortion that now nearly everyone shares. We are, White claims, relentlessly anthropocentric. He observes, "Our science and technology have grown out of Christian attitudes toward man's relation to nature which are almost universally held not only by Christians and neo-Christians but also by those who fondly regard themselves as post-Christians. Despite Copernicus, all the cosmos rotates around our little globe. Despite Darwin, we are *not*, in our hearts, part of the natural process. We are superior to nature, contemptuous of it, willing to use it for our slightest whim." No matter what we've learned about how tiny we are in the universe, or how much DNA we share with other creatures, we cannot shed our self-centeredness and arrogance. We are happy to abuse nature because we think of ourselves as distinct from it, in power over it. And White alleges that "Christianity bears a huge burden of guilt" for this.[11]

Well, the essay hit a nerve, unsurprisingly, among both theologians and ecologists, so that anyone writing about ecology in the last fifty years—religious or not—has felt the need to respond to the essay, qualifying White's analysis, insisting that post-Enlightenment secularism is actually to blame, reexamining and evaluating the Christian theological tradition, or otherwise trying to figure out to what extent White was right or wrong. When I finally read the essay myself, I expected to encounter an old curmudgeon lobbing generalizations, even plausible ones, as a religious skeptic. Instead, I was astonished to discover that White refers to himself as "a churchman." It turns out that White is critiquing Christianity from the inside. And at the end of the essay, he essentially calls for theological reform. If we're going to address the ecological crisis, he writes, Christians are going to have to "find a new religion, or rethink our old one."[12] In a brief final flourish, he champions Saint Francis as a possible model with which to begin that rethinking.

Sometimes a curmudgeonly statement is exactly what we need to get people moving on a big and important reform movement. White gave ammunition to critics of Christianity, but he also set off a rash of soul-searching among Christian thinkers, and that's a good thing. Obviously, a five-page essay is not going to account for every nuance of a two-thousand-year-old faith tradition, but most of us don't live long in the land of nuance. We operate by simplified, reductive ideas whose roots in history are long forgotten. And we typically have swirling in our heads several ideas, some of them contradictory, and we draw from this swirl as needed, depending on the occasion.

When it comes to humans and "nature," the foundational ideas that operate in the Christian contexts I've known—what we say in worship, what we're taught, and how various Christian groups actually behave in the world—might be boiled down to an assortment of nature notions like this:

Nature is

a. a temporary bunch of clay from which humans eventually evolve / get rescued / get redeemed into spiritual beings;
b. the scenery against which humanity's redemption drama gets played out;
c. another book, besides Scripture, that we can read to learn about God;
d. goods and services God supplied for our use, including aesthetic enjoyment and "recreation"; or
e. fellow beings in the household of creation.

I find it curious how we move among these ideas as needed. When someone dies after a long struggle with cancer, you might hear saccharine evocations of the first option: "At least she's free of that body. God needed another angel!" Christians are supposed to believe in the resurrection of the body—we profess that in the Apostles' Creed, our oldest, most ecumenical creed. Even so, it's surprising how often Christians imagine an afterlife of disembodied spirits. An entirely spiritual afterlife is one way to make sense of the evident facts before us, that dead bodies end up in graves or ash-filled urns.

Most of the time, though, I think we operate with the second option: nature is the scenery, and we are the stars of the show. God is the ruler of history, and history is about *us*. In church, we're too busy thinking and singing and praying about the dynamics of human salvation to ponder the scenery much, except perhaps in a hymn of praise on a summer Sunday. Meanwhile, the third option—nature as revelatory book—serves as a helpful theological support for Christians studying science as well as for people enjoying the outdoors. Option d is a tricky one. On the one hand, nature-for-our-use validates our aesthetic response to beauty, allowing us to ponder a starry sky and ascribe that glory to God: "How great thou art." We might also cite c and d as the reasons we ought to care for creation. But d has also, historically and today, been used to justify our consumer habits. If nature is for our use, then why not use it however we please?

That last perspective, that humans are fellow beings in a whole, vast household of creation, is the one I've come to believe is the fundamental scriptural witness. This is the principle against which all the other nature notions must be tested. But I infrequently hear this last perspective lifted up, celebrated, or pondered—not until recently, and then only among ecotheologians or nature writers, many of whom are people of other faiths or no faith.

All the ideas in my list can be derived to some extent from Scripture, and thus all of them are present in the Christian theological tradition. Since this leads to confusions, inconsistencies, and the troubles Lynn White warned against, many philosophers and faith leaders agree that it's time for a theological housecleaning. It's time to reinterrogate our nature notions and reprioritize. One way to think about the history of Christian theology, and we're relying on sweeping generalizations here, is that, until the early modern period, the Christian church—and other faiths, too, to some extent—focused its reflection on divine-human relations. In Christianity, that meant, for example, establishing the ecumenical creeds and sorting out the niceties of atonement theory. With the European Renaissance, the Reformation, and then the Enlightenment, attention shifted slowly toward human-human relations, with a growing emphasis on individual rights, political theory, and social equality (at least aspirationally). No one imagines that the work on human-human relationships is done—far from it. But we also have urgent business now on the human-nature axis. All three axes of reflection—among God, humans, and nature—are interrelated, and we can't neglect any one of them. In fact, focusing on the human-nature relationship has helped amplify voices of marginalized people, and thus actually aids in the work to repair our human-human abuses. Reflection on the human-nature relationship is now a global, interfaith project. So Christians, too, are now called to reckon with our "ambiguous" theological tradition and seek the deeper understanding that God is asking of us.[13]

Glory to God in the Lowest

We might find a promising entry point into that theological reckoning by reflecting on a doctrine distinctive to Christianity: the incarnation. During the Christmas season of the church year, Christians ponder the mystery of God uniting Godself to this world of created matter, this world God loves.

When I was a kid, we had a shabby old nativity scene, or "crèche," that my mother hauled out every year at Christmastime. The figures came from two or three different sets. Some were painted in soft colors, and others had gotten so chipped that my dad spray-painted them gold to cover their flaws. They varied in scale so that the shepherds towered over poor Mary and Joseph, and the shaggy gold donkey looked as if it could snack on the sheep. I loved to arrange the animals around the haloed infant, fetchingly posed and nestled in matted "hay" on the wobbly little wooden manger. My older brother and I would carry out clandestine battles over the exact arrangement of the figures. He would sneak into the living room and move the figures around, and then I would come back later and reposition them the way I wanted them. I liked to take the pink-robed angel with dove-gray wings and balance her on the stable's pointed rooftop so that she could preside precariously over the crowd scene below.

Everyone loves a good nativity scene, but the whole tradition is a fancy. The nativity narrative in Luke mentions the manger, of course, but says nothing specific about animals being present. (The ox and donkey may appear in our manger scenes thanks to Isa 1:3.) Luke tells us that shepherds show up to see the baby but does not mention sheep trotting along with them. And of course, the magi do not visit the manger at all. They arrive a couple years later to offer their exotic gifts to a toddler. And anyway, they're in Matthew, not Luke. Also, sadly, there is no mention anywhere of angels hovering over the manger scene. As far as Luke is concerned, the angels appear only to terrify the shepherds abiding in the fields by night. After a birth announcement and choral performance, the angels recede into the starry sky.

Even without specific biblical warrant, though, the nativity scene tradition offers abiding wisdom. According to legend, Saint Francis was the first one to stage a live nativity scene in 1223. The tradition quickly caught on, and the crèche, whether with carved figures or live sheep, is a beloved element in Christmas celebrations worldwide. This suggests there's something in it we need to pay attention to, and indeed, the crèche actually portrays a powerful theological truth. Gathering an international cluster of humans and a whole crowd of creatures at the manger reminds us that the birth of Jesus is not just about getting Jesus strategically stationed on earth so that later he can die on the cross and save human souls. Instead, the birth of the child is the focal point of God's communion with the whole of creation. This is the deep wisdom of the doctrine of incarnation: the person Jesus is the crucial stitch uniting heaven and earth, spiritual and physical, entirely and forever. All creation communes with God in and through the person of Jesus. Maybe the livestock do not require atonement for their personal sins, but in a very real sense, Jesus came for the ox and sheep and donkeys too.[14]

My motley old nativity scene, it turns out then, made perfect sense. Shabby, broken, assorted. A refugium. Amid the long crisis of the universe's history, a diverse little microcosm forms around that manger. The refugium of Mary's womb expands into that tiny shelter, and from there the whole ecosystem of the cosmos is transformed in every direction—from the highest to the lowest in all creation, backward and forward through time. The incarnation, as Christianity has come to understand it, reveals that the essence of divine energy—divine love—is never separate from the damp cave or the grassy hillside or the sheep or angels or birthing mother but is "with us," all of us. Even before any atoning crucifixion event, Jesus is eternally united to matter and energy and the vast processes of death and renewal embedded in the created world. Jesus as God-with-us confirms how God loved the world into being, holds it together, and reveals the transformed fulfillment toward which the whole creation is headed.

How an ordinary human baby could also be the very person of God is both the difficulty and the genius of the Christian faith. We call Jesus "Christ," the anointed one, to express the dimension of his person that transcends the teacher of Galilee and is, as Paul writes in the great hymn of Colossians 1:15 NIV, "the image of the invisible God, the firstborn over all creation." All creation is the emphasis here. Ta panta, in the Greek, "all things." Christ is "before all things, and in him all things hold together. . . . For in him all the fullness of God was pleased to dwell, and through him God was pleased to reconcile to himself all things, whether on earth or in heaven, by making peace through the blood of his cross" (Col 1:17, 19–20). God reconciling to himself all things implies that humans and donkeys and spiders and chokecherries are all swept into the divine project together. A few verses later, Paul concludes the passage by urging his readers to remain "steadfast in the faith, without shifting from the hope promised by the gospel that you heard, which has been proclaimed to every creature under heaven" (Col 1:23). Every creature? Maybe we humans need to check ourselves whenever we fall into the habit of acting as if God's love story is only about us.

The assortment of creatures at the manger microcosm suggests the diversity woven into the fabric of all creation. All biological systems, vast or tiny, require difference in order to survive and grow. As I have learned more about biological refugia, I've noticed that biodiversity is always at the center of concern. The basic definition of refugia cited earlier assumes biodiversity is the equilibrium that natural systems seek: refugia are "habitats that components of biodiversity retreat to, persist in and can potentially expand from under changing environmental conditions."[15] When a mountainside or meadow exhibits "coarseness" of terrain—that is, a variety of shade and sun, mesic (wet) and xeric (dry) soils—that area serves as a better refugium. Coarseness means that in a relatively small space, a variety of conditions pertain, so that more plant and animal species can find a microrefugium suited to their survival, thus promoting biodiversity and ecosystem health. Natural systems often seek out a "portfolio strategy," in other words. Within the ecological conditions given, the more biodiverse the refugium, the more resilient it is, and the more potential it holds to persist and grow.[16]

What is true on the local scale is true of the whole earth. The crises we now face make painfully evident that humans and other creatures sicken or thrive together. The insidious effects of environmental injustice demonstrate that the abuse of creation and the abuse of other people are linked to the same careless, sinful arrogance. To countervail the power of human arrogance and division, the gospel offers a profound, humbling perception of kinship. We are kin not only with other humans but with all fellow creatures of God. We share our biological life, and we share our belovedness in God. A refugia faith is therefore radically inclusive, not only of different kinds of people, but of the whole created world. The best nativity scene would represent the whole created world, a family gathering of cosmic proportions.

Motifs in Tension

If testimony about the belovedness of all things has always been available within the Christian faith, how did so much of the Christian tradition fall into hierarchical anthropocentrism, the damaging ideology that Lynn White and many others rightfully criticize? To answer that question requires more than citing a few Bible verses. We have to think about how the stories we have told for centuries shape our imaginations.

We have to think about how mythological structures across cultures and traditions have cross-pollinated with Christian theology. Then we can understand how, in recent centuries, some parts of the Christian tradition have overspiritualized and overindividualized the Christian faith. This spiritualized individualism has in turn worsened our alienation from the more-than-human world. In other words, if our stories tell us that existence is all about the trials and triumphs of individual souls, then there's little room for attention to the physical world.

When I teach world literature, my course focuses on epics, those fundamental stories that fold into their characters and plotlines what their cultures of origin most deeply valued and also what they feared or despised. My students and I get to Dante's medieval Christian epic, the *Divine Comedy*, in the middle of the semester. We have time for only excerpts, of course, so we read a good deal of the first part, the *Inferno*, then jump to the end of the *Purgatorio*, and finally get to the end of the *Paradiso*. The poem begins with our hero, the pilgrim, in the middle of his life, lost in a dark wood, trapped by three ravening beasts who represent sin. With the guidance of Virgil's ghost, the pilgrim embarks on a harrowing journey through the salaciously gross-out circles of hell, then through successive levels of purgatory and paradise, meeting repentant sinners and saints, getting schooled in spiritual virtues. (That's the part we mostly skip, sadly.) Finally, in the very last cantos, the pilgrim experiences a beatific vision of God. It's a mystical and moving scene, and the whole thing prompts useful reflection for students. Dante's poem, however, exemplifies what theologian H. Paul Santmire calls "the spiritual motif" in Christian theology and practice.[17] The spiritual motif is the idea that existence is organized on a scale of being, and the spiritual is "higher" than the physical. Our human task is to work up that scale of being and become more and more spiritual, eventually—one way or another—leaving the physical behind. After all, God is spirit, yes?

Actually, to present Dante as a proponent of the spiritual motif is a little unfair to Dante. He is quite concerned with bodies and careful to account for their place in his afterlife schemes. Moreover, the pilgrim's culminating beatific vision does embrace all creation: the pilgrim perceives all creation as a single book, bound by God's love and contained within the divine being.[18] Nevertheless, Dante's keen interest in geography falls away as the *Paradiso* progresses, and the mystical language of the final vision treats creation as a concept more than a tangible experience.

However guilty of overspiritualizing we decide Dante might be, he at least illustrates the difficulty of negotiating the spirit/matter distinction, a conceptual distinction pervasive across cultures and across faiths. There is *stuff* and then there is the *numinous*, a reality beyond matter, a mystical perception of divinity or at least some kind of transcendence. Huston Smith, the great scholar of religions, observes that across cultures and faiths, we find similar conceptions of three realms: heavens, earth, and below. Unsurprisingly, heavens = up = spirit = divine = superior. Since "down" is the opposite of all that, one certainly wants to avoid the below as much as possible.[19] As we study epics in world lit class, my students and I observe that epic heroes are liminal figures who move among the realms, including the down-below. In fact, a *katabasis* (going down) of some kind is a necessary aspect of the hero's journey. Epic heroes are also connected somehow to the divine realm, often literally as the offspring of a god. However, most of the epic drama in the poems gets played out in that ambiguous realm in the middle: earth, matter, the physical. In fact, epic heroes are fascinating in part for the way they dramatize our own struggles to negotiate among the three realms. How does the stuff of earth "mix" with the numinous? Is earthiness always inferior? Should we aim to leave it behind? If not, how do we stay connected to that divine realm? And wait: Are there *really* three realms, or is that just an invention of human imagination?

H. Paul Santmire observes that in Scripture and throughout Christian history, the "spiritual motif" is in tension with what he calls the "ecological motif." The ecological motif assumes that the physical world is a "theological *fundamentum*."[20] Theological reflection, in other words, should never merely focus on God and human souls, but must always attend to God, humans, and the created universe. In the ecological motif, the created world is beloved by God for its own sake, not merely as a stage for human drama. In biblical stories and prophetic texts featuring this motif, God's blessing of God's people is persistently connected to a flourishing land. The two foundational stories of the Old Testament—the exodus from slavery to a promised land and the exile/diaspora and return—are permeated with the Bible's ecological motif. Redemption in these strands of scriptural story is not only about the rescuing of people but also about the renewal of this world of matter. Redemption is depicted literally and symbolically through what

Santmire terms "migration to a good land." "Rising above" the physical is not the point at all. It's not even an option on the table.

Throughout Christian history, the struggle between the spiritual motif and the ecological motif has played out. In the earliest centuries, orthodox Christianity rejected the "gnostic heresy," which proposed (among other things) that the world of matter was created not by God but by a being called a demiurge (seriously). Thus matter is dirty, inferior to spirit, and the sooner we leave it behind the better. Gnosticism is the most extreme, "dyspeptic" version of the spiritual motif.[21] Early church leaders believed that Gnosticism's rejection of the physical did not comport with the scriptural witness and especially with the emerging doctrine of the incarnation, in which God took on flesh in the person of Jesus. When navigating orthodoxy, we might say, the Annunciation defeats denunciation: Mary conceiving the Christ child defeats—or ought to defeat—any temptation to denounce the physical world. "Lo, he abhors not the virgin's womb," the Christmas carol pithily points out, and therefore none of us should abhor this physical world. But as seminarians learn in Church History 101, heresies never die. They just sneak around in different guises. One can trace throughout theological history the continual struggle to guard against creeping Gnosticism. The spiritual motif, in other words, has a tendency to assert itself to the detriment of the ecological motif.

I've been surprised to discover a range of positions throughout the Christian tradition on that spiritual/physical duality. The tradition includes many people who reflect carefully on the ecological motif—Irenaeus, late Augustine, Saint Francis, Pierre Teilhard de Chardin. For them, in one way or another, the more-than-human world has inherent value apart from its utility to humans. Other figures in the gallery of theological giants turn out to be, on this topic, the bad guys—Origen, early Augustine, Barth. Others get mixed reviews. Aquinas, for example, had plenty of appreciation for the more-than-human creation as evidence of God's plenitude and a cornucopia of blessings for humans, but he also believed that, at the culmination of history, nature will just disappear. Sic transit gloria mundi. Poof! Calvin and Luther, by contrast, are responsible for numerous rhapsodic passages about nature as the omnimiraculous "theater of divine glory," in Calvin's famous phrase.[22] They saw proclaimed in Scripture the eschatological fulfillment of nature rather than its evaporation into a spiritualized end point. Since the Reformation period, Enlightenment philosophy gets blamed for dragging theologians into an overintellectualized ether, with censure heaped especially upon the villainous Descartes and Kant. In the past sixty years, however, Christian reflection on nature has eased back toward integration of matter and spirit. Western Christian theology has benefitted especially from the rise of non-Western and Indigenous voices from all over the world as well as from a deeper engagement with other religious traditions.

In particular, the ecological motif is a rich layer in liberation theologies arising from people deeply connected to land and struggling to resist colonizing forces that would take their land or take them from their land. Liberation theologies have prompted a reassessment of the overspiritualized Western tradition. Willie James Jennings, in his brilliant and devastating work *The Christian Imagination: Theology and the Origins of Race*, goes far beyond Lynn White's brief essay in demonstrating how Christian theology has been leveraged in subtle and blatant ways by colonial powers.[23] Jennings carefully examines the historical record, particularly theological writings of the colonial period, to expose how early modern Europeans developed a version of Christianity that decoupled race and identity from place. Instead, race and identity came to be seen as carried in the body. Jennings investigates the precise historical moment in the history of the Americas when this shift took place. The decoupling of identity from place justified not only racial hierarchies and the enslaving of darker-skinned people but also the dispossessing of these peoples from their land. This distortion depends on the false principle that Christianity is only about the soul, and therefore land is just land—it is not inherently connected to anyone, it has no meaning in itself. As a result, land is open to claim by those with the biggest swords or guns or trunks of gold—all justified, of course, by the mandate to convert the heathens. Today, African Americans, Indigenous peoples, Central American peasants, South Asian and African peoples colonized by Europeans, and many others displaced or disinherited from their land live with the legacy of this distorted theology.

Errand Boy Jesus

While it has always been tempting to overspiritualize the faith, an equally difficult and related problem is overindividualizing faith. When

I teach that world literature course on epics, I also teach excerpts from Milton's *Paradise Lost*, but I'm wondering now whether Milton needs to step aside. Students find it surpassingly difficult to read Milton's dense, syntactically tangled poetry, though I can get them through that. The more concerning problem is Milton's depiction of God, particularly God the Son. In book 3, Milton presents a scene of God the Father brooding over the earth down below, where Adam and Eve are about to succumb to Satan's temptation and eat from the forbidden tree in Eden. God the Father delivers a coldly defensive speech—at least that's how I read it—in which he explains how the fall is not his fault, even if he knows about it ahead of time. Man, he insists, is "sufficient to have stood though free to fall."[24] (This raises the question of whether Woman is sufficient, but that's another issue.) God the Father then calls for a volunteer to carry out a plan of salvation he has already cooked up, thanks to foreknowledge. Naturally, the Son volunteers. The angels sing their hallelujahs, and ambrosial fragrance fills the heavenly realm.

As we work through this scene in class, I challenge students to think about how Milton's poetic drama does or does not comport with their understanding of the Trinity. The Holy Spirit, in Milton's poem, is not presented as a character like the Father and Son. The Holy Spirit is basically Milton's muse. The Son, meanwhile, turns into an errand boy for the Father. His task: head down to earth, fix things down there, and return to stand around in the heavenly throne room.

This is, I admit, a reductive reading. And I'm not giving poor Milton any credit here for his lavish descriptions of "this pendant world,"[25] particularly Eden, for which he musters every resource of the entire literary pastoral tradition. Even so, Milton's focus in the poem is squarely on the question of human moral choice, obedience or disobedience. In this, *Paradise Lost* is not far off from how the drama of redemption is often presented in a variety of Christian contexts, including worship. God the Father judges human sin from the throne in heaven. Jesus the errand boy, descending to earth, takes care of business by paying the bill for sin, then ascends back to heaven. Our job is to thank Jesus for this task completed, then make correct moral choices as free, independent, rational humans. The Holy Spirit serves as a kind of placeholder, a divine-human communication service while Jesus is gone, until he comes back and sorts humans into their heavenly or hellish eternities.

I realize this reductive sketch does not contradict biblical and theological tradition, not precisely. One could even claim that the Apostles' Creed follows roughly the same outline. And surely the claim that Jesus's incarnation, crucifixion, and resurrection somehow atone for sin is central to the faith, though it is not the whole of the scriptural story or the worship life of the church. However—without dismissing the seriousness of human sin—when errand-boy Jesus becomes the dominant image in the Christian imagination, we have made God and the redemption story far too small. A Jesus who performs a brief mission on earth and then waits to see which individuals will and will not believe in that mission—this is a formula for putting too much weight on individual sin and individual choice.

Father Richard Rohr is right, I think, when he observes that some strains of Christianity have regarded faith as mostly a matter of "sin management." Rohr observes that the Judeo-Christian tradition certainly contains a robust view of sin but also a robust declaration of original goodness. Rohr contends, however, that since Augustine, Christian theology's obsession with sin has truncated our understanding of Jesus: "The shift in what we valued often allowed us to avoid Jesus's actual life and teaching because all we needed was the sacrificial event of his death. Jesus became a mere mop-up exercise for sin, and sin management has dominated the entire religious story line and agenda to this day."[26] Focusing on Jesus's atonement for our personal sins, we spend our lives thanking him for that and otherwise go on with our business. This collapses the cosmic scope of God's communion with the universe into a deeply anthropocentric, individualistic view of salvation.

Apparently, overindividualization is not an issue only in Christianity. Marilyn Evelyn Tucker suggests that reducing religious faith to fixing human individuals is a problem across the great religions: "Worship, prayer, and meditation are often directed at purifying the soul, praising God, or getting rid of ego in order to advance toward the goal of personal salvation."[27] Getting rid of ego, purifying the soul, and praising God are all noble purposes, ones that all religions share in their own way. But when religion is only an individual salvational program, then we have two big problems. The first is that this reduces sin to individual missteps and thus provides convenient cover for all kinds of sinful systems. We need never question systems so long as we can claim our personal "sin canceled" stamp. This view of religion certainly appeals to those who wish to continue benefitting from unjust systems. The second problem is this: If religion is about individual human sins, then what is the point of the more-than-human creation? We're back to options a and b in our list of nature notions: creation is reduced to the stage on which a spiritual drama plays out. If the rest of creation is nothing but an elaborate set, then during the millions of years before humans even arrived on the scene, what was the Creator God caring about it? As Rohr puts it, "Did the Divinity need to wait for Ethnic Orthodox, Roman Catholics, European Protestants, and American Evangelicals to appear before the divine love affair could begin? I cannot imagine!"[28]

Our task now, as people who claim the Christian faith, is to draw on the resources we already have for resisting the overspiritualization and overindividualization of the faith. We need to lean into the Scripture's ecological motif and listen harder to those voices who can help us repair our alienation and gain anew a humble sense of our interconnectedness, with each other and with the more-than-human world.

Wild Goats and Leviathans

Christian reflection on the human-nature relationship, as I have studied it, tends to return incessantly to a suite of biblical greatest hits. I suppose this is natural. Genesis 1 and 2 dominate the discussion, of course. Then we go on to certain Psalms, especially 104, then Job 38–41, maybe a few verses from Isaiah. In the New Testament, we focus on John 1, Colossians 1, Philippians 2, and then Revelation 21. These passages lily-pad their way through the scriptural story, beginning with the origins of all things and concluding with images of history's destination. Along with many writers seeking biblical wisdom for our age, I have been pondering these passages, wondering how to understand them today. Soon enough, I'll try to untangle the knotted notions of what it means to be made in the image of God and what the creation accounts present as human vocation within creation, for example. But sometimes it's more instructive to dwell, not on mythic origins or visionary destinations, but smack in the middle where we can ponder life as it is, in the now. Psalm 104, for example, seems to zoom out and present a wider view, even a God's-eye view of ordinary days on this earth.

The psalmist marvels at the earth's teeming life, praising a creating and sustaining God who is "clothed with honor and majesty" (v. 1).

The thirty-five verses of the psalm make a sweeping survey of skies, winds, mountains, and heaving oceans. We glimpse donkeys drinking from a stream, wild goats cavorting on the mountains, storks nesting in pine trees, the magnificent "leviathan" frolicking in the deep, all of these creatures going about their business. God provides for all their life cycles, the psalm declares. They live, they reproduce, they die. All of them are gathered into God's provision. Humans are there too, but we feature in only a few verses. There we are, cultivating our crops, drinking wine that gladdens the heart, and eating bread that sustains the heart (v. 15). We're just another kind of creature for which the Lord enjoys providing. The last few verses of the psalm return from this vast perspective to the intimate. The psalmist wishes the wicked would stop spoiling things (v. 35). And the psalmist declares praise: "I will sing to the Lord as long as I live; I will sing praise to my God while I have being" (v. 33).

Passages such as Psalm 104 draw our attention away from our human concerns—and our inflated notions of human importance—and present an exuberant vision of the earth, one in which the more-than-human creation has a relationship with God entirely apart from humans. They have their own inherent value to God. God does not need humans in order to "rejoice in [God's] works" (v. 31). The trees will clap their hands and the hills will skip whether we're around to notice and comment or not. In fact, people have long proposed that maybe the other creatures are actually better at praising God than humans are. The Anglican churchman Godfrey Goodman wrote in 1622 that creatures "have a truth and sincerity in their service, without hypocrisy or dissimulation; they are not troubled or disquieted in their own thoughts (as we are) that they should be admonished by outward ceremonies; but they are like the angels in heaven, wholly intent to their service. I would I could say as much for ourselves."[29] Blessedly free of all the stormy weather that self-consciousness inevitably brings to humans, creatures do not need the whole apparatus of religion to get them praising God. They do so simply by being what they are.

Lynn White was correct when he proposed that Saint Francis offers one good starting place for imagining what living into our kinship with the rest of creation might look like. Saint Francis is among the most beloved and well-known Christian figures who model respect for other created beings, calling the sun "brother" and the moon "sister" and preaching to the birds. His sense of kinship arose from his ability to perceive the essence of the incarnation: *kenosis*, emptying. Jesus, as Philippians says, kenosised himself (*heauton ekenosen*), taking the form of a servant/slave (*doulou*; Phil 2:7). In imitation of Christ, Francis emptied himself of his wealth and of human arrogance. He became childlike in his gentle love for other creatures, including other people. It's no surprise that he is the one who came up with the idea of a live nativity scene. He perceived intuitively that the antidote to anthropocentrism is kenosis. Rather than imagining ourselves as the only creatures that matter in the whole universe, we instead imitate the self-emptying love of Christ. The Christmas season invites us to ponder that radiant incarnational moment in history, the crisis point that gathers all creatures into kinship, embraced by the kenotic love of God.

Fungi and the Fire of Love

The doctrine of the incarnation ought to make Christians more attentive than anyone to the kinship of all creation. Yet I have found the most beautiful reflections on the kinship of all life among philosophers and scientists who aren't talking about faith at all. Recent scientific work has revealed that even the distinctions between species—or even between taxonomical kingdoms—are less clear-cut than we have imagined. Since forest ecologist Suzanne Simard published an astonishing 1997 scientific paper in the journal *Nature*, we have known about the "wood wide web."[30] Beneath the forest soil, Simard discovered, a whole world of fungi creates a complex underground network through interfaces called "hyphae." Fungi receive sugars that trees produce through photosynthesis, and in return, the fungi provide phosphorous and nitrogen to the trees. This is called the mycorrhizal network—a term derived by combining the Greek words for fungus and roots. Even more marvelous, this network allows trees to share resources with each other. A mother tree can supply sugars to saplings. A dying tree can release its resources into the network for the healthier trees to gather up. Trees can even warn each other, through their roots, to increase resistance to marauding pests.

This discovery has profound implications. Rather than imagining a forest as a bunch of species competing for resources, we more accurately think of a forest as a "superorganism." Yes, there's competition, but there's also astonishing cooperation.[31] The wood wide web provides further evidence of what we already know about biological systems: they rely on interrelated diversity to thrive. This is why clear-cutting a forest does more than remove trees: it creates cascading failure for insects, birds, mammals. It causes microclimate disruption. This is also why monoculture planting—the overgrown red-pine plantations I can see from US-131 on the way to northern Michigan, for instance—will never thrive like a diverse forest will. Now with growing knowledge about mycorrhizal networks and their differences across regions, we may be better able to restore ruined forests or support those threatened by climate change.[32]

We humans might imagine ourselves as theoretically distinct from "nature," but the more we understand biology and physics, the less plausible our claims to distinctiveness and superiority. We exchange oxygen and carbon dioxide with trees and plants. We take in the fruits of the land and sea and the flesh of other creatures. And each of our bodies is a whole ecosystem of microbial life, inside our guts, in our mouths, even on our eyelashes. We are "holobionts"—life bundles composed of a host organism as well as all the viruses, bacteria, and fungi living on and around us.[33] We have extraordinary ingenuity and power, it's true, but we are also entirely dependent on a swarm of other living things simply to exist. And the more we learn about this earth, the more we realize how everything is interrelated on the micro- and macrolevels. We share large percentages of DNA even with plants. The same kinds of atoms and molecules compose all living things, arranged in infinite variety. Quantum entanglement, the bizarre theory that Einstein described as "spooky action at a distance," has now been verified; subatomic particles can become "entangled" such that they influence each other, even at great distances.[34] As the poets like to say, we are all made of stardust.

In ecologist and philosopher David Abram's rhapsodic essay on animal migration, he imagines the gorgeous interconnectedness involved in salmon migrating through living waters. By swimming from inland waters into the ocean and back again, the salmon are a flowing gift, linking mountain trees to ocean whales. He writes, "Think again of the salmon, this gift born of the rocky gravels and melting glaciers, nurtured by colossal cedars and by tumbled trunks decked with ferns, fungi, and moss, an aquatic, muscled energy strengthening itself in the mossed and forested mountains until it's ready to be released into the broad ocean.

Pouring seaward, it adds itself to that voluminous cauldron of current spiraling in huge gyres, shaded by algal blooms and charged by faint glissandos of whale song." The passage continues, sending the salmon back up the river, and Abram observes that this natural wonder is like the systole and diastole of the rivers and ocean, or perhaps like the breathing of the earth, rhythmically inhaling and exhaling creatures along their migratory routes.[35]

Perceiving interconnections stretches our imaginative capacities, especially when we consider the vastness of the universe in one thought and, in the next thought, the intricacies of microbial life on earth or even subatomic physics. What unites the vast and the intimate is the wonder of existence itself. The Abrahamic faiths share the conviction that the foundation of existence is not an impersonal force but emanates from the divine person. So we seek this divine being in the star nursery nebulae as well as in the tiniest seed. As Santmire puts it, Luther imagined that "if we truly understood the growth of a grain of wheat, . . . we would die of wonder."[36] Among the many theologians and mystics who invite us into this perception of God, one of the greatest is the medieval abbess Hildegard of Bingen. She heard the voice of God declaring divine energy in all things: "I, the highest and fiery power, have kindled every living spark. . . . I am . . . the fiery life of the divine essence—I am aflame above the beauty of the fields; I shine in the waters; in the sun, the moon and the stars, I burn. And by the means of the airy wind, I stir everything into quickness with a certain invisible life which sustains all."[37]

For Christians, that revelation of God's being is most fully given in Christ—Christ is the "exegesis" of God, as the Gospel of John declares (John 1:18). The incarnation of God in Christ thus reveals an astonishing secret: the three realms—heavens, earth, and under the earth—are not distinct after all, but interpenetrating. Even the "down below" is gathered into the divine reality through Jesus's suffering and death. Christ, then, is the focal point of all that exists, the "love magnet" toward which all things are drawn.[38]

When I am filled with doubt, when I need to find some handhold on the unfathomable mystery of God, I try now to think of Christ as the nexus between the divine source of all life and the person of God speaking to me in my unique, infinitesimal flash of life on this earth. When Jesus feels abstract and distant, I can feel my own heartbeat and look up toward a tangle of branches with their trembling galaxies of new green leaves. I hear the birds sing and know: *this* life, all of it, *this* is where Christ-in-whom-all-things-hold-together is revealed. Entangled in this kinship, how can I help but empty out my human arrogance and learn to rejoice?

Brother Cottonwood

Once we removed most of the major buckthorn stems, the restoration work in our little backyard ecosystem could begin. We had to have the buckthorn stumps ground and then figure out how to amend the depleted soil before trying to plant anything new. Even while that was going on, the four spruce trees formerly crowded by buckthorn already began to breathe easier. They seemed to stand up straighter and look happier. Over the next couple springs, my favorite spruce, the twenty-five-footer visible out the back deck, grew positively regal. "You're so welcome!" I told it.

Now I started getting to know the grand old fork-trunked cottonwood right on the property line, also formerly swathed up to its arboreal waist in buckthorn. Our relationship started out rough. "Crap in All Seasons" I dubbed this tree. Over the winter, I soon learned, a sixty-foot-tall cottonwood sheds hundreds of knobbly, snaky sticks. With the spring ground still muddy, we gathered up at least three wheelbarrows piled high with sticks from a small strip of lawn. As the weather warmed and the days lengthened, the next stage of the cottonwood's assault began: glueys. Cottonwoods produce thousands of sticky little arrowheads that open to release shaggy catkins, all of which drop from the tree. Actually, the tree doesn't just *drop* these things: it *spews* them, with considerable force. The arrowheads are coated with neon-green glue—*resin* is the polite botanical term—and they stick to everything, especially socks, carpets, and dogs. The catkins, once they fall, turn brick red and disintegrate into limp mats of debris that leave stains. More sticks shed over the summer, and then there's autumn, and guess what? Loads of leathery leaves. Leaves blanket the ground and bushes below, they clog the gutters, they fly over the house and alight on the front walk and blow into the garage and entryway. They do not decompose easily. What about the thickets of seed fluff that cottonwoods are known to fling like snow on spring neighborhoods, the fluff for which the cottonwood is named? Ah, but that's the *female* tree. We were dealing, it turns out, with a *male* tree.

At first, I had thoughts of tree violence. I muttered curses. It's a good thing the tree grows just on the far side of my lot line, limiting my legal rights. I thought of it as "my" cottonwood anyway, linked as the two of us were in an epic battle of wills.

One day, I was complaining about "my" cottonwood to my friend Ken, and he observed, "Yes, but the leaves make such a beautiful sound in the wind."

That pulled me up short. Had I ever *listened* to this tree?

Ken was right. Those leathery nuisances make a *patta patta* sound in the wind, whispering a soothing, leafy music. When the light comes through the leaves, their silvery undersides alternate with their darker tops, and the whole tree seems almost to glitter. I started to wonder if I was approaching my relationship with my tree all wrong. Besides creating a big mess, this tree might be giving some gifts to me and to our little ecosystem. What could I appreciate and be grateful for?

OK, a list. It sings wonderful leaf music. It flashes with a pattery glitter. Its crown shades the house. Its knobby trunk and abundant branches make an excellent habitat for birds. And anyway, the tree was here first. The cottonwood is the native here, not me. Eastern cottonwoods (*Populus deltoides*) are wonderfully adaptable and fast growing, common all over the Midwest. They're tough—they can handle muddy, clay soil, like on our property, as well as the scouring dryness of a dune. Indigenous peoples use their bark for canoes and for medicines. How could I disrespect this impressive citizen of my tiny domain? The only reason I considered it a "problem" is that I want a modest lawn and some pretty plantings. All right then. Once I developed a better attitude, the cottonwood and I reached detente. We agreed to be neighbors.

Relationships take work. So this spring, as usual, the tree flung its sticks, and my husband, Ron, and I raked and gathered them from the lawn. Now that I have some shrubs planted beneath the cottonwood, I have to pluck shed sticks from the branches of the little lilacs and ninebarks struggling below. The cottonwood demands its space, and I planted a couple shrubs too close, so one of my ninebarks is a pathetic fountain of deadness this year. And the spruce right underneath the cottonwood still can't grow any top branches on its cottonwood side. "Crown shyness," that's called, though in this case, I would call it "cottonwood bossiness." When we set up our deck for the season, we spent a couple days dodging the resinous arrowheads while the tree went through its spitwad phase. Then I spent an afternoon sweeping and power washing the deck to clean up all the catkins and dislodge probably two thousand gluey arrowheads from between the deck boards. I'll never get all the neon residue off completely.

It's still an ornery old tree, but it has my respect. As for my squirrel neighbors: there I have some work to do. They rudely steal my birdseed, the little monsters. I have yet to make my peace with them.

BLACK-CAPPED CHICKADEE
POECILE ATRICAPILLUS

April
Douglas, Michigan

Summers, 1970s
Holland and Grand Haven, Michigan

The lake is working its magic. I came out here resistant, sad, anxious. I did not expect the lake to change that. But the rippling waves meet the shore and fold their edges under like a rocking cradle—*shhh, shhh*. The knots in my soul are loosening.

A little boy squats down and digs at the water's edge, absorbed in his project. He stands, toes sunk in wet sand. I watch him while drinking in the soft air laced with the smell of water, sand, wet plants. Does sand have a smell? I think so. Something lifts me back to my young teenage years. I am connected with this place through memory, through the body. If I could bundle together the smells of sand and lake with musky jasmine perfume, coconut sunscreen, peppermint lip balm, and straw-berry shampoo, I would be constructing a time machine back to those days when I first learned to love the Michigan lakeshore.

My family did not have a cottage while I was growing up, but we vis-ited friends' cottages often, and my mother and I camped at Grand Haven State Park on the big lake for two weeks every August along with all her friends from church. To call it camping is an exaggeration. Like the other campers, we parked RVs and trailers on numbered asphalt lots arranged around three intersecting ovals, just steps from the vast public beach. The campground is walking distance from the pier, the marina, and the nearby town's shops and restaurants. For my mom and her friends, our two-week sojourn was about coffee together, beach lounging, shopping, visits from children and grandchildren, late afternoon happy hour, and fun and laughter away from their home responsibilities.

For me, summer was about being in a body, being a girl. Innocent sensuality. Lying on Michigan's beaches with girlfriends as a young teenager, the weight of our bodies in the warm, sugary sand, the heat of the towel, the smell of sunscreen, the shy pride we took in being young and smooth and exposed to the blazing sky. Determinedly cultivating our fashionable tans while Top 40 radio murmured from a boom box. Managing bikini tops to avoid tan lines. Clomping around in the wooden sandals everyone was wearing. Getting our periods, the fuss and bother and curious embarrassment about tampons and pads. Swimming on lucky days of warm lake temperatures in the satiny soft water, sometimes glassy calm, sometimes swelling with waves. The bright sun blackening our vision. The whooshing of relentless waves in our ears, or on calm days, a quiet lapping. The glow of a lightly toasted body at the end of the afternoon, the heat and sweat and the dusting of sand on the back of the calves. We placed ourselves on the edge of these wild forces—wind, water, sand, sky—and felt a visceral assurance that the world we barely understood was bigger than boys and grades and the relentless teenage calibrations of social status. The world was vast and magnificent and full of mystery.

After a day at the beach, that feeling of languid exhaustion. A shower felt so good—unless you were fool enough to get sunburned on your shoulders. Then the water pounded and stung. Lotion smoothed everywhere, clean hair, a fresh T-shirt and shorts. Sand in hair, sand in shoes, sand under bare feet on ancient linoleum floors of cottages. Sand emptied from socks and pockets. The smell of charcoal grills. Later, back on the beach to watch the sun blaze diamonds of light on the lake surface, then spread a shimmering sunset trail of teal, violet, salmon pink. Sitting on cooling sand as the light softened and clouds low on the horizon leapt alive into peach and magenta. We gathered around driftwood fires, our voices and laughter rising as night crept over us and the lake whispered on in the dark.

Chapter 3
_____

From Consuming to Healing

You visit the earth and water it,
you greatly enrich it;
the river of God is full of water;
you provide the people with grain,
for so you have prepared it.

—PSALM 65:9

knew almost nothing about Great Lakes maritime history until the summer Ron and I visited the Sleeping Bear Point Coast Guard Station Maritime Museum near Glen Haven, Michigan. One can find this attraction "up north," near Sleeping Bear Dunes. If you're holding up your hand, as we do, to simulate the "mitten" part of Michigan's geography, Sleeping Bear is at Michigan's pinkie tip.

Initially, the museum seems unimpressive. It's just a clapboard house, a boathouse, and a couple of other historic buildings perched on a narrow spread of grass just a few hundred feet from where Lake Michigan laps the shore. From 1902 to 1942, however, this was a station of the US Life-Saving Service, which became the US Coast Guard in 1915.

Why a station at this spot? Shipping. The station demonstrates that people will deploy remarkable ingenuity and endure extreme danger in order to extract the earth's treasures and build human prosperity. When White settlers poured into Michigan from the 1820s onward, and investors and industrialists started extracting lumber, iron, copper, and other commodities from these "virgin" lands, somehow these raw materials had to be moved around the Great Lakes basin or out the Saint Lawrence River. This required boats, lots of them, and later trains. To avoid the open waters of the big lake, sailing vessels and steamers would slip between Sleeping Bear Point and the Manitou Islands several miles offshore. The passage was tricky, with shoals and finicky winds, and ships frequently got into trouble, especially during the stormier periods of the April-to-mid-December shipping season.

In 1870–71, 214 people died in shipwrecks on the Great Lakes alone. That year, Congress addressed the nation's shipwreck problem by establishing the US Life-Saving Service. Eventually, there were 64 stations around the Great Lakes (with 140 on the Atlantic coast). Three of the Michigan stations—Sleeping Bear Point, North Manitou, and Point Betsie—were specifically designed to monitor ships attempting the Manitou Passage.

There was no radar, no radio yet. So rescue operations required a combination of diligence, bravery, and clever contraptions. Each station employed a keeper and seven "surfmen." Keeping an eye out during daylight was fairly straightforward, but nighttime watch required feats of athleticism. All night, the surfmen on duty walked two miles from the station in each direction, watching for ships in distress.

Let's say you're the surfman on duty, you're walking along, it's dark and probably cold and stormy, you're almost to the end of your two-mile stretch, and you spy a ship in distress. Now you have to turn around and run—run! and remember, this is on sand—all the way back to the station. Ring the bell! Wake up the guys! And join in a rescue operation that would make the fittest CrossFitter faint with exhaustion.

The rescue involved dragging a wheeled wooden beach cart down to the beach and along the shore till they reached the endangered boat, then shooting a rope onto the boat using something called a Lyle gun, then setting up a sort of gigantic zip line from the boat to a quickly assembled support system on shore. The zip line held the "breeches buoy," a pair of roomy canvas shorts with a life preserver ring at the waist. The surfmen would run this contraption back and forth on a pulley system, fetching the endangered crew one by one. Each poor sailor got the zip-line adventure of his life. Apparently, the procedure was remarkably effective.

In 1931, the crew of the Sleeping Bear Point Station had another problem to deal with. The sand dune was encroaching on their buildings, as dunes will do. So they propped up the two buildings, put them on rollers, and moved them a mile down the beach, using two Percheron horses walked in from town. Both buildings were plopped safely down in their new location without so much as a broken pane of glass.

I learned all this and more from the nicely curated materials in the old station house and from the volunteer interpretive guides. One of the guides was especially eager to answer my questions. "Most people aren't all that interested in what I have to say," she said ruefully. She was sweeping the sand out the front door of the station house as we chatted. "We have to keep this sand dune where it belongs," she remarked, as if it were a naughty outdoor cat.

Sadly, we did not visit the museum at the time of day when a group of volunteers stages their reenactment of a breeches buoy rescue, employing the assistance of visiting children to save the hapless Raggedy Ann and Andy from deadly peril. Despite missing this spectacle, I came away from our visit impressed with two abiding thoughts: People are so ingenious. Also, people are crazy.

You have to marvel at the courage, stamina, and inventiveness of those who devised these tools and procedures and those who actually did this lifesaving work. According to the museum's website, "From the time of its establishment in 1871 until it became part of the U.S. Coast Guard in 1915, the U.S. Life-Saving Service rescued over 178,000 people. Its success rate was an astounding 99%."[1] Amazing. On the other hand, my admiration is tempered by the knowledge that, at least in Michigan, this was all in service of a more ambiguous goal: building industry, business, and wealth to support White settlement and Manifest Destiny. As with the lumber industry, the shipping industry at the time seemed obviously wholesome and heroic to the folks involved, a means to a better life—for some anyway. I doubt it all seemed so wholesome and heroic to the Ottawa, who had ceded a huge chunk of northern Michigan to the US government in 1836. People didn't *have* to run ships through the Great Lakes in all weathers, risking lives and accepting the inevitable losses of vessels. But when it comes to building wealth, we don't like to think about limits.

House Rules

We are creatures of desire, imagination, and creativity. That is our divinely ordained nature, a magnificent gift. Yet we are also creatures of greed, foolhardy in our resistance to limits. In this age of crisis, when our human technosphere is taxing our biosphere beyond its limits, how can we use our cleverness in new and better ways? As refugia biology suggests, a crisis entails loss, but a crisis is also an opportunity for healing and for new kinds of growth. What is being revealed to us as we look for signs of that new growth, as we seek to become healers?

Theologian Sallie McFague has argued that Americans—including American Christians—have fallen too hard for the mythology of "neoclassical economics."[2] This is the term she uses to describe an economic model originating in the Enlightenment, of which Adam Smith is the most famous proponent. This model presumes a particular view of human nature and purpose: humans are individuals who compete for limited resources, using reason to act on their own self-interest. If everyone does this, this economic model proposes, then eventually goods and services will circulate and everyone will prosper. While it's true that capitalism has been the economic system most effective in lifting millions out of poverty, unfortunately, the simple neoclassical model is patently false. It correctly acknowledges people's basic selfishness, but it also underestimates the voracious hunger of greed. In addition, it fails to recognize that people do not always make rational choices, nor do we see ourselves only as individuals. We have strong bonds with various groups or communities, to which we can be remarkably and irrationally loyal—for good or ill. Moreover, the neoclassical model ignores the needs of the biological systems it commodifies. This is why a cursory survey of recent history turns up plenty of evidence that neoclassical economics does not, in fact, lead to everyone's prosperity. This economic model, even with some restraints, has created wealth but also underwritten a history of racialized plunder and severe wealth inequality. Yet some American Christians—with the active encouragement of those who protect the fossil fuel industry—persist in imagining that the neoclassical economic model is somehow God's ordained design.[3]

As an alternative model, McFague proposes what she calls "ecological economics."[4] The term is somewhat redundant, since *ecology* and *economics* come from the same Greek root: *oikos*, "household." In this model, humans and all the other creatures are roommates in the household of the planet. This way of thinking assumes a very different view of humans: we're not competing individuals, stepping all over each other to satisfy our raging consumer preferences. Rather, we are housemates who need to cooperate. As anyone who has shared an apartment knows, living together requires good "house rules." And those house rules have to take into account everyone's differences and needs. As roommates in the household of creation, humans have a number of advantages over other creatures—highly developed frontal lobes and opposable thumbs, among other things. We have used our advantages to create magnificent art and craft, humor and music, but also to become terrible bullies. We have been destroying the place. If any of us are going to survive well, we're going to need new house rules.

McFague is not the first modern thinker to evoke the household model. Agrarianist and philosopher Wendell Berry has been writing along these lines for decades. Aldo Leopold, the University of Wisconsin conservationist, wrote foundational essays on how biological science reveals not just a collection of entities but natural systems, and so we should think in terms of systems, devising ways to work together with other creatures for the thriving of the whole. As Berry and Leopold observe, an ecological economy model is based more accurately on the interrelatedness of biological and earth systems and our embeddedness in them. Moreover, a household-of-life model is closer to the ways in which many Indigenous peoples have understood themselves as belonging to their lands and waters, a belonging that undergirds principles of sustainable use. Finally, this model is also truer to a biblical vision of life on the planet. If anything, the household model is an ancient way of thinking, not a new way.

But here we are in the twenty-first century, centuries of civilizations behind us with all their plunders and marvels, and now with almost eight billion people on a globalized planet. The household model is a far greater challenge than ever before. Figuring out and practicing new house rules is not going to be easy. Should we turn back the clock on our industrial infrastructure, unravel our technological achievements, tear down our cities? Should we all become off-the-grid subsistence farmers or hunter-gatherers? Live in happy harmony with cockroaches and never swat a mosquito? What is the purpose of our genius, our curiosity and inventiveness, if not to create snug homes and magnificent concert halls and high-tech hospitals and all the other glories of civilization?

An ecological economy need not devolve into unrealistic visions of barefooted, harmonious communes for all. Markets, commerce, banking, investing, and the familiar structures of capitalist society have their place. But these structures must be tempered by an honest accounting of what they take and whom they serve. Tempering capitalist structures makes the business game more complex, since businesses have to take into account not only quarterly shareholder profits but all the "externalities" of their operation. What is the cost of spewing waste fluids into the nearby river to everyone and everything downstream? Who pays that cost? What is the cost of producing single-use plastics that cannot be recycled and end up either shipped to Asia and dumped or incinerated locally? Forward-thinking businesses are now attempting to calculate those costs and work toward a "circular economy." This means figuring out how to move away from the linear system we're all used to, a take-make-waste system in which you extract some resource, make something with it, and let someone else worry about what happens to the materials after the consumer uses it. Instead, a circular economy seeks to create a no-waste system along the entire supply chain. Businesses design products that use sustainably sourced materials—or better yet, materials already in the "loop"—plan for longer product durability and repairability, and also plan for retrieval of the materials after the life cycle of the product. One expert estimates that only 9 percent of the global economy is currently circular. If we could double that, it would already make a huge difference in emissions and waste.[5] This means that business leaders and policy makers are among the most important figures in any transition to a new set of house rules. Their power over other people's lives and over our planet's future is soberingly enormous.

Maybe the purpose of our genius now is to work out these new house rules, so everyone can live well without destroying the planet and exploiting each other. Overall, we've gotten the rules wrong. It seems clear enough that we need to reimagine what it means to live well, setting our sights on something more morally and practically sound than limitless, individualized consumerism. We will need every bit of curiosity, persistence, and ingenuity we can muster to focus on healing and on sustainable prosperity for all, especially now that we're dealing with a planet in extraordinary flux.

Healing Stories

During the weeks following the feast of Epiphany, stretching from January 6 until the beginning of Lent, the church reflects on the life and ministry of Christ. Through Scripture reading, preaching, art, and song, we consider the mystery of God-with-us in the person of Jesus as teacher, prophet, and healer. Epiphany means "moment of appearance," and this season is about how God's character and purpose are revealed through Jesus. In the life of Jesus, in other words, we are presented with the quintessence of how God works in the world. In recent years, as Epiphany season has brought us around again to the familiar stories of Jesus's ministry in the Gospels, I have been marveling at how Jesus's ministry follows the refugia pattern. Jesus, born to a low-status family from an unremarkable town, begins small with a few healings, a little preaching, a few disciples. As Jesus's notoriety grows, he preaches about the kingdom of God using earthy examples—the mustard seed, leaven, a wheat field—to remind listeners that in the earth, too, God works from small, sometimes hidden things that become astonishingly transformative. God's healing purposes begin small, and by the Spirit's power, they grow.

Pastor and Keetoowah Cherokee Randy Woodley observes that according to Luke 4, when Jesus inaugurates his public ministry, he shows up at the synagogue in his hometown and reads Isaiah 61. The passage begins, "The spirit of the Lord God is upon me, because the Lord has anointed me; he has sent me to bring good news to the oppressed." The passage goes on to describe a prophetic vision in which God heals not only people but cities, lands, and waters in an outpouring of divine love and purpose. By choosing this text for his inaugural sermon, Woodley argues, Jesus announces himself as the fulfillment of God's promise of *shalom*, that rich Hebrew term encompassing peace, flourishing, and delight. God has promised shalom not only to the people of Israel but to all the nations, and we know from the persistent ecological motif in the Old Testament that in God's economy the flourishing of people and the flourishing of the earth are inseparable.

As I consider those healing stories in the Gospels, I marvel that Jesus heals body, mind, and soul in a mere moment with a look, a gesture, a word. But I also wonder, What about all the people who *don't* get healed? A mother's daughter gets raised, but of course many other mothers' daughters simply die. A man's demon is cast out, but many other people live in torment for decades. And for that matter, why does Jesus seem unconcerned with healing land? In fact, one incident in the Gospel of Mark makes one wonder what Jesus had against the poor fig tree (11:12–14), not to mention a certain herd of pigs (5:1–13). Yet it's clear that Jesus is intimately familiar with the Sea of Galilee, the vineyards and grain fields, the sparrows and lilies, the olive trees. In his teaching, he constantly uses illustrations that depend on his listeners' understanding of the farms and rivers and animals that support their lives. We know that Jesus attends to and understands our human interdependence with the earth. So what about all the people and everything in the world that do not get healed and fixed and made whole?

I read these stories with wonder and longing—and then impatience. Jesus preaches a kingdom coming, a kingdom already here, jolting his listeners into seeing God at work even while they live under the oppressive thumb of the Roman Empire. I understand that Jesus's miraculous healings are supposed to be signs of that kingdom on its way. Well, we're still waiting for its full arrival. How do we manage the gap between what Jesus's life and ministry promised and what we still await? I suppose the only way to manage that gap is to point to God's affection for the refugium way. As with the Old Testament stories of Israel, where God works with a small gathering of Semitic tribes as sign and seed of a larger purpose, Jesus's ministry, too, is a mustard seed: tiny but potent. We describe the church, at its best, as the body of Christ, carrying out through the Spirit the ongoing project of bringing that kingdom to fulfillment. So the only way I can bear the aching mystery of all that still needs healing is to imagine God sending us all a perpetual invitation to follow in Jesus's way. God's invitation says, Now *you* become healers.

Biological refugia are places where healing begins and where the capacities for growth and resilience rebuild. After a fire ravages a mountainside, burned grasses and dead wood refertilize the soil, preparing it for seed. The surviving trees and shrubs reseed the area; mycorrhizal networks rebuild. Surviving creatures seek out nesting and den spaces and begin reproducing again. A refugia faith, likewise, seeks out whatever life-giving, kingdom-promising elements persist and strives to nurture them.

As we consider what kingdom-promising elements might look like, it might help to reevaluate that word *kingdom*. As Woodley acknowledges, the word needs some translation for our times. "Kingdom" (Greek

basileia) was meaningful to Jesus's listeners, who had experienced nothing but kings and imperial rule. Jesus was trying to evoke a radical
alternative, an upside-down version of the empire they knew, where
the poor and hungry and meek and mourning are blessed. Woodley
wisely suggests that today, we could benefit from setting the word *kingdom* aside. Some have offered the term *kin-dom* as an alternative, which
is charming and useful. But I like Woodley's idea better. He proposes
that we replace the word *kingdom* with *community of creation*. This phrase
removes militaristic and monarchist associations and, more important,
triggers our imaginations to include all creation, not just human political entities. It also fits with Indigenous worldviews. Woodley writes,
"The phrase 'community of creation' is specifically infused with biblical
and indigenous meaning because it assumes all of creation is participating in the new community, not just humans."[6] The community of creation is within you. The community of creation is at hand. I like the way
this phrase jars the imagination.

In particular, I appreciate the way "community of creation" invites
us to acknowledge that we are not the only healers available. God works
through human agency but also through the force of life everywhere
pulsing through creation. At best, we humans are merely wise and gracious partners with God and with plants, animals, microbes, oceans,
rivers, winds, sun—all the more-than-human world. In one short parable in Mark 4, Jesus describes a farmer who sows seed, and then, while
the farmer goes about his other business, day and night, the seed
grows. The farmer does his part, but the earth—through metabolic
and chemical processes in the seed and the soil—brings growth from
seed to harvest (Mark 4:26–29). Jesus is making a point here about the
kingdom—I mean, the community of creation—and it's an ecological
point. People can be agents in healing work, but renewal depends on
the miraculous ordinary that God has built into the world and continues to sustain.

Now as we face the overwhelming task of devising and managing
new house rules for a whole planet, the invitation of God feels weighty
and vast: *you*—not only people but all of this planet—*you all* become healers. If only, like Jesus, we could say a word, offer a gesture, and it would
be so. Calm the storm, wipe out the disease, return to the right mind. We
can't, but we are not exactly helpless. We have those large frontal lobes
and opposable thumbs. We have centuries of knowledge building and

experience behind us. We have a resilient earth, with built-in healing powers. We have pockets everywhere of people already doing the work. If we want to follow Jesus and become healers in the community of creation, we cannot assume the process will be automatic or easy. We have to work at it, praying for everything we need: discernment, compassion, skill, power, willingness, and knowledge.

Back to Class

I've been reading and learning about the climate crisis, its causes and possible mitigations, for several years now, and I never stop feeling overwhelmed. Too many powerful structures are involved, too many people and places, too much to learn and know. There's no end to the books and webinars and email newsletters and calls to urgent action. I know what activists say: join with others, pace yourself, connect locally. I am doing all that, as best I can manage. But still.

Not all the learning is grim and discouraging. I've actually found it invigorating—and dare I say, fun?—to learn more about this place where I live. Though I grew up here, I am not native in the ancestral sense; my immigrant grandparents chose West Michigan around the turn of the twentieth century, joining waves of immigrants from their countries (the Netherlands and Hungary in their cases) and many other countries. I am one tiny story among billions in the human history of migration, forced or voluntary or somewhere in between. But here I am now, connected by affection and experience to this woodsy, watery region bordered by the big lake and sinuous sand dunes. I realize that if I'm going to dwell here, cooperate well with this land, then I've got to know more about it. There are numerous ways of knowing a place, of course, but I thought I should at least try out some serious science.

Fortunately, I work for a university well populated with knowledgeable scientists, including Deanna van Dijk, one of the world's few experts on aeolian geomorphology. That lyrical term refers to a subfield of geography that focuses on, among other things, how coastal sand dunes move. All landforms are dynamic to some degree, but dunes, they move before your very eyes. At least the active ones do. Dunes on Lake Michigan's eastern edge shape-shift especially in the autumn, when strong west winds blow off the lake, into and up and over the largest freshwater dune system in the world.

For an entire fall semester, Deanna graciously allowed me to sit in on her Geography 181 course, a course designed to give first-year students experience doing field research. I became a student again, showing up for class with my notebook, taking notes during Deanna's carefully organized and illustrated lectures on wind-carved landforms and aeolian processes. We learned about the exact mechanisms by which grains of sand lift and tumble in the wind, along with the formula for the rate of sand movement in relation to wind speed. We learned about dune forms, vegetation and succession, and the tricky challenges of dune management in Michigan. We learned terms like *saltation, reptation, creep, deposition,* and *deflation.* New words, unsurprisingly, were my favorite part. I gathered new terms and stuffed them in my pockets like shells collected on the beach.

Mostly I enjoyed joining Deanna and her students as they practiced a scientific way of knowing. After years in the literature and writing world, where words are the only currency of exchange, I tried out sketching and taking measurements and reading graphs and charts. It was awkward to feel so stupid, especially at first. On our first day "in the field," on Dune 5 at P. J. Hoffmaster State Park near Muskegon, we were supposed to write down measurements in our field notebooks for the weather conditions that day. The instructions that we taped into our Rite in the Rain lab notebooks suggested that quantitative data are preferable to qualitative, but qualitative data are better than no data at all. Well, there it is, I thought: the distinction between science and poetry. In science, you measure things. In poetry, you imagine and feel and metaphorize. Science and poetry share, though, the same quest for keen observation and precision. In my notebook on our first day, I wrote, "Wind speed = 1.4–1.7 m/sec." Then for good measure, I wrote, "Gently breezy."

I found the epistemological culture of science class both foreign and exhilarating. I found field research both refreshing and tedious. Field research on dunes involves complicated gadgets and a great deal of patience. Guided by Deanna and five experienced student-mentors hired to assist, the first-year students spent long hours learning how to use devices like a "total station," a handheld GPS mapper, an anemometer, and various types of sand traps used to capture slugs of sand for later weighing. We drove an hour each way to our field sites, where students would spend several hours counting the number and species of plants in a quadrat or taking dozens of elevation measurements with a hand leveler, writing it all down in their field notebooks for entry into Excel spreadsheets later. The students would then crunch the data into charts and graphs for their poster presentations at the end of the semester. Most of the time collecting data in the field, it seemed to me the students enjoyed the work. But it was still work.

Out on the dunes, I mostly watched all the measurement taking, marching around behind the intrepid Deanna as she checked in on each group. It was hard to keep up. Deanna is cheerful, practical, and unstoppable. "Deanna of the Dunes," I call her, which makes her sound like the heroine of a novel, and she certainly could be. In class, on the day before each Thursday field outing, she would announce the weather for the next day. If wind was in the offing, she visibly rejoiced, much to the students' amusement: wind means sand is moving, thus enhancing the learning opportunities. One day late in the semester, Deanna announced, "Tomorrow there's a possibility of very scenic snow showers. Think about Christmas!" Sure enough, the day turned out icy, windy, and miserable. We went to our research sites anyway, and the shivering students counted Pitcher's thistle plants and took GPS readings in a sleet storm. Despite Deanna's frequent admonitions to dress for the weather, some students showed up in flimsy shoes or without gloves. Eventually, Deanna and her student-mentors called it a day, and the students all went out for hot chocolate. Science does have its rewards.

At the end of the semester, I watched the students attempt their first professional-style poster presentations. They did a great job. But all those hours yielded the most basic responses to their research questions. Do sand fences help prevent foot traffic and promote the growth of vegetation that prevents erosion? Well, we have three weeks' worth of data, and the answer is yes, at least in these two small areas, unless the fences are damaged, in which case, not so much. This is not to say anything against the students or Deanna. On the contrary, Geo 181 is a brilliant course, and the students learn a great deal about the process and ethics of research. But perhaps what they learned most fundamentally—I know this was my takeaway—is that building even the smallest morsels of scientific knowledge requires extraordinary skill, patience, and determination.

Stewardship and Other Shorthands

Continuing to build and communicate knowledge is one of the great challenges we face finding our way to new house rules. Meanwhile, for people of faith, inadequate theology presents another challenge, even a barrier. Rather than participating fully or providing leadership in the project of devising these new house rules, healing the damage humans have done, joining in the Great Work, we can rest too easily on familiar theological ideas. Easy references to "being made in the image of God" and being "called to stewardship" or "creation care" can mask our indifference. In fact, I would argue that we have allowed these biblical ideas to become cliché, flabby, and to some extent counterproductive.

During the summer of 2018, I spent a few lovely days of intense discussion with eighteen colleagues from a variety of disciplines, including the sciences. We were trying to work out together why it has been so easy for North American Christians to ignore or even deny the climate crisis. In particular, we interrogated the idea of stewardship. For some, stewardship of the earth has been an enormously helpful theological principle, but mostly the idea hasn't seemed to "move the needle" and get regular churchgoers much involved in climate action. We wondered, Is stewardship just not the right motivator? What are we missing?

As we talked with each other and developed our separate chapters for the book we were writing together, most of us reexamined in one way or another traditional interpretations of Genesis 1 and 2. Genesis texts inevitably appear in Christian discussions of human relationship with the rest of creation, and the typical pattern today is to navigate through these texts in order to conclude that the distinctive human vocation is benevolent stewardship. To reach this standard conclusion, we first establish that Genesis 1:26–28 NIV, the "creation mandate," declares that humans are made in the image of God and commanded to "rule" and "subdue." While this verse has long been leveraged as a justification for humans (well, humans with power and agency) to exploit and ruin the earth, we are now obliged to deplore this previous interpretation and instead declare that "dominion" actually means "creation care." We then point out that creation care / stewardship is supported by Genesis 2, the second creation account, especially verse 15: "The Lord God took the man and put him in the garden of Eden to till it and keep it." The Hebrew words *abad* and *shamar* are actually best translated as "serve and protect." So there we have it: We balance "rule" with "serve and protect," and we arrive not at domination but at the noble project of stewardship. We are called to care for God's creation. We are called to be, in my friend Steve Bouma-Prediger's lovely phrase, "earthkeepers."[7]

It's all sound interpretative work. "Stewardship" and "creation care" are pleasant-sounding terms and, as shorthand terms go, not inaccurate. The idea that humans are stewards of creation has helped moderate some Christians' tendencies to participate eagerly or simply unknowingly in an unsustainable extraction economy. Unfortunately, however, stewardship and creation care can easily become toothless concepts. For one thing, the metaphor itself is problematic. An owner (God) only needs a steward (us) if the owner plans not to be present. When we subtly assume God is not everywhere present, we are more likely to see what we can get away with. Overcome with our cultural idolization of growth and luxury, it's easy for Christians, along with everyone else, to turn "being good stewards" into "using resources efficiently for maximum profit (for some)." We can mouth the words and go right on doing whatever we please. A developer in Michigan has been fighting for years to dig up the Kalamazoo River channel in order to build luxury homes and a marina—over the protests of the community, Potawatomi groups, environmental groups, people concerned about preserving a nearby historical site, and the laws about altering waterways and designated critical dune areas.[8] I'm sure this guy imagines that he merely wants to be a good steward of that wedge of land he owns, positioned between a state park and a nature preserve. He's "stewarding" it to make a profit. Even former Environmental Protection Agency chief and climate-change-denier Scott Pruitt managed to use the word with a straight face when he announced the United States' withdrawal from the Paris Agreement: "We owe no apologies to other nations for our environmental stewardship," he said.[9]

Our group of scholars was well aware of how "stewardship" can become a self-deluding piety. Each of our essays wrestled with the problem, and we even titled our book *Beyond Stewardship*. Since that summer I have continued to wonder whether repeatedly trotting out verses from Genesis 1 and 2 is even all that helpful. Deriving ethical guidance from the creation accounts in Genesis 1 and 2 is always a hazardous business. These are ancient Near Eastern creation texts, not legal codes or ethical guidebooks. We wish we could torque these texts with hermeneutical pliers and get them to pop out the answers we want on any number of questions, but that's not how stories operate. If we come at them demanding answers, they have a tendency to turn into mirrors, reflecting back what we want them to say rather than revealing a challenging word for our moment. I do hold "a high view of Scripture": I do believe these are stories we are meant to cherish, to sit with, to listen to. They always speak anew, if we can listen well and with the guidance of the Spirit. So perched as we are, atop centuries of often contradictory interpretation and commentary, we have to ask once again: What do we need to hear from these stories in this place and time? What do they say to us now?

Old Testament scholar Walter Brueggemann, in his commentary on Genesis, insists that the creation accounts are meant neither as *history* (accounts of what happened) nor as *myth* (stories to represent what is always true) but as *proclamation.*[10] The Genesis 1 creation account dates from the time of Israel's exile under the Babylonian Empire; this account was meant to serve as an antidote to despair. An elegant liturgical poem attributed to the priestly strand in the Torah, Genesis 1 is a counterstory over against the Babylonian creation myths. It declares that the God of the Hebrews is the God of all creation, and this God has established a relationship of joy and delight with all creatures. It is a counterstory, too, over against the fear of abandonment the exiled Israelites must have felt. Genesis 1:26–28, in that context, reads as an affirmation. You who feel abandoned: You have dignity and vocation. *You* are my image in the world, says God, not as opposed to the other creatures of the earth so much but as opposed to the idols of your conquerors. It's sobering to consider that this passage, containing those strong Hebrew words for "rule" and "subdue," arises from a time when the storytellers were not ruling anything, not the birds or beasts or their own land or even themselves. Speaking into fear and anxiety, this creation account is a proclamation of God's passionate relationship with creation. To be my image, says God, be like me: God does not dominate with violence but makes space for other creatures, blesses them with the freedom to flourish, delights in them, rests in that delight, and remains in relationship with this creation.

The Genesis 2 account, Brueggemann says, is older, perhaps from the Solomonic period, and thus it can be imagined as a check on monarchal arrogance. This account, attributed to the Yahwist strand, focuses on humans as soil creatures, with *adam* made from the *adamah* ("soil"). God places the soil creature, *adam*, in a garden where the human can learn to serve and protect the humus, in partnership with the animals and a cohuman. This fellow doesn't even have a proper name, despite what our modern translations imply. He's just a generic *adam*. As I read this text now, I realize that the garden was, in a way, the world's first refugium. In fact, let's coin a term and call it a "prelapsarian refugial substructure." The Eden refugium is not necessitated by a crisis but designed as an initiating microculture, a place to create capacities at a manageable scale. Notably, those capacities depend on both human continuity with and distinctiveness from the rest of creation. Humans are made of the same stuff as the rest of creation but are also given distinctive moral responsibility. Brueggemann breaks down this moral responsibility into *vocation, permission,* and *prohibition*. The cohumans have great freedom to flourish, but also limits. The thriving of the little refugium depends on the humans respecting those limits. Thus for Brueggemann, the two creation accounts proclaim together, in dialectic. You who are in despair, remember you have dignity. You who seem to rule, remember you are dust. We need both these proclamations, today and always.

Brueggemann ignores in his commentary the little story in 2:19–20 of *adam* naming the animals, but to me this is the oddest and therefore the most interesting story element. Why include this curious detail? It's actually a charming moment in which God seems to enjoy the suspense, waiting to see what *adam* will name the animals. The human is given freedom to play with language, and God accepts what the soil creature comes up with: "Whatever [*adam*] called each living creature, that was its name" (Gen 2:19 NIV). This story element has sometimes been seen as confirming human dominion over the creatures. After all, naming is often an expression of power in the Hebrew Scriptures, as it is today. That view doesn't seem to fit the playful tone of the passage though. Instead, I wonder if prelapsarian language here serves not as an assertion of power but as an establishment of relationship. Naming can be a loving act too, a form of attention and connection.[11] For example, tiny children often defy all suggestions and find their own names for their beloved grandparents.

Reformation theologians, taking their cue from earlier biblical commentary, proposed that Adam had a kind of prelapsarian superpower: an intimate knowledge of each creature. Martin Luther imagined that Adam, "as soon as he viewed an animal, came into possession of a knowledge of its entire nature and abilities." Adam could give the animals their "right" names, then, because of this intuitive knowledge. The animals, according to these commentators, were obedient and cooperative in their pre-fall state. Calvin remarks that this gentleness would have remained in animals if not for the fall. Instead, says Calvin, when Adam disobeyed God, he lost his original, God-given authority over the animals. Adam "experienced the ferocity of brute animals against himself. Indeed, while some can be broken with great effort, others always remain untamed, and some inspire us with terror by their fierceness, even when unprovoked."[12] Both Calvin and Luther, I've noticed, as much as they rejoice over every whale and blade of grass, also express persistent anxieties about insects, ferocious beasts, prickly plants, and other worrisome aspects of the natural world.[13]

In proposing that Adam originally enjoyed a profound, innate knowledge of the creatures, Reformation theologians offer a fanciful conjecture. But it's a thought-provoking idea. If we imagine the first human in the Genesis story beginning with deep knowledge of the other creatures, then the first human use of language would echo God's use of language in the first creation account: God speaks a world into being, entering into a relationship of delight with that creation. Similarly, *adam*'s relationship with the creatures, enhanced through naming them, is also characterized by attention and delight. In fact, the text portrays God joining into that delight while watching *adam* come up with names. In some interpretations of the passage, the animals are seen as a kind of failed experiment: God attempts to salve poor *adam*'s loneliness with a bunch of animals, but alas, it doesn't quite work. Here I much prefer biblical scholar Theodore Hiebert's reading, in which Hiebert points to the agrarian mindset of the story's first tellers. In that context, the animals are not a false start but a necessary set of partners in *adam*'s vocation of serving the land.[14] In his comments on the naming story, Orthodox theologian Alexander Schmemann confirms the joyful view of relationship the story offers, writing, "To name a thing is to manifest the very essence of a thing, or rather its essence as God's gift. To name a thing is to manifest the meaning and value God gave it, to know it as coming from God and to know its place and function within the cosmos created by God."[15]

When *adam* does receive the cohuman he needs in the next few verses, he offers an effusion of language, a little poem:

This at last is bone of my bones and flesh of my flesh;
     this one shall be called [isha] for out of [ish] this one was
     taken. (Gen 2:23)

In this very first piece of direct human dialogue in the Bible, *adam*
manages to make a pun, connecting the Hebrew words for "man" and
"woman" (words whose etymologies, interestingly, are from separate
Hebrew roots). In the woman, our soil creature sees a mirror image of
himself; he knows her because she is like him. Our up-till-now gener-
ically named *adam* finds a name for himself and for the woman at the
same time: *ish* and *isha*. Their coordinating names signal their relationship of mutual regard. These verses are therefore consistent and continuous with the previous verses about the animals, suggesting that
naming derives from knowing and creates relationship.

The naming story in the Genesis 2 account, then, might suggest
to us that the right relationship between humans and the rest of creation is one of deep knowledge for a greater purpose: partnership in a
world that gives praise to the Creator. Perhaps this is what the "listening community"—as Brueggemann likes to call the faithful—needs to
hear in this text for today.[16] In the Bible's story of the world's first refugium, humans and creatures together are blessed by a loving Creator
to flourish together. Humans in particular are given vocation, permission, and limits. They are instructed to cooperate with the creatures in
the thriving of the garden, serving it, protecting it. This work—and it is
work—depends on deep and loving knowledge. Here's another reason,
then, that the term *stewardship* is inadequate: stewardship implies duty,
and duty is never as effective a motivation as love.

Brueggemann and other scholars suggest that the two creation
accounts fit into the broader story arc of Genesis 1–11, which includes
the fall as well as the flood story and its aftermath. These texts were
pieced together in a pattern of creation, uncreation, re-creation. The
famous fall narrative in Genesis 3, an account of human resistance to
limits, sets the world on a course of progressive uncreation. Even in the
midst of uncreation, though, God is working toward re-creation. Notably, after the humans are "caught" in their violation of limits and told
that they will now experience difficult labors both agricultural and
reproductive, God also hints at the importance of their descendants in
verse 15, a verse Christians have interpreted as the first promise of a

Redeemer. Adam seems to pick up on this hint, because he immediately gives the woman another name: Eve, "living" or "one who gives life." Despite this promising moment, the pattern of uncreation accelerates in the next chapters, culminating in the flood story. Here, too, we see God working creation out of uncreation. In the postdiluvian covenant with Noah, God insists on remaining in passionate relationship with the whole creation. Human wickedness is not cured, not by any means. Even so, God renews the covenant relationship, renewing vocation, permission, and prohibitions for humans, though with some differences. God therefore persistently invites humans to participate in the ongoing process of re-creation. This re-creation, Christians believe, is deepened and fulfilled in the life of Christ.

Uncreation in dialectic with re-creation—that dynamic has only intensified throughout history. Human disregard for our limits has grown now to grotesque proportions as we clear-cut forests, strip-mine vast territories, dump tons of plastic waste, drive other creatures to extinction, and even alter the planet's climate. Likewise, the scale of our earth-healing task today is overwhelming. For this task, the Genesis creation accounts cannot give us all we need, but they do perhaps still provide some reference points. As image bearers of God, we imitate God's form of rule: creative self-emptying so that all can thrive. This requires deep and loving knowledge, ingenuity, and humility. Absent our prelapsarian superpowers, that knowledge comes only slowly and painfully, but the work of building knowledge is redemptive work. For this reason, we need to move beyond what the Genesis accounts suggest as our human vocation. We no longer inhabit a prelapsarian garden. We live instead in a damaged, uncreated world. So as lovely as the term *earthkeepers* may be, I think it's not quite precise, since "keeping" implies maintaining things in some current state. Today, instead, it's more urgent to understand our vocation as one of repair, re-creation, healing. We need to be "earth healers." Or better yet, "partners in earth healing."

If we are partners in earth healing, we need to ask different questions about any place that we own or live on or love. For millennia, humans have mostly asked, "What do we want and need from 'nature'?" In this age of the Great Work, we need to ask instead, "What healing does this place need, and how can I help?"

From Stewardship to Reciprocity

During the same fall when I sat in on Deanna's dunes class, I was also teaching a first-year writing course for science majors. I had students read a number of chapters from Robin Wall Kimmerer's beautiful book of essays, *Braiding Sweetgrass*. Kimmerer is a botanist—a moss specialist—and also a member of the Citizen Potawatomi Nation. I assigned the chapter "People of Corn, People of Light," in which Kimmerer recounts the Mayan creation story.[17] In this story, the gods have to try several times before they get humans "right." They first create humans from mud, but those creatures are too crumbly; they fall apart. Then the gods try wood. The wood humans are lithe and clever but heartless. They destroy other creatures, and the rest of the earth rebels against them. Next, light. These humans are "dazzling" but arrogant. Finally, the gods make humans from corn. These humans are conscious—they dance, sing, tell stories—and they are humble. They show respect and gratitude for the rest of creation. They are the ones who last.

My students *loved* this story. Partly, I think, they were thrilled to read other creation accounts for once besides the biblical one. Partly they recognized what Kimmerer also points out: the story presents us with a question. What kind of people are you in this world? The students appreciated the clarity and simplicity of the story's implications: be humble, be grateful, for you are made of the same biological materials as the rest of creation, and you have a role in it, like everything else. Kimmerer's essay goes on to consider the particular knowledge and contribution of other beings. Plants make air, light, and water into sugars and oxygen. Animals breathe oxygen from plants and produce carbon dioxide, which the plants need. Buffalo help grasses thrive by grazing on them, birds know how to fly, salamanders can "read" magnetic lines in the earth. Everything has its brilliance, its beauty, its skill and contribution. These days, writes Kimmerer, scientists are the ones who best carry this knowledge, the stories of other creatures: "The practice of doing real science brings the questioner into an unparalleled intimacy with nature fraught with wonder and creativity as we try to comprehend the mysteries of the more-than-human world. Trying to understand the life of another being or another system so unlike our own is often humbling and, for many scientists, is a deeply spiritual pursuit."[18] The essay concludes with an encouragement for scientists to tell these stories and to regard other creatures as our teachers. Humans are, after all, "younger brothers" on the earth. Evolutionarily speaking, other creatures have been here longer. Plants, for example, "were here first and have had a long time to figure things out."[19]

As many have observed, the time has come when we all need to listen to Indigenous wisdom. Kimmerer describes the Anishinaabe prophecy of the Seventh Fire, a time of crisis when the young must gather scattered fragments of ancient knowledge and help heal the land.[20] How astonishing that peoples whose cultures were systematically and brutally destroyed, whose knowledge survives only with great determination and dedication—how astonishing that these people carry wisdom full of healing balms that all of us, including the colonizers, need in order to survive. Kimmerer is an ideal translator of that wisdom, since she is also proficient in the language of Western science. She fully acknowledges that "science polishes the gift of seeing,"[21] but she also carries stories and ways of knowing that provide vital correctives to Western ways of thinking.

I was especially struck in her essays by the theme of reciprocity. Kimmerer tells of teaching a graduate writing workshop full of students who professed a deep love for the earth. "Do you think that the earth loves you back?" she asked them.[22] They were stunned. So was I, when I read that. I know I haven't loved nature enough, but I've never even imagined that nature could somehow love me back. Yet this mutuality is exactly what Kimmerer explores throughout her book. All creatures have gifts, we all give to one another. This is the next step beyond recognizing that we are kin with other creatures: understanding that we all give gifts to one another. Certainly, other creatures contribute to each other and to us. But what do we contribute to them? We are relentless takers, consumers, extractors. Our wildlife refuges and botanical gardens and zoo-based breeding programs are only meager compensation for what we take. Many passionate people have committed their lives to the study and preservation of flora and fauna, including of the most fanged and fearsome of creatures. Even so, our taking far outbalances our giving.

While reading Kimmerer's book, I was distressed and ashamed that these themes of reciprocity and gratitude were not stronger in my own Christian tradition. We talk about gratitude to God all the time—true. We thank God *for* pleasant weather and, on occasion, for other creatures. Some of us remind one another that we must be good stewards.

But I can't recall ever hearing about reciprocity. Reciprocity is distinct in crucial ways from stewardship or "creation care." Stewardship and creation care assume we are in control, we are in charge, and we get to choose our benevolence. The earth gives us things, and we "take care" of it so it can continue to give us things. This feels comfortable—too comfortable—because it keeps us squarely at the center. Reciprocity, on the other hand, acknowledges that humans and the more-than-human creation all take care of each other. Perhaps our modern alienation from the rest of creation has muted themes of reciprocity where they have appeared in Scripture and the Christian tradition. Twelfth-century abbess and mystic Hildegard of Bingen, for example, believed that the earth not only provides for human needs but is also "touched by" human actions, so that when we sin we do violence to the world around us.[23] In any case, Kimmerer calls us to consider what reciprocity can mean today: "I've heard it said that sometimes, in return for the gifts of the earth, gratitude is enough. It is our uniquely human gift to express thanks, because we have the awareness and the collective memory to remember that the world could well be otherwise, less generous than it is. But I think we are called to go beyond cultures of gratitude, to once again become cultures of reciprocity."[24] In environmental science circles, the things that creatures and terrain elements provide within their ecosystem—food for other creatures, water filtering, oxygen respiration—are sometimes called "ecosystem services." Sometimes that phrase is used in economic contexts to translate the work of natural elements into monetary terms, to put a cash value on air and light, since cash value is, for some, the only measure of importance. Kimmerer just calls these ecosystem services "gifts." In many Indigenous ways of thinking, humans and the more-than-human world are all part of a gift-exchange economy. Or we could be.

If humans didn't exist at all, life would continue on earth. Let's not flatter ourselves: biologically speaking, the earth does not need us to tend and care for it. Life on earth existed for eons before we arrived. Have we made the earth better by our arrival? Theologians have long interpreted Genesis 1:26–28 as God's instruction to humans to unfold the potential of creation. Very well, but in our unfolding of potentials, we can also destroy, especially now that we have become so very fruitful and multiplied to so many billions. "Stewarding" and "caring" are only necessary because humans take things from the earth to survive.

We know it's possible that our existence can do more harm than good to the earth, yet I've heard some Christians shunt off responsibility for our actions to God. "Well, even if climate change is real," they say, "God won't let us destroy the planet. Don't worry about it. God will do something." What follows is usually a reaffirmation of free-market economics as the solution to our problems. I have more faith in the power of God than in the unfettered market; I also note from the evidence that God allows people a great deal of freedom to do evil and ruinous things. Giving humans moral responsibility entails allowing us to act immorally and to suffer the consequences of our actions—or in the case of climate change, to let other people suffer the consequences, at least at first. Do we really want to find out just how far God will let this go before God "does something"? Or could we instead perceive that God is indeed doing something, through the knowledge and work of people and through the self-healing powers built into the planet? The question for each of us is whether to resist or cooperate.

All right, then: What can we give back through a pattern of reciprocity to a planet that gives us so much? What will make the more-than-human creation glad that we are here? I wonder about that now as I read about efforts to protect critical dunes and mitigate the polluting of Lake Michigan and our local watersheds. I wonder as I drive the highways out of my city, past cornfields and office parks. I wonder as I try to rescue my own small piece of land from the dreaded buckthorn invasion. If my spruces are glad that I helped them by freeing them from the buckthorn, how could I even know?

Refugia Tracking

Of all the people acting as healers right now, some of the most exciting to me are those working in the field of restoration ecology. Modern restoration ecology is a full-on academic subspecialty and worldwide practice, with academic journals and professional associations and the whole bit. The point of restoration ecology is not to return every piece of land to some pristine "original" state. What would that even be? Ecosystems are dynamic. In Michigan, for example, we could "return" the area between Lansing and Grand Rapids to a pre-White-settlement state by ripping out Interstate 96; planting oaks, maples, and beeches; and hoping for the best. We would have to somehow convince today's overabundant deer not to gobble up the seedlings. And anyway, humans "interfered" with the land long before Europeans arrived. The Anishinaabeg of the late Woodland period managed the region with carefully planned burns to open up some areas for better hunting, for example.[25] That's what created the oak openings that thrilled the first White settlers—these areas looked to them like the open forests of Europe.

Rather than seeking some pristine originary state, restoration ecologists are engaged in the practical work of healing—often from damage humans have created—toward a resilient future state. To do this, they have to approach their work more as pragmatists than romantics, answering two extremely difficult questions: Which land and water do we heal, and to what state? Refugia turn out to be crucial in answering those questions. If researchers, managers, and stakeholders can identify places where a particular species has been surviving well, especially under stresses like drought, fire, insect proliferation, alterations to water flow and temperature, and so on, then they might be able to plan better for a changing climate, focusing conservation efforts on places with "high refugia potential."[26] Refugial conservation biology, in other words, is a method for partnering with natural processes to support the persistence of threatened species and help preserve—or even restore—biodiversity. The June 2020 issue of the journal *Frontiers in Ecology and the Environment* features nine articles about this practice that describe a variety of studies.[27] One article considers the particular challenges of ensuring the survival of freshwater fish that prefer colder water temperatures. Creatures that move around or migrate, such as salmon, sea turtles, and waterfowl, this article points out, need "a suite of habitats and resources over a species' life cycle that are relatively buffered from contemporary climate change" if those species are to survive across time.[28] For creatures like these, we have to identify, protect, and even create "stepping-stone" refugia—a series of suitable places where the creatures can survive along their migratory routes. Another article presents a series of maps that model "consensus vegetation refugia" in California under two main climate scenarios for forty-three species, such as chaparral and Douglas fir. The idea is to find spots where a plant species is likely to survive "under both wetter and drier future projections," hence "consensus." The authors of this article are attempting to determine how much of this vegetation is likely to survive, and where, to the end of the century.[29] Refugia, in this field of biology, operate as "biodiversity slow lanes." They give us time to get smarter about how we partner with the more-than-human world, helping us set priorities for management and support resilience. The work is difficult, with an enormous number of factors to consider: terrain, feeding habits, sensitivity to change, water sources, weather patterns, human impact, genetic diversity within a species—and all of this for multiple interacting species across varying scales of space and time, as conditions change.

This scientific work suggests another important reason casually tossing off the terms *stewardship* or *creation care* is a form of arrogance. Perhaps the terms can prompt our attention to this work. But restoration ecology demonstrates how difficult it is to know how to care for even a limited sector of a single ecosystem. How can we possibly steward the whole earth? Theologian Richard Bauckham notes that "the image of stewardship is still too freighted with the baggage of the modern project of technological domination of nature. Can we entirely free [the term *stewardship*] of the implication that nature is always better off when managed by us, that nature needs our benevolent intrusions, that it is our job to turn the whole world into a well-tended garden inhabited by well-cared-for pets?"[30] To find both the urgency and the limits of our healing role, we must build knowledge as a redemptive process, and the more the better, not only for professional researchers and managers, but also for ordinary people. We can listen to the understanding of particular ecosystems built over many generations by peoples indigenous to those regions. One of the things both scientists and Indigenous peoples know is that sometimes we need the humility to back off and leave the more-than-human world to its own healing work. Some land regions, some rivers and lakes, and some parts of the ocean need relief from human demands for the sake of the various species that can survive only without our meddling interference. Respect for other members of this household, in other words, requires giving them some space, some large-scale refugia.

National Geographic recently featured the work of several environmental research groups that are pushing to preserve 30 percent of the planet by 2030 and 50 percent by 2050. (In 2018, about 15 percent of the earth's lands were formally protected, along with about 7 percent of ocean area.)[31] These groups have gotten together to create a composite map, combining analyses of the human footprint, various biomes, and hot spots for biodiversity. The map, published in June 2020 in the journal *Global Change Biology*, is intended to support evidence-based

recommendations on exactly which areas of the world must be priori-
tized for preservation in order to provide maximum carbon sequestration and species biodiversity.[32] The dream is to convince governments,
private institutions, and conservation groups to work together in order
to "dedicate 30 percent of [our] land and sea to a robustly financed,
locally supported, ecologically representative mix of areas managed for
the benefit of nature."[33] High-priority areas include, for example, peat-
lands south of the Hudson Bay, the Amazon Rainforest, Southeast Asian
rain forests, and Red Sea coral reefs. The groups are also working on the
next tough problem: designating what preservation means for each area.
Some ought to be "Strict Nature Preserves"—no human interference—in
order to create space for species that require large, undisturbed habitats. But many other regions could continue to be "anthromes"—places
populated by humans but wisely managed.[34] Making space for human
management is especially important to Indigenous groups who live in
sensitive areas—or who used to and want to return to their lands.

Intelligent Tinkering

If we are going to be earth healers, planet-scale agreements about limits
on our human activities will be a vital dimension of our new house rules.
However, equally vital are the rules we devise for farms, cities, suburbs,
gardens, and backyards. It's hard to imagine all of us living by the Indigenous subsistence practices Kimmerer beautifully describes, gliding
canoes through watery wild rice fields or shaving black ash to make baskets. And I admit I sometimes grow impatient with Wendell Berry, whose
work always seems to gravitate back to the small, temperate-climate farm
as the ideal pattern of human life. But although we do not have all the new
house rules figured out, we do have some clear ideas now about what *not*
to do. After several generations of increasingly aggressive agribusiness,
we now understand the ecological outcomes of monocropping and heavy
fertilizer use in soil erosion, degradation, runoff pollution, and pesticide-
resistant bugs. We now understand the ecological costs of massive animal
feeding lots too. We also know what's possible: It is possible to farm in
ways that actually improve the soil, not degrade it. It is possible to eat far
less meat and raise animals humanely. It is possible to green up our cities,
turn more areas into gardens and parks. People are doing all these things
already.

For those of us not on distinguished international conservation boards, our healing work can start small, with refugia. Bill Jordan and John Aber, the founders of modern restoration ecology, built on the legacy of the Curtis Prairie restoration project through the University of Wisconsin–Madison Arboretum. The project began with only sixty acres, which university faculty, students, and the Civilian Conservation Corps set out to restore to tallgrass prairie. In the decades since, the project has not only continued to provide invaluable knowledge about tallgrass prairies and how to re-create them but also inspired a whole branch of ecology.[35] Among the originators of the project was the great conservationist and writer Aldo Leopold. Witty, humane, practical, and wise, Leopold grappled in all his writings with the question of how to heal the places he loved. He understood that we can't "go back" to some pristine wild state, and he understood that there are always limits to what we know. We will make mistakes. But we can still become earth healers. The first rule, he surmises, is to do our best to preserve all the parts: "To keep every cog and wheel is the first precaution of intelligent tinkering," he writes.[36] This presumes careful observation and study of what the parts might be, from plants to insects to fungi, even if—especially if—we aren't sure how they work together. In his famous essay "The Land Ethic," Leopold offers his most succinct and influential statement on how to make judgments about restoration goals: "Examine each question in terms of what is ethically and esthetically right, as well as what is economically expedient. A thing is right when it tends to preserve the integrity, stability, and beauty of the biotic community. It is wrong when it tends otherwise."[37] Judging whether something meets those metrics—integrity, stability, beauty—is more challenging than it might at first seem. These words sound, in fact, like aesthetic or philosophical measures more than biological ones. Maybe even measures with a theological weight. Leopold wasn't making a directly theological statement, but he might have been. Those words match up pretty well with a restored community of creation envisioned in the covenant promises of Scripture and heralded in the life of Jesus.

Despite putting every effort we can into conservation, restoration, and healing, ultimately humans will not bring about that healed and whole community—that is the work of God. We can witness to that divine work, though, and participate as much as we can, leaning toward the community-of-creation vision with all the knowledge and love we can summon.

Ugliness and Meanwhile Grace

One spring day during the Covid-19 quarantine, I invited my daughter to go with me to a park across town for a short birding expedition. The Highlands is located right off Leonard Street, almost directly across from the street where I grew up. As I remember it, The Highlands was a golf course, but I only ever saw it from a distance. As far as I knew it was accessible only to an exclusive clientele. My friend Amy's family were members, la dee da. But I never set foot on it.

Now it's a public nature preserve. The golf course owners eventually succumbed to the inevitable and sold the land to developers who wanted to build condos. But in 2017 the Land Conservancy of West Michigan (LCWM) joined with Blandford Nature Center—a long-beloved educational nonprofit right next to the golf course—to arrange a purchase of the property. In 2019 they began a restoration project that will turn these 121 acres into a refugium right in the city, with wildlife habitat, nature trails, and educational programs.

Mia and I arrived midmorning, equipped with warm jackets, sunglasses, and binoculars. We pulled into the gravel parking lot and noticed immediately the spot where the clubhouse used to be, now an expanse of dry dirt. We started walking, not quite sure where the paths were supposed to be. They were barely evident, only faintly outlined.

In fact, what struck me most was how messy it all looked, like nothing more than an abandoned golf course. You could make out the old fairways, now weedy and dry. You could see the water features, now muddy and edged with dried grasses. Since it was early May, the deciduous trees were barely leafing out, and some of them looked rather rickety. Some of the spruces were just standing there dead, as if someone had stuck thirty-foot Christmas trees in the ground and left them to decay.

And yet. The birds were singing. Before even stepping on a "trail," we spotted a heron and a hawk overhead. Mallards and Canada geese pairs calmly sunned themselves at the edges of the ponds, one pair with gosling fluff balls waddling nearby. Tree swallows swooped and circled. We heard red-bellied woodpeckers and tufted titmice. Before long we spotted a beautiful pair of Eastern bluebirds. Of course there were robins, cardinals, blue jays, starlings, and crows. Later we saw a hermit thrush, a palm warbler with golden belly and little rusty cap, and a northern flicker with her stylish stripes and spots. Mia also got good photos of brave little chickadees who seemed to enjoy the spotlight, posing in spruce branches for her. "Small bundles of large enthusiasms," as Aldo Leopold fondly describes them.[38]

Besides razing the clubhouse and putting up a couple signs, the LCWM had done . . . what? It was hard to tell. Later, I went to their website and learned that much more was happening than an amateur like me could spot with the naked eye. The Highlands operated as a golf course for over a hundred years. That meant a hundred years of coddling turfgrass with heavy watering and fertilizing, pumping pesticides and other toxic substances into the surrounding watershed. As a first step toward new life, the LCWM removed the turfgrass. Just scraped it right up. Then volunteers helped plant scads of native wildflowers. We won't enjoy those for another couple years, though. The flowers will spend their first two seasons putting down dense, deep root systems that absorb water and hold the soil. The LCWM also dug out wetland areas in places where the land already dipped. So some of those ponds the critters were enjoying were not just water hazards gone wild. They were new.

The LCWM is finding ways to help this land heal, to create a resilient, sustainable place that provides hospitality for more-than-human life right in the city, with residential neighborhoods and busy streets nearby. A whole master plan has been developed, by a team of experts with plenty of community input, to turn this land into a native prairie and savannah ecosystem. Each phase of the plan requires the rains and seeds and creatures to do their work before the next phase can begin. There's no rushing the process, not if you want to do it right. And the first stages look like a mess. As the LCWM website points out, "In restoration, ugliness is often the first sign of progress."[39]

While we wait and watch, though, we recognize that the transition period has its own graces. Birdsong and sunning turtles, for example. A killdeer, with broad black bands across its breast like a sailor-stripe shirt. I wonder what this suggests for us, right now, in this time when so much seems ugly, unkempt, neglected, unhealed. A lot seems dead. We wonder about God's promises. Are enough seeds planted to start healing the planet? Could we ever agree on a master plan? Even if we all help, do we have enough time?

Waiting, transition, in-betweenness. I am trying to look for the meanwhile graces.

PITCHER'S THISTLE
CIRSIUM PITCHERI

August
Sleeping Bear Point, Michigan

We walk backward through time. From the trailhead, shaded with eastern hemlocks and white pines, we work our way closer to the lake and through earlier stages of plant succession. The softer trees and ferny underbrush soon give way as the sandy trail undulates into areas more exposed to wind and sand movement, places where only pioneer species can survive.

Here are a few twisting cottonwoods, those crotchety and determined citizens of this region's flora. Cottonwoods don't mind being buried by moving sand, so they can grow closer to the lake, where the wind is stronger and the dunes more active. To beat moving dunes, they'll send out root shoots if they have to and pop up stems a little farther on. What looks like a stand of a few trees is actually a clump with connections underground. We spot one bent old cottonwood with one trunk dry, sand scoured, and barkless; one trunk that looks recently dead; and one trunk in the middle topped with a pom of healthy green leaves pattering in the breeze. Lots of scrubby ground-cover plants thrive here too—sand reed grass, little bluestem, bearberry, sand cherry—all of them tough enough to tolerate dryness, extreme heat, and winds that carry scouring suspensions of moving sand.

We chuff down slopes, labor up soft sand hills. Then: the lake! The water shines sea-glass turquoise out to the depth drop, then shifts to royal blue. We are high on a perched dune system now, high enough for a view of the Manitou Islands about seven and ten miles offshore. Open dunes surround us, bristling with beach grass like stubble on a chin. Beach grass clings to the crests surrounding bowls of bare sand, the first plant that can establish on the very edge of constant, rapid change.

Disturbance prompts renewal, movement, life. *Ammophila breviligulata*, American beach grass or marram grass, *needs* to be buried by moving sand every year. Burial of up to three feet per year is ideal, prompting the plant to spread rhizomes horizontally and to grow upward, thus building a thick tangle of deep, interconnected roots. You can tell where a dune is moving by looking for lush, healthy beach grass.

We spot a good deal of Pitcher's thistle too—*Cirsium pitcheri*, that prickly darling of dune conservationists. It grows only in the Great Lakes region, only on open dunes with just the right amount of marram grass and moderate disturbance. Thanks to human impacts, the Pitcher's thistle is a federally threatened species, hence the affection of conservationists. Even as thistles go, the Pitcher's is not exactly a beauty. It's grayish, papery, and frankly rather stubby. It would never grow in your garden, but if it did, you would probably pull it out without remorse, maybe even with satisfaction. It's finicky too. It takes five to eight years to bloom, then flowers and produces seed once, then dies. The Pitcher's thistle has its place, though. Goldfinches, sparrows, and bees visit it for their groceries. The artichoke plume moth, when artichokes are in short supply, seems to consider it an ideal bed for incubating larvae, although we're not entirely sure whether that benefits or drains the plant. One of this little prickler's tricks might solicit some respect: it plunges a six-foot-long taproot into the sand to anchor it and siphon up water.[1]

We walk on, following blue-painted signposts across pathless dunes. Gauzy clouds and a breeze soften the blazing sun, but heat rises from the quartz-feldspar sand. In a vast bowl of bare sand, we cross through a "ghost forest." Sometimes, disturbance is too much. Here, moving sands long ago buried a forest alive. The trees died. Eventually, the dune receded again, exposing still-upright gray skeletons. Nothing but jagged, desiccated, barkless trunks remain, leaning from the memory of old winds, pocked with circular scars where branches once grew.

Chapter 4

From Avoiding to Lamenting

Deep calls to deep in the roar of your waterfalls;
all your waves and breakers have swept over me.
—PSALM 42:7 NIV

I n Christian tradition, the season of Lent sets each of us
squarely before a bracing truth: you will die. On Ash Wednes-
day, the first day of Lent, a priest or pastor or elder smears
ashes in the shape of a cross on the foreheads of the faithful, saying
to each person, "Remember that you are dust." Thus begins a period of
soul-searching, self-discipline, and repentance in preparation for the
culminating dramas of the church year: Holy Week and Easter.

I tend to welcome Lent when it comes. In Michigan, Lent coincides
with the sleety, slushy weariness of late winter. Damp, icy winds chill
to the bone, clouds brood low and heavy. Melancholy comes easily,
especially for those of us who tend toward it anyway. Self-discipline,
limits, meditating on Jesus's words of judgment, plodding on despite
everything—that's the sort of religious observance I can manage. I'm
still young enough that for myself, mortality seems mostly theoretical.
I can indulge my melancholic tendencies within the safe confines of
Lent's start and end dates. It's just an exercise.

During the Covid-19 pandemic, though, Lent felt amorphous and
perpetual. The more liturgically minded people on my Twitter feed

started referring to this time as "Coronatide."[1] Days and weeks passed undistinguished from each other. Absent our usual routines, we lost the rhythms and patterns that steadied us. We felt adrift. Mortality, always nearer than we like to imagine, became quantifiable, as we watched statistical curves rise and death numbers mount. We endured more limits for a longer period than any of us would have guessed we could tolerate. Meanwhile, social earthquakes kept the ground shaking beneath us: continued police brutality and racial inequities blatantly exposed, plus the daily traumas of political news. The proposed end point of our isolations kept extending further and further into the future. Some people bucked and fumed. We are lousy at limits in America.

The Covid-19 crisis forced us to set aside any tacit assumptions we might have cherished about progress and think instead about impending doom. What if global pandemics continue to seize us, becoming the new normal? What if the Republic really does fall to pieces? People reached for the most preposterous of conspiracy theories to explain the confusion. But I imagine all of us had our moments when we wondered, What if this is all just one piece of a greater cascade of disasters that means: the end?

I once attended an art exhibition of early sixteenth-century woodcuts and engravings, commemorating the five hundredth anniversary of the Protestant Reformation. Martin Luther, I learned, did not imagine that his efforts at reform were awakening the dawn of a new, more enlightened age. He and his compatriots in those early years were more like the prophets running for the hills while yelling over their shoulders, "Repent! The end is near!" In the exhibition book, art historian Robin Barnes notes that when Luther entered the European scene with his calls for ecclesiastical reform, the "atmosphere was already heavy with queasy forebodings." The prints of the period were full of monsters, witches, debaucheries, and what was evidently considered the ultimate indicator of divine judgment, hailstorms. These images demonstrate vividly that Luther and his contemporaries expected the apocalypse any minute. Why not? So much was happening at once: diseases and plagues, astronomical and meteorological weirdness, witches, Ottoman Turks, class unrest, a shockingly corrupt church establishment, and all these technological and political upheavals! How could the world survive? Better to repent and get ready. Barnes writes, "Luther saw his own movement to revive the gospel as the last act in this great conflict."[2]

Some modern Christian traditions seem to have organized their entire religious practice around vivid imaginings about the end times. My experience has been quite the opposite: the "no one knows the day or the hour" approach. No feverish renderings of the daily news as fulfillments of Revelation's prophecies, no planning for tribulation. I was taught to focus on faithful service here and now, leaving the future to God. Someday, sure, there would be a culmination of history, but meanwhile, we were exhorted to assume the world would wobble on long past our own momentary walks upon it.

I still mostly believe that it will. I do not spend my hours trembling before images of apocalyptic pyrotechnics—except when I watch disaster movies, which I love. I'm more worried about slow, painful decline. Climate science presents its own apocalyptic predictions, and a whole subgenre of science fiction imagines a vivid variety of climate-disaster-induced dystopias. Even if we do everything "right" in this moment to transition our infrastructure and slow climate change, life could continue to get much harder even for the most privileged. Survival has already gotten even harder for the most vulnerable, both humans and more-than-human creatures.

During the long Lent of Covid-19 quarantine, we found refugia in our own homes if we could. Refugia, I realized then, are not impermeable safety bunkers, protected from the crises around them. Instead, the surrounding conditions of disrupted equilibrium penetrate into every safe space, into the spirit. Our weary spirits made it difficult to fall into healthy new routines in our pandemic refugia. Instead, after the initial stage of attempting new hobbies, there was a long stage of floundering. As the pandemic wore on, we had to take stock: What is most important? What must we let go? We tried to keep our spirits up but found grief unavoidable. We had to lament what we and others were losing.

Refugia faith, it turns out, requires a sturdy capacity to grieve, lament, and repent. It requires the humility that comes from feeling helpless and small. More important, refugia faith compels us to grieve along with others, to build empathy and compassion for those whose griefs we may never have bothered about before. Lenten practices over the years have helped me understand the spiritual necessity of facing one's own and others' grief, ritualizing that grief through lament. However, lament remains a less familiar spiritual practice than repentance, from which it is distinct. Repentance assumes guilt; it is about accepting one's own responsibility and changing one's ways. Lament, meanwhile, does not necessarily entail guilt. Lament simply allows grief some space. Lament allows us to ask why, feel our sorrow, and sit with the lack of answers. In this way, lament binds us together, reminding us that when one member of the group suffers, the rest should carry that suffering too. Lament, then, is one way of respecting others, loving our neighbors. Acknowledging grief through lament can sometimes lead, appropriately, to repentance. And repentance can bind us together too, by repairing the rifts between us.

I'm not sure there's a suitable biological analogy for the importance of facing these negative feelings. Perhaps it's enough to say that when an ecosystem is stressed, the creatures have their own ways of signaling their distress and responding. In any case, in human refugia, we must be willing to acknowledge one another's pain and loss if we hope to find and create refugia spaces that can genuinely help us rebuild and renew. Failing to acknowledge pain is disrespectful to those who suffer most and, ultimately, renders any action less effective.

Christians, along with people of other faiths, should not be afraid of grief, lament, or repentance. Ideally, our religious practices have given us tools for understanding and managing sorrow and guilt. Lenten practices in particular—such as meditation, fasting, prayer, reflections on Scripture passages describing Jesus's suffering, calls to self-exam-ination and change, and reflections on mortality—all of these are useful exercises. But exercises only go so far when trials actually buffet. I won-der how many of us have exercised our capacities for grief, lament, and repentance sufficiently in order to undertake the Great Work ahead. I don't think I have.

Nature Red in Tooth and Claw

My favorite chapter in Annie Dillard's classic *Pilgrim at Tinker Creek* con-siders and almost celebrates the centrality of death in nature. Dillard notes that according to one of her reference books, "ten percent of all the world's species are parasitic insects."[3] She marvels at a world so designed that a good share of all creatures can only exist by "harassing, disfiguring, or totally destroying" other creatures. In fact, she observes, everything is nibbled, tattered, frayed, and infested with parasites. We creatures eat each other. Disturbances come. Things die. That's how nature moves forward. Dillard writes, "I am a frayed and nibbled survivor in a fallen world, and I am getting along. I am aging and eaten and have done my share of eating too. I am not washed and beautiful, in control of a shining world in which everything fits, but instead am wandering awed about on a splintered wreck I've come to care for, whose gnawed trees breathe a delicate air, whose bloodied and scarred creatures are my dearest companions, and whose beauty beats and shines not in its imperfections but overwhelmingly in spite of them, under the wind-rent clouds, upstream and down."[4] Death and disturbance are central to existence. Plants and mammals, insects and reptiles, fish and birds are designed to tolerate it, even to depend on it. The world survives because, for the most part, reproduction keeps ahead of death. For the most part, disturbances are not so great as to completely wipe out an ecosystem or species. For the most part.

Paleontologists have identified, through the fossil record and geological studies, five previous periods during which disturbances were so massive and rapid that a huge percentage of species was wiped out. The most famous of these periods is the one that apparently occurred sixty-six million years ago, evidently catalyzed by an asteroid impact near the Gulf of Mexico. The impact vaporized calcium carbonite and sulfur, blasting into the atmosphere a noxious blend of carbon dioxide and sulfate aerosols. The resulting climatic changes wiped out perhaps three-quarters of all species, including almost all the dinosaurs. Thus ended the Cretaceous period. (Crocodiles, fungi, ferns, and avian dinosaurs, among other groups, survived to evolve another day.)[5] Obviously, our understanding of events millennia ago can only be speculative, based on what evidence we have. But paleontologists have concluded that refugia were crucial to the persistence of life on earth during these massive upheavals. The concept of refugia, in fact, comes originally from paleontological speculation and study.

Recently, scientific consensus is growing that we are living amid a sixth extinction period. When I read Elizabeth Kolbert's 2014 book, *The Sixth Extinction*, I was surprised to discover how recent the sixth extinction theory is. Kolbert describes the scientific paper that first proposed this theory, which was published in 2008 and based on the sudden and bewildering die-off among Panamanian golden frogs and other amphibians.[6] The paper served as a kind of wake-up call, prompting the scientific community to consider the gravity of all the accumulated species losses we had been observing for decades. Already in 1962, Rachel Carson had published her book *Silent Spring*, calling attention to the effects of DDT and other pesticides, especially on birds. Her work eventually led to the founding of the Environmental Protection Agency in 1970 and the passing of the Endangered Species Act in 1974. Since the 1970s, thousands of scientists and concerned citizens continued observing, with scientific protocols, in real time, the rapid reduction of individuals and species all over the world and across plant and animal classes. Kolbert wrote in 2014, "It is estimated that one-third of all reef-building corals, a third of all freshwater mollusks, a third of sharks and rays, a quarter of all mammals, a fifth of all reptiles, and a sixth of all birds are headed toward oblivion."[7] Those approximations are more than confirmed by the most recent, rigorous data from the International Union for Conservation of Nature and Natural Resources. They classify as threatened species—which includes anything from "vulnerable" to "critically endangered"—41 percent of amphibians, 34 percent of reptiles, 34 percent of conifers, 33 percent of reef-forming corals, 26 percent of mammals, and 14 percent of birds. Those are just a few categories. Happily, it looks as if octopuses and squids are doing all right, with only 1.5 percent threatened.[8]

It's true that in the course of life on earth, species go extinct even apart from major extinction events. There is such a thing as the "background rate" of extinction—that is to say, the rate at which species naturally die out.[9] Survival of the fittest, you know? Nevertheless, current conservative calculations estimate that species are going extinct at one hundred times the background rate, some say one thousand times.[10] We can see it happening; that's the thing. We are living through a period of such great disturbance that a huge number of creatures can't adjust fast enough. Nature is ordinarily "red in tooth and claw," as Tennyson points out, but this—this is not ordinary.[11]

This time the disturbance is us. Humans. There are so many of us, and we disturb everything. Mostly we destroy habitat by burning rain forests to create palm plantations or grazing areas for beef cattle. We destroy and break up habitat with our cities, highways, suburbs, and vast monoculture farms. We dam rivers, disrupting habitat for fish and birds. We pollute air and waterways with our emissions, industrial runoff, fertilizers, toxic waste, and garbage. We have created huge swirls of plastic garbage floating in the ocean. We have filled the world with so much plastic waste that seabirds feed it to their young. We carry plastic in our own bodies.[12] We hunt animals to extinction for pleasure or for the supposedly medicinal powders we can make from their parts. We travel around and move goods around and thus scramble patiently evolved and balanced systems, bringing invasive plants, insects, and fungal infections where native inhabitants have no defense against them. We have changed the climate so that breeding grounds are now underwater or ravaged by fire or stressed by heat and vulnerable to insect infestations. We have loaded the atmosphere with so much carbon dioxide that the ocean absorbs 2.5 billion tons of it per year, lowering ocean pH and making the ocean more acidic.[13] We have replaced wild creatures with ourselves and our livestock. Today, it is estimated that 96 percent of mammals, by weight, are humans and our livestock. Only 4 percent are wild creatures.[14]

Most people are aware of endangered species. We've heard of save-the-whales campaigns and tried to spot a rare snow leopard at the zoo. Focusing on attractive, "charismatic megafauna" is meant to arouse people's sympathies for those quirky owls or gorgeous tigers or spectacular rhinos or adorable pandas or whales or polar bears. This works to some extent. The downside is that it tends to extract each species from its whole context, both the diverse ecosystems on which every creature depends and the systemic causes of biodiversity decline. Destroy an apex predator or reduce its population significantly, and you are likely to cause "trophic cascade," which means everything down the food chain suffers, right down to insects and ground-cover plants. It works the other way too. Acidify and warm the ocean, and you disrupt the foundational zooplankton that support the entire food web "above" them. Spray whole crops with pesticide, and you kill the insects that feed the birds as well as the bees that pollinate the flowers in the meadows next door.

The more-than-human world tries to adjust to our human disturbance. The problem is that we humans are now so many and so powerful that our disturbance is too pervasive and rapid. Creatures will seek refugia from all this disturbance, but they can't always find it. Forests will migrate north by inches as their habitat gets too warm for them to survive, but that takes decades. Black bears will try to survive in fewer hectares as their former habitat gets chopped up by roads and developments, but they need enough space and enough mating pairs for genetic diversity. Little brown bats and Panamanian golden frogs have no defense against the imported fungal infections that wipe them out. Literary scholar Robert P. Harrison coined the term *species loneliness* to describe our sense of loss as we cripple the earth's biodiversity, shoving other creatures aside to make more room for our growing population.[15] Robert McFarlane defines species loneliness as "a sense of isolation and sadness arising from human estrangement from and extinction of other species."[16]

So some of us, having heard these cries of distress, imitate Noah and try to create arks. Dedicated and passionate people labor heroically in wildlife refuges, zoos, preserves, rescue operations, and land conservancies, and through all kinds of scientific research and activism. These arks can serve as kinds of refugia, but we can't operate thousands of arks forever for every threatened species. Even the arks we have cannot and will not save everything. The whole point of an ark is to provide a temporary, "relative refugium"—that is, a place where conditions are somewhat more suitable than those outside the refugium. We can never keep up with an arking strategy because we *are* the flood. We are creating the conditions that prompt the need for refugia. And we are not a temporary disturbance. How do we reckon with the losses we have caused, with what we have already done?

Scientific Sorrow and Solastalgia

On our first night at the Au Sable Institute to visit our friend Tim Van Deelen, the wildlife biologist, Tim invited Ron and me to the faculty potluck. The summer faculty and their families gathered at one of the larger cabins clustered on Big Twin Lake, where faculty live while teaching at the institute. We heaped our plates with potato salad and broccoli slaw, and Tim grilled up some amazingly tender venison steaks he had brought with him—certified free of chronic wasting disease, he assured us. After dinner, I chatted with Bill Deutsch, a fisheries biologist from Alabama whom I had met the previous summer on the Beyond Stewardship project team. Bill and his wife, Janet, were at Au Sable on a birding expedition—they wanted to see the endangered Kirtland's warbler, a gorgeous little bird that nests only in young jack pines, which in turn reproduce only when fire opens their seed cones. Areas around Au Sable are among the few places that still meet the Kirtland's particular requirements. Only a few minutes into our conversation, Bill was talking about climate change, about species loss, about the temptation to despair. "But we have a duty to hope," he said, seemingly reminding himself. He had been reading Frederick Douglass's autobiography and was amazed by Douglass's life, his resilience. Bill drew parallels to coping with the ongoing discouragement of the climate crisis and repeated, "We have a duty to hope amid exhaustion and cynicism."

Later that evening, Ron and I walked thirty steps from our cabin to Dave Warner's cabin. Dave is a plant biologist and a colleague at Calvin University who also teaches at Au Sable in the summer. Dave and his wife, Terry, welcomed Tim and Ron and me, and we all settled on the old sofas, passing around beers we technically weren't supposed to have on Au Sable's dry campus. Within minutes, we were talking about loss.

"Have you got ash borer in Wisconsin?" Dave asked Tim.

"Oh, yeah," said Tim.

They discussed beech bark disease, caused by a scale insect that makes room for a fungus that then curdles the bark into lesions that eventually kill the tree. They talked about oak wilt and the woolly adelgid that is killing hemlocks. Finally, they apologized to Ron and me for all the negativity.

"Now you know what biologists talk about at night," laughed Dave.

The more time I spend with my science colleagues, the more I feel their sadness. They are living the frequently cited line from Aldo Leopold: "One of the penalties of an ecological education is that one lives alone in a world of wounds."[17] My friends in the biology and ecology fields shoulder the burden of these wounds. Mostly they cope with sadness by burying themselves in their work: their research, their teaching, their advocacy. They are not alone, because they do have each other and their students. But they see loss and ecological dysfunction close up and understand their intricacies. They quantify them in graphs. As Robin Wall Kimmerer notes, science professionals enjoy an "unparalleled intimacy with nature fraught with wonder and creativity."[18] The greater their intimacy and wonder, though, the greater also their capacity for grief.

I have been dwelling on species loss simply because the more-than-human creation is easy to ignore. It's somewhat harder to ignore the headlines emphasizing current and predicted human suffering. The field of environmental justice reminds us all to listen to the griefs and losses of other people even if we ourselves feel as if climate stresses haven't hit our region yet, or if we are buffered from those stresses by privilege.

Those who are already vulnerable, both here in North America and around the world, tend to suffer first and suffer more. Fossil fuel emissions and toxic waste have already caused skyrocketing rates of cancer, asthma, COPD, preterm births, and other maladies, unsurprisingly hitting Black and brown people the hardest.[19] Industrial pollution and aging infrastructure cause water pollution in lakes, streams, and aquifers, as well as in city water supplies, hitting the poorest people hardest. The Flint, Michigan, water crisis, for example, in which the city's residents endured deadly levels of lead poisoning, occurred because of systemic racism and determined neglect.[20] Extreme weather, such as floods, fires, and droughts, drove over forty million people from their homes in 2020, and that kind of disruption is hardest on people with the fewest resources.[21] As climate stresses become more extreme, we are likely to see more permanent migrations. In 2005, Norman Myers of Oxford University calculated that we can expect two hundred million climate migrants worldwide by 2050. That number is commonly cited, though hard to confirm, of course. A background paper for the United Nations Development Programme's 2008 report notes Myers's number but acknowledges that so many factors are involved, predictions are difficult. Even so, the paper warns, we can expect mass upheaval in the decades ahead.[22] Already the people of the Maldives, whose low-lying South Pacific islands are severely threatened by rising seas and severe storms, are struggling to raise the millions needed to save their islands with geoengineering schemes. They may need to resort to their former president's plan: move a half million people elsewhere.[23] Already, the citizens of Isle de Jean Charles in Louisiana are agonizing over how long they can stay where their families have lived for generations, while their wetlands succumb to ocean rise, causing fish and vegetation to die from too much salt.[24] Already, the National Oceanic and Atmospheric Administration is reporting a rapid increase in "sunny day" flooding, when high tides push ocean water right over streets of coastal cities and overwhelm sewer systems.[25] Writer Mario Alejandro Aliza ponders his beloved Miami, admitting that even if some form of the city survives, it will look very different. People will have to "retreat intelligently from certain neighborhoods," he says. Some areas of the city will have to be "responsibly abandoned."[26] What will that feel like?

In addition to the challenges to physical survival faced by people on the front lines of climate change, imagine the emotional challenges of loss, trauma, and grief. Australian environmental studies professor and philosopher Glenn A. Albrecht has proposed we do not have sufficient words for the griefs we are feeling now, and that more people are likely to feel in the decades ahead. So Albrecht has invented a suite of new words, assembling them mostly from familiar Latin and Greek roots. He has coined the term *psychoterratic*, for example, to describe the full range of human psychological responses to place, responses ranging from rapture to affection to sorrow. The feelings you experience as you turn off an exit on the highway toward your home neighborhood or walk through a sun-warmed wildflower meadow are psychoterratic responses.

In particular, Albrecht endeavors to describe the feelings of loss we experience when places we love are altered and diminished. As an Australian, he has witnessed the devastating effects of climate warming on that continent, especially the destruction caused by fires sweeping hotter and more widely through wild areas and human settlements. To describe this grief, Albrecht invented the word *solastalgia*, a combination of Latin words for solace and for pain. The term means a "melancholia or homesickness" for the way a place used to be.[27] This is what you feel when you visit Grandpa's voluptuous garden, formerly kaleidoscopic with vegetables and flowers, now neglected by the next homeowner and nothing but thistles and garlic mustard. Or when you try to visit the wetland where you used to spend quiet hours watching herons lift, their stilt legs dangling, and find it's now a Walmart. Or when you see formerly verdant mountain slopes transformed by pine beetles into an upright cemetery of brown tree corpses. Or when you watch your island homeland slowly sink under a rising sea. The solace you once felt in your beloved place has evaporated, replaced by hopeless desolation.

Where's the Outrage?

The professional scientists I know best are also Christians, and they wonder, Why aren't more Christians sad? Or angry? Why aren't Christians the most outraged people on the planet over the destruction we have caused to one another and to the community of creation? Right in the pews of their home churches, my scientist friends feel alone indeed in that world of wounds, because so many of their coreligionists prefer, if not denial, then at least avoidance. They avoid looking straight on at the climate crisis, place loss, and species extinction. They should be lamenting, fuming, working, but instead they're avoiding.

Tim told me that he's deeply tired of Christian people piously intoning about "creation care." The pleasant phrases "creation care" and "stewardship," besides allowing us to imagine ourselves still comfortably in charge, also allow us to avoid painful feelings. We can dwell in the satisfaction of our own easy, benevolent feelings toward "nature," all while avoiding the sorrow and guilt we don't want to feel. I understand that sorrow and guilt are not the most effective ways of winning people to a cause. If persuading people to take action on climate change is our most urgent and primary goal, then making people feel sad and guilty is not exactly the most effective motivator. But at some point along our journeys, we have to face the hard parts. As people of faith, we should understand that sorrow and guilt are honest, appropriate, and necessary if we want to respond with compassion and justice to the world's groaning—and to our own.

So why do we close our ears to the groaning, and why do we avoid accepting our own complicity? "Let everything that breathes praise the Lord," says the Psalmist (Ps 150:6). In the Psalms and throughout Scripture, the more-than-human creation—the depths of the earth and the seas, the fields and forests—all join in a cosmic song of praise. "Praise God you creatures here below," we sing. "Praise God above you heavenly hosts." Do we really mean it, though? The praise of God, emanating from all created things in heaven and earth through the sheer ecstasy of their existence—this praise is not our doing. It does not happen because we exhort the world to praise, like a choir conductor. Instead, we are invited to join in a chorus of praise that began long before us and would go on quite well without us, thank you. The humpback whale song has praised God for millennia. So has the unfurling of fern fiddleheads and the rattle of pileated woodpeckers and the jaw power of the crocodile. What does it mean, then, if we humans, by our actions and inactions, have diminished that chorus of praise? The accelerating cascade of species extinctions is our fault. Maybe we didn't understand the extent of it before, but now we do. I doubt that our human praise songs, however earnestly sung by however many millions, make up for what is lost. We are, by neglect and indifference, dampening the glory of God revealed in creation. Wendell Berry, with his usual bracing candor, names this for what it is: "Our destruction of nature is not just bad stewardship, or stupid economics, or a betrayal of family responsibility; it is the most horrid blasphemy. It is flinging God's gifts into his face, as of no worth beyond that assigned to them by our destruction of them."[28] Where is the outrage at this blasphemy? Where is our lament and repentance? These questions well up from within Pope Francis's 2015 encyclical, which features no shortage of sharp statements. "The earth, our home, is beginning to look more and more like an immense pile of filth," writes the pope.[29] He refuses to soften what we're facing: "Dooms-day predictions can no longer be met with irony or disdain. We may well be leaving to coming generations debris, desolation and filth."[30] He deplores biodiversity loss, insisting on the inherent value of every creature: "Thousands of species will no longer give glory to God by their very existence, nor convey their message to us. We have no such right."[31] At this moment in history, the pope declares, we need nothing less than an "ecological conversion."[32]

I read efforts at lament and repentance over the earth's ruin in official denominational statements from across the Christian spec-trum. Occasionally, I hear lament and repentance in pastoral prayers at my own highly eco-aware church. But I have to say, I find the most potent expressions of anger and sorrow outside the organized church altogether. I find the most potent anger and sorrow in nature writers of no religious creed or of some other creed or of careful distance from a church that has disappointed them with its indifference. No one does outrage or lament more eloquently, for example, than Kathleen Dean Moore in her book *Great Tide Rising*. Moore draws on her skills as a moral philosopher, nature writer, and great lover of wild places to create a vivid moral analysis of "why it's flat-out wrong to wreck the world."[33] The climate crisis, she argues, is a violation of human rights, a failure of reverence, and a violation of justice. Though she writes for a general audience and thus does not depend on specifically theological reason-ing, everything she writes is perfectly consonant with the deep currents of the biblical witness.

Moore works through reasons to commit our energies sacrificially to repair of the world, organizing those reasons according to the clas-sic ethical categories: reasons based on consequences, reasons based on our duties and obligations as humans, and reasons based on the virtues. This is illuminating, but to me, her tone is even more import-ant, as she combines rational clarity with moral passion. "I believe in

moral outrage. I claim it as my right," she declares.[34] With full attention on justice among humans, Moore also insists on the inherent and
undeniable value of all creatures. In describing a snorkeling expedition, she reflects on the gorgeousness of all life: "This is a different
point of view, from inside this sea of living things, from this swirl of
creative energy, generative systems of generative systems. There are
hierarchies of size and power in the splash and struggle, but there is
no hierarchy of value. Each thing is worthy."[35] At the end of the book,
Moore quotes from the remarkable Earth Charter, a "global consensus statement" endorsed by two thousand organizations representing
millions of people. The first words of the charter's first "pillar" affirm
the value of all life as well as the dignity of human beings. The charter
calls us to do the following:

a. Recognize that all beings are interdependent and every form
   of life has value regardless of its worth to human beings.
b. Affirm faith in the inherent dignity of all human beings and
   in the intellectual, artistic, ethical, and spiritual potential of
   humanity.[36]

The document is meant to include people of all faiths and no faith, but
it seems to me that believing in God, loving God, would make one only
more passionate about each of those statements and more outraged at
their betrayal.

Ostriches and Behemoths

People do get stuck on this point: How can we have time and energy for
lamenting animal suffering when there's so much human suffering to
worry about? A good question. It is hard to whump up anger and grief
about a beast I've never seen in the wild, like a polar bear. However wondrous polar bears seem on the nature documentary, and however sad
the soundtrack makes me feel about their starvation as polar ice melts,
they're still so far away. I can care in an abstract way, because I understand the importance of biodiversity for the survival of all life. I can
also care because of the inherent beauty and wonder of every created
thing. Maybe I can afford to care about polar bears because I'm sitting

there on my comfortable sofa watching a documentary, not worried about how I will pay the bills or whether I need to move my family away from our homeland.

If it's true that all creatures have inherent value, how are we supposed to weigh that against the human suffering that seems to demand our priority attentions? It's fascinating that in one of the world's most famous texts about human suffering and lament, the book of Job, God's response to Job's suffering is to celebrate the wildness of more-than-human creatures. This ancient parable, magnificent in its philosophical depth and poetic art, is basically an ornate gold frame around one of the darkest and most ancient questions of all human existence: Why? Why do the innocent suffer?

Job asks this question by laying it directly at the feet of God, almost accusingly. That opening prologue in chapters 1 and 2 portrays God as impassive and even cruel, willing to take the bet that "the accuser" proposes. This God is willing to torment the righteous Job just to see, just to find his breaking point. It's a literary expression of what suffering can feel like—that we are being tormented by some cosmic power. In chapters 3 through 37, Job's three friends appear and attempt to comfort him, but they keep insisting on repentance. They are convinced Job has done something to deserve his miseries, because that is the way the world works. That's what makes sense. Virtue is rewarded, evil is punished. Obviously. Job insists that this cannot be so because he is innocent and yet he suffers. Why?

The book of Job refuses to relent on any point. God is in power. The righteous suffer. Yet God is in power. Yet the righteous suffer. Well, one could simply eliminate God from the equation. But Job refuses to do this, refuses to "curse God, and die" (Job 2:9). Instead, he flings down a shocking statement of faith that echoes through the ages: "Though he slay me, yet will I trust in him" (13:15 KJV). Job's stubbornness in faith always takes my breath away. Rather than turning away from God, Job turns toward God, turns the tables and becomes the accuser. Why, God? Why have you let this happen? That is the essence of lament: asking the question why, putting it before God. Lament entails both feeling the sorrow and leveling the protest.

For thirty-five chapters, God provides no answer. Finally, after all those tiresome debates between Job and his friends—finally—God answers Job "out of the storm":

Who is this that darkens counsel by words without knowledge?
Gird up your loins like a man, I will question you, and you
shall declare to me. (Job 38:2–3)

Not exactly the "there, there" we might have hoped for. Instead, this
God is imperious, sarcastic: "Where were you when I laid the earth's
foundation? Tell me, if you understand" (Job 38:4 NIV). In other words,
"Who do you think you are, mister?" In the following four chapters,
God ignores Job's particular sufferings altogether and launches into
what Bill McKibben calls "the first and greatest piece of nature writing in the Western tradition."[37] The divine words from the whirlwind
lift our imaginations from Job's troubles to a God's-eye view in which
human beings, in the vast scheme of creation, are small potatoes. Instead,
God revels in the wild energies of the created earth—the springs of the
sea, storehouses of hail, constellations and clouds. We enter the wilds
to witness the freedom of creatures over whom humans have no control. A lioness hunts her prey, mountain goats give birth, the ostrich
flaps her ridiculous wings. God is on a roll with this poetic disquisition,
completely absorbed in the delights of hawks on the wing and eagles
on craggy cliffs. God spends an entire chapter and a half extolling the
wonders of "Behemoth" (Job 40:15) and "Leviathan" (41:1), frolicking in
the deep.

It all seems completely off point. Yet Job gets the gist. This "whirlwind" of divine speech overwhelms Job with humility. The vast scale of
creation, the deep time of God's perspective—it's all too much for Job.
"I lay my hand on my mouth," he says (Job 40:4). "I had heard of you
by the hearing of the ear, but now my eye sees you" (42:5). In focusing on
the creatures of God, Job perceives how glory and terror go together.
Wildness—that is the way of creation, that's where we see the nature of
God beyond our systematic theologies and philosophical inquiries. We
humans do have a tendency, as my friend Josh puts it, to act like "persistent cosmic prima donnas."[38] There's comfort in a whirlwind that rips
that pretension out of our grip. I know people who have experienced
much suffering who find in the book of Job a great comfort, because
there they find freedom from needing an answer. Their suffering does
not need to make sense. It just is. As the words of God sweep us over
mountains and oceans, forests and savannahs, we are jolted into awe
and then humility, and that humility is a gift.

In the words of theologian William P. Brown, Job moves from "wound to wonder." He receives a "crushing dose of wonder," and his lament concludes with repentance: "Therefore I despise myself, and repent in dust and ashes" (42:6).[39] Righteous Job, even though he is righteous, repents anyway, repents of underestimating the terror and beauty inextricable in the person of God and in this world. After this climactic moment, God turns tender, scolding Job's friends for their wrongheaded pestering, restoring to Job more camels and oxen and beautiful daughters than he ever had before. It's a pat ending—too pat in some views. But this, I think, is meant to signal the artificiality of the story's frame. The frame is merely a cheeky setup, designed to raise the question of suffering and then immerse that question in the wild glory of God.

The Agony of God

From a posture of humility, we can more honestly transform grief into lament. Lament is simply grief brought before God, carried in a vessel made from even the smallest shred of faith. This is what I appreciate about Kathleen Dean Moore's approach. She not only gives me permission to lament both human suffering and the suffering of all creation but obliges me to it, calling us all to bind up anger and sorrow into genuine lament. Without true lament, I don't know how we can engage in repentance and turn toward new ways of living. One of Moore's most evocative phrases for me is "the moral power of . . . sorrow."[40] As I reflect on the phrase, it seems to me that this moral power vectors in several directions. Sorrow has the moral power of teaching *orthopathy*, right feeling. To value something rightly entails grieving. To love something—to love what God loves—is to feel anger and sorrow when it is lost or threatened. Indifference, then, is the symptom of insufficient love. It stings to say this, but insufficient love for this world is insufficient love for God.

Lament leverages that moral power of sorrow toward repentance. During Lent, Christians practice repentance in order to prepare for one of the most difficult things we do in the Christian life: look upon the crucified Christ, the very face of God. On Good Friday, more than any other day of the year, we cannot turn away from the agony of God, an agony spent on our behalf, on the world's behalf. "Christ died for our sins," we say. This includes our sins against one another as well as against creation itself, whether by intention or neglect or indifference. "God so loved the world," we say. Not just human souls but the whole cosmos. God is not indifferent to any suffering, so when we speak of God's "judgment" for our sins, we can think of judgment as divine love compelled to anger and sorrow over the suffering we cause. This divine anger and sorrow are concentrated into the love we behold in the crucified Christ: a love so deep it is willing to absorb not only our human moral offenses and sinful condition, but all suffering and death, all of it braided into creation itself.

In that soaring and beloved passage in Romans 8, Paul describes a creation "groaning in labor pains until now" (Rom 8:22). This chapter is full of groaning. We ourselves, Paul continues, "groan inwardly while we wait for adoption, the redemption of our bodies" (Rom 8:23). The Spirit is groaning too, interceding for us beyond all words. The passage concludes with one of the most beloved and reassuring phrases in all of Scripture: nothing "will be able to separate us from the love of God in Christ Jesus our Lord" (Rom 8:39). The conclusion to be drawn from Romans 8 is not only that God is with us in our own suffering but also that we need not fear the agony of either sorrow or guilt. When we face squarely what we have done in the world, we enter into the agony of God, but also into God's compassionate love. This is the love revealed in Christ, the one in whom—as Colossians 1 declares—all things hold together, the love that longs to reconcile all things. The whole creation waits in longing, says Paul, "for the revealing of the children of God" (Rom 8:19). Perhaps it is only in feeling true sorrow and repentance, in truly groaning with the whole creation, that we fulfill our calling as God's children.

Radical Evil

Is all death in nature a result of sin? That's one puzzling question that arises at the intersection of theology and ecology. I was taught that anything "bad" in creation—not only human suffering and sin but also predation, icky parasites, death itself—is all the result of sin. When Adam and Eve ate the wrong fruit in the garden, all that stuff was the result. Mosquitos carry diseases now, and beeches die of disease, and crocodiles snatch wildebeest calves as they cross the Mara River during migration. The creation-fall-redemption narrative creates a neat explanation for the violence and tatteredness of the more-than-human world. However, it's hard to square this narrative with evolutionary science, which concludes that nature has been a frenzy of predation and death for millions of years, long before humans entered the scene to add their moral irresponsibility to the mix. Recent theological reflection, such as the works of Matthew Fox and Pierre Teilhard de Chardin, has tried to grapple with the apparent conflict between creation-fall-redemption theology and the fossil record by suggesting that death and predation are not, in fact, the result of human sin, but were built into creation. Fox proposes that we need to lay off our obsession with original sin and instead consider our "original blessing." By following Jesus's example and communing with the created world, Fox believes, we can live into that blessing and realize our essential divine nature. Meanwhile, Teilhard proposes that evolution is how creation has moved toward human consciousness and how it will continue to evolve toward its culmination in "christogenesis." That is, the cosmic Christ will draw all things to himself, just as Colossians 1 describes, like a kind of love magnet. Humans developed consciousness, Teilhard thinks, in order to help bring that telos about in the universe. This is our purpose, and one day all created things will be subsumed into the "white spiritual heat of ultimate charity," as H. Paul Santmire puts it.[41]

It seems a grand and glorious vision, but as Santmire points out, neither Fox nor Teilhard reckons fully with radical evil. It's true that Genesis 1–3 does not say the world was "perfect" and death-free before the fall, as if no fern ever withered or no fawn died. It's lovely to imagine that, but that's not what it says. The creation is "very good" in Genesis 1:31, and it seems as if God persists in that same opinion in Psalm 104 and Job 38–41. Anyway, as Brueggemann points out, we need to read the Genesis texts not as historical accounts but as proclamations of faith. And surely, among the many things all of Scripture proclaims is the reality of human rebellion. Thus as Santmire summarizes, "While death and suffering are given with the created goodness of the cosmos, self-conscious rebellion against God, the arrogance of humanity's will-to-power, is not. And that is precisely the existentially congenital condition of humankind: to exist, by its own doing, in a state of radical alienation from God."[42] Santmire goes on to modify Teilhard's vision by reclaiming the need to repair this radical alienation through Christ's death. Yes, Christ becomes incarnate in order to stitch God and creation together in intimate love. But Christ also becomes incarnate to repair the breach caused by human rebellion. Only because Christ repairs that breach can humans do their part to undo some of the damage, anticipating God's renewal of all things. Santmire—along with many others throughout the Christian tradition—insists that the biblical vision of that anticipated fulfillment calls not for an ultimate telos of blazing pure energy but for a redeemed physical creation with Christ at the center. A vision culminating in Revelation 21, with a green city, centered on a river and tree, whose leaves are for the healing of nations.

This reclaiming of the need for atonement seems essential to me. I don't know about some prelapsarian state of death-free perfection before human rebellion. What I do know, without doubt, is that humans have been capable of grievous evil. Nature has its fill of death and violence, but we humans choose violence, choose cruelty, choose destruction. Our sins become embedded in our institutions and organizations and ways of life to create systemic sin, systemic evil. No need to reiterate proof. Our cruelty is not merely a passing stage while humans evolve toward a higher consciousness. Every century vomits up evidence of radical evil. There is therefore no way around the cross and the atoning blood of Christ. Nor is there any substitute for repentance.

Facing our own evil is perhaps even more difficult than facing our grief. Some of us know well how to exercise both lament and repentance; some of us know exactly how it feels to endure the radical evil humans are capable of. Jews, Indigenous peoples, and Black Americans are among those who by necessity have much to teach about the art of lament and survival. Many White Americans came to understand this, perhaps for the first time, in the wake of George Floyd's murder at the hands of a Minneapolis police officer in early 2020. The protests and even riots that followed, the reawakening of the Black Lives Matter movement, the flurry of book sales as White people struggled to educate themselves—all of this resulted from hearing anew or even for the first time the keening lament that has been rising from African Americans for centuries and has never ceased.

There is much to repent from. There is also much to learn from those who have endured cruelty and know how to create refugia amid terrible suffering. In a searing essay, Mary Annaïse Heglar writes that the existential fear arising from the climate crisis is not the first time humans have felt such fear. Hardly. She describes what her own family members felt under Jim Crow in the South, living every day in terror of what hysterical and cruel White people could do. She writes, "I want you to understand how overwhelming, how insurmountable it must have felt. I want you to understand that there was no end in sight. It felt futile for them too. Then, as now, there were calls to slow down. To settle for incremental remedies for an untenable situation. Black people of the not-too-distant past trembled for every baby born into that world. Sound familiar?" Heglar wants to remind people who are now awakening to fear of the climate crisis that African Americans and others already know plenty "about building movements, about courage, about survival." They know what it feels like to reach a point when you must ask, "What else can you be but brave?"[43]

The Discipline of Limits

Coping with sorrow and grief is difficult, and repentance is harder yet. At least that's been my observation. As I've aged, I think I've gotten better at holding sorrow, not being afraid of it. Having lived through a few sorrows of my own helps. So does walking with students, colleagues, friends, and family over the years as they have passed through dark valleys. So does listening more consistently and deeply to people who know what it means to suffer and endure. As a Wendell Berry poem proposes, the older you get, the more you feel like a composite of "those lives and deaths / that have belonged to you."[44] Repentance, however, never seems to get easier. Repentance requires both inward contrition and outward action—it requires a turnaround, a change. In response to the climate crisis, to species extinction, to the wreckage we have wrought on the earth and therefore on each other, repentance is not complete without changed actions, both as individuals and as societies.

A few of us are able to participate in earth healing quite explicitly by, say, tramping out into forests and scraping DNA samples from whitebark pines in order to determine pockets of genetic diversity and therefore help identify likely refugia where conservation efforts should be concentrated.[45] Not all of us are conservation biologists or even citizen scientists, though. For the rest of us, our role is to find our own "little work," in the usual ways people recommend: learn to know and love the places entrusted to us, keep voting for leaders who will prioritize climate action, keep reducing energy consumption, keep getting involved in groups working toward a transition to a new energy infrastructure, keep learning more and using less. The bottom line to all of this work, it's clear, is that we all have to accept limits. For those of us used to affluence, the limits—on energy use, on travel, on meat eating, on consumption and luxuries, at the very least—will be hard.

I struggle with this. I don't need *more* than I have right now, but I don't want *less*! I wrestle in my mind with all the typical rationalizations:

Other people live more luxuriously than me! Let them reduce their luxuries!

That won't be nearly enough. And remember that billions are living with far less than you, and all this is not their fault.

I worked hard for this life!

No, you didn't. You worked, but every advantage was handed to you.

My parents worked hard to improve their children's lives.

True, but that doesn't matter now.

I can list some things I can do without: lots of restaurants, lots of clothes, lots of meat, fancy cars, boats . . .

That's nice. It's a start.

OK, well at least let me keep air-conditioning, potato chips, and chocolate. And tea. And hot showers. And live music.

Well, we'll see.

Let me live out my life in reasonable comfort and let the next generations adjust.

Really? Seriously?

And there it is. In facing my own resistance to the limits that will come, I come face-to-face with my own roaring selfishness.

I should know better. All religious traditions commend a wise spirituality of limits. The decentering of self, the practice of serving others, the surrendering of one's desires to God. Jesus isn't the only one to preach the love of God and neighbor, or to observe that if we wish to make room for God, we must empty ourselves: "For those who want to save their life will lose it, and those who lose their life for my sake will find it" (Matt 16:25). Christian Lenten practices of fasting and prayer, of "giving something up," are meant to serve as little formation exercises in curbing our appetites and making space for God. Unfortunately, one of the greatest weaknesses of American churches is our dismal record of forming people in the spirituality of restraint, whether individual restraint or communal restraint. We're very good at praising God for our abundance, far less good at limiting abundance for the sake of others and the earth. Those of us who loom large on this planet will have to become smaller. We will have to make more space for other species. We will have to give up power and let previously disempowered people lead. When climate leaders advocate for a "just transition" to new energy infrastructure, new ways of doing business, new foodways, they are seeking fairness and consideration for all, especially for those who have been disempowered and disadvantaged before. For those of us used to affluence and advantage, the changes we must make constitute a form of *kenosis*, self-emptying, and Christ is our exemplar. We can choose to accept these limits, on behalf of one another and the more-than-human creation. Back in 1989, Bill McKibben observed in *The End of Nature* that more-than-human creatures have many gifts and wondrous abilities, but we humans have reason: "Should we so choose, we could exercise our reason to do what no other animal can do: we could limit ourselves voluntarily, *choose* to remain God's creatures instead of making ourselves gods."[46] We are the only creatures who can consciously choose self-restraint.

One of the common discoveries for those who observe Lent is that self-restraint and limits bring unexpected joys. Emptying can lead to deeper fullness. I was walking on my college's campus one day during the pandemic quarantine, and after weeks of relative quiet in the house, the roar of traffic on the nearby highway felt unbearably loud. Imagine if all those fossil-fuel engines were fewer in number and electric and much quieter, I thought. I began to muse on a cleaner, quieter world, the world we glimpsed ever so briefly during those first weeks in March and April 2020. Pollution visibly reduced, a clear view of the Himalayas, the sweeping away of Los Angeles's smog. Adopting limits has its benefits. In the second half of his 2010 book *Eaarth: Making a Life on a Tough New Planet*, McKibben sketches a rough picture of the limits we might face in future generations, assuming we are able to mitigate the climate crisis enough to find some equilibrium. Life will be more local, he predicts. Our foodsheds and energysheds will be more regional, even microregional. We will travel much less. We will depend a great deal more on our neighbors for resilience. This is not all bad, McKibben argues, though he does not pretend we won't feel the losses. Radical mobility and independence have helped ease difficulties for a lot of people for whom parochial life would be stifling and even toxic: "The process that made us anonymous to our neighbors carried real benefits, not just costs," he acknowledges.[47] During the pandemic, we all got to experience a taste of these sorts of limitations. Some of us found some blessing in it, but it was not easy.

The truth is, we've given up so much already in the modern era. We have sacrificed clean air, clean water, biodiversity, and a great deal of beauty for the sake of the conveniences, wealth, and power some of us enjoy. Every ugly, weedy lot in the city, every blasted mountaintop, every clogged and smelly river represents a sacrifice someone has made for something else. We know how to sacrifice. It's just a matter of what we're giving up and for what.[48]

Even if we summon our better angels and accept the limits that will help heal what we have destroyed, even if we graciously receive the limits forced upon us, we still may not "succeed." The more pessimistic climate models indicate that we may reach tipping points that bring more chaos than we want to imagine. It is highly likely that many millions of people will die from floods, major storm events, starvation, and epidemics. And war. It will take miracles of mercy to prevent wars over resources, exacerbated by migrations. We may be fighting what J. R. R. Tolkien's Lady Galadriel describes as "the long defeat."[49] The challenge will be to choose virtue even amid this descent, to choose what is right. Faithfulness, despite the outcome. Whether things go relatively well or badly in the next decades, we will need refugia, and those refugia will have to be places where we can grieve honestly, practice lament, and learn repentance. Doing these things well together will strengthen our bonds with one another and with the more-than-human world, helping to sustain for the work ahead.

Among the works I viewed at that art exhibition of early sixteenth-century woodcuts and engravings, I recall in particular an engraving by Albrecht Dürer, *St. Jerome in His Study*. There sits Jerome at his desk, crowned with a halo that looks as if scholarly work has set his head on fire. At his feet sprawl the usual symbolic lion (courage) and dog (loyalty), both sleeping contentedly. Light pours in from the window, illuminating

Jerome's work. On the windowsill sits a skull, as if to say, Death is always near, memento mori. But directly in Jerome's line of vision, between himself and that skull, stands a small crucifix. If Jerome were to lift his head and look straight at the skull, the crucifix would block his view. Christ comes, always, between us and the specter of death.

In the end, as gruesome as many of those prints were, I found the whole exhibition oddly comforting. Maybe the world is always ending. Maybe fear and upheaval are always part of the deal. Maybe what seems like an end can become the beginning of a new age, should God extend sustaining mercy a little longer. If our pious forebearers, in despair about corruption and disaster, could keep their eyes on the cross, well then, so can we.

In the Shade of the Dogwood

A robin had built her nest in the dogwood outside my window before I even noticed. It was a thing of wonder: a good ten inches of foundational dried grasses wedged into a branch fork, topped with a whirl of sticks and grass, at once sturdy and soft. Once I noticed her, I wondered why she wasn't sitting on the nest. She seemed to flirt with it, flitting in and out of the shadowy leaves. I learned that robins lay one egg per day, up to four eggs, and then they start incubating them. Sure enough, after a few days, she settled in.

I've gained new respect for robins in recent years. They're common as dandelions around here and always have been. I've taken them for granted since childhood. But lately I've noticed their song—every morning, every evening, a full-throated rill: *verily verily truly truly*. After all these years it finally dawned on me that robins are songbirds. Now I appreciate their beauty and resilience. They've figured out how to survive and thrive among humans. They sing and raise their young, and they look hilarious as they run across sidewalks and streets like sprinters on wiry legs.

Every day as I worked at my desk, I checked for my mama robin on her nest, and there she was. I greeted her often, and we were companionable in our respective work. Even in her shady alcove, it was hot. She opened her beak and panted, as birds will do.

Then at 10:40 a.m. on a Tuesday, I heard a fuss: a squirrel was ravaging the nest. The mother robin was frantic. Another robin came to help.

They flapped in and out, trying to dissuade the intruder. I rapped on the window and swore at the squirrel, as if that would help. I ran outside. By the time I got out there, it was too late. The robins had shooed the squirrel away, but the nest looked disheveled. It was too high in the tree for me to see into it, but what now? Were the eggs gone, cracked, ruined?

Now several robins had gathered on the scene, perhaps in solidarity. The mama came back to the nest and perched over it for a bit. She kept trying to sit on the nest but couldn't get settled. That's it, I thought. It's over. The eggs are ruined. I felt an ache in my stomach, grief in my body.

Why it hit me hard, I don't know. It was just one clutch of eggs—it's not as if robins are endangered. It's not as if I don't know how nature works. Circle of life and all that. When I told my friend Gayle about the incident, she was philosophical: "Well, squirrels' nests get attacked by raccoons," she observed. *Yeah, well, the squirrels deserve it*, I thought.

Later that day, sure that the robin had abandoned the nest, I went out and got a ladder and lifted the ruined nest from its perch. It was holding together, if disheveled. A neat mud ring trimmed its rim. Below the tree I found the empty, broken eggs. A beautiful rich blue, like Persian tile.

That evening I sat outside on the back deck, and as night fell, I heard a robin's full-throated song: *verily verily truly truly*. I wondered if it was my mama robin, rejoicing anyway, praising. Or maybe it was another robin, rejoicing on her behalf. *Life life life*. Death and loss, but *life life life*.

SWAMP MILKWEED
ASCLEPIAS INCARNATA

February
Grand Haven, Michigan

One unseasonably warm, bright February Sunday, I drove out to Grand Haven to give a talk at a church. After the service and the education hour, I drove the mile or two from the church to the state park, just to feel what I might feel there. The campground was closed, of course, but people were everywhere, easing their winter cabin fever, walking their dogs on the pier, buzzing drones on the chilly beach, clambering over the huge rocks abutting the base of the boardwalk. Everything looked friendly and familiar to me, even after years away. The pier, the ovals of pavement where the campers and RVs park in the summer season, the vast beach, the bathhouses.

Places hold our memories and histories. If we're lucky, through repeated encounters with a significant landscape, we create ties of affection to a place. Or maybe we store fragments of ourselves in places we have loved, like leaves that gather in a corner, so when we return to that place, we recognize some trace of our past selves. Ecomemory, some people call this.[1]

I know that many people have loved this particular stretch of sand and water and sky. Maps of native lands and historical accounts tell me that Ottawa clans of the Anishinaabe peoples lived in this region, but I was never taught that history in school. I've only recently followed my own affection down through history, learning more about Native peoples and about White settlement. Grand Haven as I know it today began taking shape in the 1850s, as the logging industry boomed. Entrepreneur hoteliers built small resort hotels around Grand Haven, drawing visitors for festive events and eventually for resort stays and dips in the health-enhancing mineral springs. Families started building cottages in the forested dunes in the 1880s, passing those cottages down to the next generations, giving them affectionate names like Sweet Lands and Bide-a-Way and Cozy Corner. Then came the public parks, the grand bathhouses on the beach with changing rooms and concession stands, the dance halls that compelled young people to climb aboard the interurban railway from nearby cities and head out to the lakeshore for an evening of fun.[2]

When my mother took me camping here each summer in the 1970s and '80s, I had the sense that she loved this place, but as a kid it never occurred to me that she had her own ecomemories here, ties of affection going back to her younger days. After she died, and I inherited boxes of her photo albums, I discovered old photos spanning decades, many of them featuring my mother with her friends, smiling in their swimsuits on West Michigan public beaches, including Grand Haven. Among the most interesting are three blurry photos of my mother and father, both age eighteen, Dad dressed in a coat and tie, Mom in a fashionable outfit, posed against a foredune. The photos are marked "V-E Day." On V-E Day, they went to the beach.

My own affection for this place seems brief and transient—settled on a shallow layer of recent cultural history, on only one generation of memory. In fact, since my teenage years, I have created deeper ties to other spots on our lakeshore, especially the place in Douglas that has become our family cottage. So it wasn't especially surprising that I felt oddly blank on that warm winter day in Grand Haven. I sat on a little hillock of sand and winter-dry beach grass and ate the lunch I had packed, the sun angling its white light on the calm water. I remembered being young here, but I couldn't feel with the intensity of those days. Layers of memory glanced against me like birds' wings, as easily gone. If my mother were alive, I could call and tell her I had been here, and she would be pleased.

On the way home, I stopped back in town at my parents' grave. Dry leaves had gathered in the shallow indentation where the ground settled over them, my parents, sharing that plot like a queen-sized bed. How can their bodies lie under there, dry and shrunken, boxed and vaulted? I wanted to dig them up and look at them again, remember that they were real. The faces and hands I knew so well. Their ways of moving and speaking.

The utter quiet. Only the sound of distant traffic and the wind. How could they be gone? For fifty years they were, to me, warm and chattery, beloved and exasperating. And now, buried in the ground and silent.

"Behold, I am making all things new," I hear in my spirit. Is this the voice of God? The wind blows, the waves crash, we lose and forget and mourn and go numb. And we wait. We wait for whatever comes next.

Chapter 5

From Resignation to Gratitude

Before the mountains were brought forth,
or ever you had formed the earth and the world,
from everlasting to everlasting you are God.

—PSALM 90:2

Early on a Friday morning in June, a truck came to the house and dropped eight yards of mulch in the driveway. The truck bed lifted and dumped and then banged back down so hard it jolted me out of bed. A few minutes later, Deanna and her crew of college students showed up to spread the entire load on the backyard area we had decided to call—naturally—"the refugium."

I scrambled out of bed and tossed on some clothes. The students didn't need my help, but I wanted to say hello and have a chat with Deanna. Not Deanna of the Dunes this time, but another Deanna, a recent graduate of the university who is now running the Plaster Creek Stewards projects. Deanna of the Swale, we could call her. This Deanna and I had been strategizing since the previous summer about how to heal the areas of our property where we had pulled out, chopped down, and otherwise beaten back all that buckthorn.

I had already repaired most of the previously buckthorn-infested areas with plantings, including three river birches I was a little in love with. I worried and fussed over these birches as they worked, season to

season, producing their remarkable peeling bark and their swaying flutters of toothed leaves. They showed signs of stress on hot summer days,
but overall they were growing a little stronger every year. In another
formerly buckthorned area, we put in turfgrass to open up the view a
little. That left still unmanaged the messy, wildish area along the back
property line, adjacent to our neighbors'.

Fortunately, these neighbors are dear friends, Trevor and Linda.
When they moved in a few years ago, we explained about buckthorn,
and they were eager to take down the thicket of it on their property
too. The fall before, Trevor had spent a few satisfying afternoons with a
chain saw, leaving a pile of cut buckthorn stems that the sparrows abso-
lutely adored all winter long. "The Sparrow Mafia Casino and Resort,"
we called it. Sparrows love a good woodpile.

Earlier that spring, a band of us—Trevor and Linda and Ron and I
and the assorted offspring we could conscript—had all gone out there
to disappoint the sparrows and haul away the woodpile to prepare for
the next stage. We agreed together that we were not going to make this
shared area into groomed suburban yard but restore it instead to something more natural and native, a stepping-stone refugium right in the
neighborhood. Our residential neighborhood in the city already curves
its streets and yards around wooded ravines where skunks and musk-
rats and other creatures live, including a band of brazen urban deer
who regularly assault our hostas. In proximity to these small ravines, our
refugium would not be the only relief from turfgrass for miles; instead,
it would be more like an island in an archipelago. Deanna had assured
us that she and her crew could take our muddy mess, with its clay soil
and poor drainage, its buckthorn stumps and creeping myrtle and who
knows what else, and help us turn it into useful habitat for native plants,
bugs, and birds.

Today's task was laying all that mulch to keep down weeds in preparation for planting. The pile of mulch in the driveway was not the
musky, fragrant cypress mulch you get from the garden store, but low-
cost mulch, which Deanna buys from a tree service. It smelled pleas-
ingly organic—green and a little sour. Like decomposing leaves, which
a good deal of it was. Among the chips and chunks of shredded wood
and leaves, the load contained, weirdly, a good-sized piece of tree trunk,
just the right size to make a low seat. The crew left it in the yard, so after
they had spread the mulch and left, I hoisted the trunk chunk into a

wheelbarrow and rolled it into the refugium myself, placing it for maximum aesthetic effect: a meditation spot.

Three days later, the student crew arrived again, this time with twenty flats of thirty-six seedlings each, plus two sapling trees, all propagated at the university's greenhouse and nursery site. We wanted a couple trees in there to accompany the already established residents—a slender, towering cottonwood and a couple white ash saplings, volunteer offspring from the surviving ash on my property. For our new trees, Deanna had given us some species choices that wouldn't mind "having their feet wet" in the muddy clay. We settled on a tamarack and a bur oak.

Deanna surveyed the area, placed the new trees, and flopped down the flats where she thought each species would do best. Even in this small area, there are shadier spots, wetter spots, areas of more or less understory. Refugial biologists would approve, as the best refugia are "rough"—they include varied terrain and conditions, which give plants and animals a "portfolio strategy" for good survival. Deanna had chosen baby native plants likely to adapt well to our refugium, but she also wanted to place them within it for maximum chance of success.

Then we went to work. This time, I got out there too, alongside the intrepid undergraduates. Planting took some muscle. The "soil" was wet from recent rain, heavy and pasty, like dark-chocolate cookie dough. It was covered with a good eight inches of mulch that had to be dug through to find the dirt beneath. And in a lot of places, we were digging into roots, tangles of creeping myrtle, crisscrossed sticks. We had to hack away to get any kind of hole. I hoped the seedlings were tough enough to do their work. They were just tender little babies, and the soil was so thick. How could they spread their hairlike roots into that mud?

I thought about how this restoration work differed from those yard-makeover shows on TV, where a bulldozer comes in and creates a completely blank slate in someone's yard before they bring in the potted palms and install the Jacuzzi. There was nothing blank about our slate. There were still buckthorn shoots here and there, especially along the back fence where Trevor's chain saw hadn't yet prevailed. Besides the tangly myrtle lingering under the mulch, some random tree seedlings I couldn't identify poked up here and there. The whole thing was bordered by a fallen box elder trunk that had sent up new shoots, as well as an old firewood pile now covered with brush and wild grapevine. We didn't have to start with perfect, though. Our job was to make enough space to give the new native seedlings a fighting chance and help them along for a while. They would take it from there, creating a thick root network that would absorb water, actually improve the soil, and provide habitat.

As we worked, the students and I chatted and joked and sweated. The students named the tamarack "Tammy" and the bur oak "Bert." Mostly we just dug and planted. Over and over, the same motions. My arm got sore from chunking that trowel into the dirt. We planted stiff goldenrod and swamp milkweed, black-eyed Susan and Culver's root, yellow coneflower and bee balm, marsh blazing star and golden alexanders. My favorites were rattlesnake master and hairy beardtongue. Who can resist plants with names like those?

Then suddenly, we were done. A few students walked the area to make sure we hadn't left any of our 720 plugs orphaned on the surface. One guy gave the area a water-down with the hose. Then they were gone. Now I would look after the place for a while. And we would look for signs of new life.

Jesus the Gardener

The resurrection of Christ is among the more difficult Christian beliefs to accept, but it's a lot easier in the middle of a garden. Which may help explain the long tradition of depicting Jesus as a gardener. Paintings from the European Renaissance and baroque periods frequently depict Jesus greeting Mary Magdalene on Easter morning while toting gardening tools or leaning on a shovel—even wearing a floppy gardening hat—as if he had gotten up extra early to get a little weeding done.[1] The Jesus-as-gardener tradition is based on the resurrection story in the Gospel of John, which describes Joseph of Arimathea and Nicodemus arranging for the crucified Jesus to be buried in a new tomb in a garden (John 19:41). On the first day of the week, when Mary Magdalene and the other women come to bring spices, they discover the empty tomb. They immediately run to tell the male disciples this upsetting news. Peter and John run back to the tomb to confirm the story, there's confusion and befuddlement, John sees and believes—whatever that means—and then everyone leaves except Mary Magdalene. She remains to weep alone before the empty tomb, still unnerved by this strange development. In her sorrow, she looks into the tomb to find two angels, who ask why she is weeping. Then she turns around to find another figure, and this person, too, asks why she is weeping. She supposes, according to the text, that this fellow is the gardener (John 20:15). The Greek word here, *karoupos*, means garden keeper or warden. But it's the risen Jesus himself, who calls her by her name.

Biblical interpreters from ancient times knew a rich metaphor when they saw one, and they were not about to pass over Mary's potent misunderstanding. Jesus *is* a gardener, of course. Italian scholar Franco Mormando, commenting on a sixteenth-century Italian painting, writes, "Jesus is the gardener of the human soul, eradicating evil, noxious vegetation and planting, as St. Gregory the Great says, 'the flourishing seeds of virtue.'"[2] In the Gospel of John's first chapter, unmistakably echoing the opening of Genesis, the writer declares Jesus to be the Word through whom all things were made. This identifies Jesus with the Creator God, maker of the first garden and the first gardeners, those creatures birthed from soil and Spirit breathed.[3] At the end of John's Gospel—here's another metaphor that's hard to miss—Jesus becomes the seed planted. Plant Jesus in the ground, and in three days, new life rises up. No stone can block its way. Paul catches on to this living metaphor, too, in his soaring chapter on the resurrection in 1 Corinthians. Christ is the "first fruits of those who have died," he writes (1 Cor 15:20). Addressing those who find a physical resurrection nonsensical, he tries to explain with a seed metaphor: "What you sow does not come to life unless it dies. And as for what you sow, you do not sow the body that is to be, but a bare seed, perhaps of wheat or of some other grain. But God gives it a body as he has chosen, and to each kind of seed its own body" (vv. 36–38). The difference between agriculture and the divine resurrection, though, is that resurrection breaks out of cyclical patterns into a new, enduring reality: "What is sown is perishable, what is raised is imperishable. It is sown in dishonor, it is raised in glory. It is sown in weakness, it is raised in power. It is sown a physical body, it is raised a spiritual body" (vv. 42–44).

As biblical scholar Gordon Fee explains, in that last phrase, "spiritual body" (Greek: *soma pneumatikos*), Paul seeks to establish between this life and the next both continuity and transformation. Basing his argument on the resurrected body of Christ, Paul insists that in the eschaton, bodies will persist, though they will be transformed (as

Christ's was) to suit, as it were, a new habitat of a fulfilled creation. The body (*soma*) will be spiritual (*pneumatikos*) "not in the sense of 'immaterial' but of 'supernatural.'"[4] Paul understands that his readers are straining to imagine how this physical world—how flesh and blood, so full of decay and suffering—could be transformed into eternal glory. Unfortunately, the spiritual body idea has perpetuated confusion for his readers ever since, helping to lean the whole Western tradition toward that spirit/matter dualism with which we are still wrangling. Yet Paul insists on what must have been for his original readers, and remains for modern readers, a mind-blowing category violation: "The dead will be raised imperishable, and we will be changed. For this perishable body must put on imperishability, and this mortal body must put on immortality" (vv. 52–53).

The tradition of depicting Jesus as gardener persists across cultures, with remarkable examples from Chinese, Indian, African, and European artists. One of the most stunning recent expressions is a 2017 work by Dutch artist Janpeter Muilwijk titled *New Gardener*. Jesus appears in overalls and T-shirt, moving toward Mary Magdalene with open arms. Mary is dressed in simple, shimmering white, veiled like a bride. Her hands are raised in a gesture of—hesitation? surprise? Perhaps this is the precise instant when she recognizes her teacher and friend, when bewilderment and despair pivot to joy. Or perhaps the artist captures Jesus saying to Mary, "Do not hold on to me" (John 20:17), while Mary offers hands-off compliance. Either way, a halo encircles her head: she is already, in this shivering and ambiguous moment, a saint. Meanwhile, Jesus's gaze is not fixed on her but beyond her, as if looking to the work yet to be done. A dogwood tree blooms behind Jesus, exquisitely detailed birds dot the scene, and bits of garden fence sweep across the painting's corners. In a lovely touch, butterflies alight on each of Jesus's wounds, "marking them as sites of transformation," according to art writer Victoria Emily Jones. Jones nicely encapsulates how Jesus as gardener points to the redemption of the whole creation: Jesus's "resurrection broke ground in this garden," Jones writes, "marking the beginning of a massive restoration project."[5]

Garden as refugia space. Of course. In refugia, miracles occur. From remnants, from fragments, from what seems like nothing, new life grows. In the Easter story, God takes this refugia pattern and breaks it wide open. Jesus is dead, then he is alive, transformed and embodied and imperishable. The Easter garden defies the usual considerations of scale; it's a hyperlocal refugium with cosmic effect. In orthodox theology, what happened in the garden constitutes a dramatic breaking-into-history of God's creative power, something radically distinct from the normal, natural cycles we know—death, decay, microbial transformation. Instead, the resurrection demonstrates a fulfillment promised to all creation, a reality beyond death in a culmination of history we can hardly imagine.

In the meanwhile, refugia faith must be cruciform. We attend to that crux where death and life intersect, deeply imprinted in the cycles of the created world, as if God wants to be sure we don't miss the point: death is ubiquitous, but life is too. Refugia faith recognizes, even amid death, the power of renewal built into creation. This renewing power points to, yearns toward, the cosmic fulfillment sealed in Christ's death and resurrection. When we say that we are "united to Christ," we mean that, while we wait for that ultimate fulfillment, we allow that pattern of dying and rising to be imprinted on our spirits, on our lives. The shape of the cross reminds us that woundedness and renewal intersect, and at that intersection, we find the very person of God.

It's easy to survey the world's decay and give in to hopelessness. How tempting to cede sovereignty to the law of entropy, to calculate the exponents on the crises we face right now, to surrender to the persistence of human wickedness and foolishness, to resign ourselves to a downward spiral. On some days that seems the most sensible, realistic posture. Yet God loves to work with scraps and remnants, the most unlikely materials possible. God loves to plant a seed when no one is looking. As Randy Woodley writes about Jesus's debut sermon in Isaiah 61, "It appears, according to Luke and several of the other Gospel writers, that when God wants all humanity to know something important, he invests his time and efforts in obscurity."[6] The familiar fact that tiny seeds become enormous plants, mustard bushes or oak trees, and that all living creatures begin as tiny spirals of DNA contained in single cells—we at once take these miracles for granted, and we acknowledge them as miracles. Refugia faith attends to the miracle of the seed.

In the northern hemisphere in temperate climates, Holy Week and Easter conveniently coincide with spring. In Michigan, Easter rarely falls on a warm, sunny day. We are more likely to have chilly wind and spatterings of rain, maybe even ice. Floral Easter frocks and summery pastels seem aspirational at best. Nevertheless, perennial daffodils and tulips push up from the ground. Buds swell on the trees. Robins tilt their heads toward the cold mud to listen for worm rustlings. Sleepy, furry creatures scuttle out from winter dens, emerging from their own little tombs. Life is resilient. Even in the darkest places of our lives, life wants to persist. Grass in sidewalk cracks. Weeds in stony fields and urban parking lots. In the hottest deserts and on the most frigid polar ice, in the deepest fathoms of the ocean, the Spirit of God broods always, and life finds a way.

Relief on the Edges

Twenty miles outside town, out among cornfields and orchards, Ron and I find the driveway marked by an unassuming sign: Plainsong Farm. As we pull in and park on the grass, I'm struck by how ordinary it all looks. Two farmhouses, a small barn, a couple of outbuildings, a hoop-style greenhouse, and fields. Cars roar by on the busy rural road. Yet Plainsong Farm represents an intentionally designed space for healing land, building community, and rediscovering faith all at once.

Emily comes to greet us, accompanied by a calico cat called Dandelion. Emily is a seminary student, now on staff at the farm. She's tall and slim, with an eager smile, wearing a long skirt and sweater. Then comes Nurya, who looks exactly like an Episcopal priest should—cardigan sweater and clogs, fluttery hand gestures. She sparkles with energy as she walks us around the farm, telling us the story.

"It was one of the only moments of vocational clarity I've had," she says, describing why she started a faith-based farm.[7] God gave her the idea, much to her own surprise. She and her husband were living on ten acres of neglected organic farmland and unmown fields, but she knew nothing about farming. She didn't even know what a faith-based farm *was*. Few people did in the early 2000s.

Many years of wrestling followed, some false starts. Nurya was discouraged but undeterred. Finally, miraculously, money and the right people came together. Nurya gathered a staff to start farming and teaching and experimenting. Today, Plainsong Farm has a community-supported agriculture (CSA) program, where people can buy a season-long subscription to the farm's harvested produce. The farm also gives away a portion of its harvest to food pantries. And the team works with churches that want to start gardens and farms of their own. Recently, they started a program for young adults who come to the farm and live for twelve weeks in community, gaining farming skills and discerning their own call to do farm-based ministry. They host a Sunday evening worship time and meal, and Emily is helping to devise meditative walks and other prayerful opportunities for people to visit the farm and connect with both the earth and God.

Plainsong is one example of a growing movement toward community-based gardens and farms meant not only to grow food but to build capacity for community. Fifteen years ago, Nurya could find only a handful of such places with Christian connections. Jewish folk, she discovered, were about ten years ahead, with an extensive, organized network of faith-based farming programs. In the last five years, though, hundreds of faith-based farms and church-sponsored gardens are sprouting up across North America. Nurya can rattle off dozens of names now, people modeling ways to do this and starting to influence others. As Emily describes it, these groups are "rethinking their faith tradition through the lenses of food and ecology. And they're rethinking food and ecology through the lens of their faith tradition."

On our afternoon visit, Emily and Nurya guide Ron and me past the barn. Here are some seedlings set out in trays on a table: basil, lettuces. In the main fields, rows of cherry tomato plants are strung up neatly on cables. Long rows of cabbage, chard, broccoli, rhubarb, and potatoes bask in the cool autumn sun. Irrigation hoses snake up and down the rows. Other areas are planted with cover crops to renew the nitrogen in the soil. One square is entirely covered with some kind of tarp, resting. Most of the property is just wild Michigan field: lots of goldenrod, some Queen Anne's lace, grasses, other wildflowers.

I ask questions about nitrogen fixing and farming techniques, but Nurya and Emily don't know all the details. "We're not the farmers!" they both remind me. "We're farmer adjacent!" They're learning, of course, but Michael and Bethany are the resident farmers. Mostly Nurya is in charge of managing the nonprofit end of things, fund-raising, and visioning. Emily works on programming. Nurya still serves part-time in a regular Episcopal parish too.

We turn the corner, around a stand of spruces, and come into the back areas. It's quieter here, and the farm is starting to work its magic on me. Now we've reached the old orchard, formerly tended by the previous owner but long neglected. It produces biennially, yielding edible but scruffy-looking apples. And here are the pigs! Several plump pink pigs are penned—with a simple, solar-powered electric fence—into an area that includes a pine grove and a few of the apple trees. These are happy pigs, downright frolicking on the well-trampled ground, their beady eyes bright. They were gifts from a large-scale ag farmer, Emily explains. Now here are the chickens. They're napping in their little A-frame roost at the moment. Their enclosure includes a big pile of vegetable scraps, a source of plant matter as well as the insect larvae chickens love. "They eat very well," remarks Nurya.

We walk farther into the back area, where they've cut some paths through the goldenrod and grasses so that people can take meditative walks. We pass the fire pit, where the resident community holds meetings and hangs out together. We end our tour in the hoop house, filled right now with tomato plants strung up on carefully engineered lines hooked at the top to a clothesline-like wire. The wire system supports vines heavy with fruits, green and orange and abundant (the ripe ones have been picked). The tomato house somehow feels bewitching, like walking through a magical forest.

Early in her process, Nurya was inspired by Fred Bahnson, who has written in his book *Soil and Sacrament* about his own experience with a church-based community garden.[8] Fred helped found and run Anathoth Farm as a way to heal his North Carolina community after a shocking murder sent everyone reeling. Fred writes honestly about the challenges of this kind of project—conflicts among stakeholders, steep learning curves, the usual difficulties of raising plants and animals. Nothing goes exactly to plan. Hard labor is rewarded with delicious food and celebrative community meals—but also with crops that die for no apparent reason and certain pesky turkeys who refuse to cooperate.

These farms and community gardens embody refugia patterns. They are places of experimentation and renewal, excellent examples of human cultural refugia overlapping with refugia for plants and animals, occupying that fertile space between wildness and a completely human-built environment. In his books, Bahnson weaves the story of Anathoth Farm with an account of his travels to four other faith-based farm communities. He describes his stays with a Trappist monastery, a community garden in North Carolina, an organic farm in Washington State, and a Jewish organic farm in the Berkshires. These farms are connected, in a variety of ways, to the usual structures of religious life, yet thrive on the edges of these structures. Nurya agreed that farms like hers provide refugia both *from* and *within* regular church life. Places like Plainsong create space for embodied practices and for the kind of community building that happens when people do meaningful work together. These farms also create space for meditation and renewal away from the routines of church programming and high-tech worship. Plainsong Farm is not a substitute for the regular church, Nurya insists. Yet young people especially, she has observed, "can't live the usual congregational grind." They need these edge spaces, "some kind of relief space."

Get Small and Jump In

Farms and community gardens connected to faith groups are participating in a broader response to the damaging effects of industrial agriculture. All over the world, people are seeking ways to wean from large-scale monocropping that depends on patented seeds, fossil-fuel-based fertilizers, and massive, gas-guzzling machinery. Industrial animal agriculture, too, is fossil fuel intensive, pollution intensive, and inhumane. Industrial agriculture has been wildly successful in producing food on a mass scale, but its drawbacks are now well known and well documented in scientific studies as well as in more journalistic, general-audience work by writers like Michael Pollan. Pollan's 2006 book *The Omnivore's Dilemma* marked a moment of growing public awareness about the politics and dysfunctions of the American food system.[9] More of us are now aware that our industrial foodways are not healthy for the earth, for other creatures, for our diets, or for our life in community.

We now understand, for example, that food production accounts for about 21–37 percent of overall greenhouse gas emissions, depending on what is included in the estimate.[10] Massive monocropping of corn, soy, wheat, and other crops depletes soil, loads land and water with fertilizer and pesticide runoff, and destroys pollinators with pesticides. Raising meat animals is a huge problem too. Ecologically minded activists and educators will often say that one of the first things individuals should do to "help the planet" is consume much less meat. Our outrageous meat consumption in the United States—a habit we have successfully exported elsewhere—creates demand that drives deforestation for grazing land as well as concentrated animal feeding operations that ruin land, pollute water, and torment the actual creatures. Livestock grazing now accounts for 25 percent of land use worldwide, which is 70 percent of agricultural land.[11] Moreover, industrial agriculture places power in the hands of big ag companies and owners of huge plantations and meat processing operations rather than with the people who work the land or tend the animals. Our massive food systems represent an old story of alienated labor and dispossession from land, and not only for Black, brown, and Indigenous people. White farmers in America's heartland—the heroes of American mythologies about fruited plains and amber waves of grain—have suffered grievous losses since the advent of fossil-fuel-based fertilizer and genetically engineered seed after World War II. Ironically, skyrocketing yields have proven the farmer's bane, forcing monocropping and increasing dependence on industrial inputs. In the 1970s, under Nixon's agriculture secretary, Earl Butz, farmers were instructed to "get big or get out." Many were compelled either to sell their family's land or to farm according to industrial practices, whether they wanted to or not.[12]

We simply can't farm and raise animals according to these industrial paradigms anymore; these practices are not sustainable, nor are they just. As with our energy systems, though, we're tangled up in the infrastructures and habits we know. Most of us depend on the industrial food system because we do not know how to feed ourselves from our own labor, and we can't all suddenly become successful farmers. Food production has always been, and always should be, a communal enterprise. The question now is whether we can move away from industrial practices that require massive fossil-fuel inputs, extensive transportation networks, and ruinous land practices and toward more localized foodsheds and regenerative practices. It is possible to farm in a way that improves soil, that takes from the land but also gives back to it.

The transformation toward new—or renewed—farming practices is happening, at least on a small scale. In North America, young people with no recent family history on the land are choosing to become small-scale farmers. All over the world, a new generation of people are creating farm refugia: tucking big gardens and small farms into urban centers, amid suburban sprawls, and onto repurposed monoculture farms. They are recovering heirloom seeds adapted to tougher conditions, training up and equipping people with little land and few resources to grow their own food, learning from Indigenous regenerative practices.[13] People are recovering practices that many of us lost only a generation ago: a kitchen garden for everyone, small allotment gardens, a few urban chickens. Many conscientious farmers are eager to learn better land and soil management. The number of certified organic farms in the United States rose over 80 percent from 2011 to 2019, to 16,585 farms.[14] Cattle ranchers, too, are learning to manage grazing so as to improve soil and carbon sequestration while raising livestock more humanely.[15] All over the world, leaders in this movement are reconnecting others to the life-giving miracle of soil, air, water, and seeds.

Practicing Resurrection

Though the earth's wild places inspire our awe and wonder, farms and gardens can be beautiful too—sculpted settings where human effort coaxes soil, air, water, and seed into the familiar alchemies that sustain us. I don't want to overromanticize farming and gardening; people involved in the current "farming moment" are often quick to acknowledge that their plots and acres are hardly utopias. Farming is demanding under any circumstances, and regenerative agriculture requires enormous ingenuity and persistence. There are endless problems to solve with pests, weather, and weeds. There are people problems too, since any cooperative human effort inevitably involves conflicts and fallings-out. Nevertheless, farms and gardens can model refugia spaces where humans, plants, insects, fungi, and other creatures establish life-giving, mutually beneficial patterns that promote thriving for all.

One of the more exciting features of the small-farm movement is the way in which Black, brown, and Indigenous leaders are using farms and community gardens to heal generational trauma connected with the land. Randy Woodley, a Christian pastor and legal descendent of the Keetoowah Cherokee, founded Eloheh Farm on fifty acres in Kentucky. He did not know how to farm; he was raised in Detroit. So he and his wife, Edith, learned. They wanted to train Indigenous leaders in farming skills as a way to reclaim, even in a small way, connection to lands wrested from their ancestors. *Eloheh* is a Cherokee word that means "harmony, wholeness, abundance, and peace," and it represents the vision on which the Woodleys' farm would be based.[16] Unfortunately, the Woodleys and their team were driven off that first Kentucky farm by White supremacists who threatened them with gunfire. The county

government refused to hold the tormentors accountable, and the Woodleys were forced to sell their land at a loss. They moved to Oregon and
started a new farm while Randy taught at Portland Seminary. They have
recently moved again, this time to a ten-acre farm in Yamhill, Oregon,
where they continue to model sustainable farming, support Indigenous
entrepreneurship, and welcome visitors and trainees. Their personal
history eerily recapitulates the history of Indigenous people in America, yet Randy and Edith have persisted and succeeded in pursuing their
refugia vision.[17]

Soul Fire Farm in Pennsylvania exemplifies land-healing initiatives with a concern for African American history and land-based
trauma. Leah Penniman, the founder, tells the story of African women
in the time of the slave trade who, kidnapped from their homelands,
quickly braided seeds into their hair—a powerful gesture of hope that
someday they could bring a tiny memory of their homeland into whatever terrors their future would bring.[18] Enslaved African people survived through generations of forced labor on other peoples' land, then
through further generations of enforced poverty in the sharecropping
system or being cornered into the least desirable urban landscapes.
Yet the memory of land connection persists. Even when African people
worked the land for slaveholders, the land itself became a refugium.
The soils and trees and crops spoke of life and resilience amid unspeakable suffering. Imported seeds whispered life out of death. Today, Penniman and her team draw on those deep land connections, striving to
raise up leaders of color who can practice and teach regenerative farming. They are recovering the wisdom of African Indigenous practices,
combining it with current, science-based knowledge in order to farm
in ways that build soil fertility rather than deplete it.

Wendell Berry's famous poem "Manifesto: The Mad Farmer Liberation Front" concludes with a single imperative: "Practice resurrection."[19] The more I learn about these refugia farms and gardens, the
more beautiful and miraculous they seem. They become hubs of healing, abundance, and communal resilience. Hillside Paradise Parking
Plots Community Garden in King County, Washington, for example,
was created from a one-acre parking lot donated by a church. World
Relief Seattle helped organize the depaving of the parking lot and created fifty community garden plots for refugees and immigrants in the
community, who are now bringing their expertise and voice to land use

in the city. Meanwhile, the farm includes rain gardens and a cistern system that not only helps with irrigating the plots but also mitigates the Seattle-Tacoma area's problems with polluted runoff. In any urban setting, when rains wash water off pavement, the oils, industrial pollutants, and other wastes sitting on the pavement get caught in the runoff and rush into the storm sewers and then into any nearby streams or rivers. So this little community garden in Washington is modeling how to absorb and filter that runoff with tolerant plants and rock areas, keeping the runoff out of the Puget Sound.[20] Here in West Michigan, Eighth Day Farm was also established on what used to be a parking lot. With the encouragement of the property manager, farm staff dug up an acre of strip-mall parking lot to create a community farm right in the city of Holland. The vision here, too, is to connect people to land and to each other, in the city, through a farm market, a CSA share program, educational programs, and informal connections among visitors and volunteers. And of course, to provide fresh and healthy food.[21]

These projects make me wonder what my own city's 28th Street would look like if half the commercial properties—especially the many abandoned ones with commercial real estate for-sale signs on them—were turned into farms or replanted into fields and forests. What if every neighborhood had large gardens, more trees, more green, so that people who don't own land, not even a tiny city lot, can still have a bit of land that feels like their own? After our visit to Plainsong Farm, Emily wrote me a note in which she described regenerative agriculture as a "living embodiment of the in-breaking of the Lord's Day." People have often used plowshares, she observed, to colonize, subdue, and poison the land—and dispossess people from it. But the people of God, even and especially in captivity, exile, and trauma, have always been promised outpourings of grace that looked, at least in part, like healthy agriculture.

We are soil creatures and seem to do better when we're closer to soil. I think of my friend Jeff, who has written about his experience at Princeton Theological Seminary working at its "Farminary." Jeff was raised in suburbia and has spent most of his life in big cities. For him, raising chickens and turning over compost piles were entirely new experiences. But he planted Chinese greens to connect with his ancestry, got used to working the soil and playing with baby goats, and soon, he says, his hours on the farm started to feel life giving. He found belonging and connection, some relief from anxiety, joy in the sound of wind and the feel of dirt in his hands. Jeff has written that compost alone taught him more about death and resurrection than anything in his seminary theology courses.[22]

After all, a good compost pile is basically a microrefugium. Throw together a pile of scraps and rejects, eggshells and fruit rinds, tough stems and grass cuttings, and at first it just looks like rotting death. But death is never wasted in the microbial world. Decay brings life; in fact, decay *is* life. A good compost pile teems with microorganisms—more than a billion per teaspoon. The bacteria, fungi, and actinomycetes feed on the carbon and nitrogen in the decaying plant matter, and these metabolic processes create heat that makes way for other kinds of bacteria to do their work. Worms and bugs are also essential in this transformational work. Thus compost represents an elegant orchestration of the tiniest, lowliest specks of life. Given time, moisture, the right temperature range, and enough churning to keep up the oxygen supply, and a pile of death transforms to living soil, ready to serve as the foundation of the whole nutrient cycle.

I'll never be a farmer. As much as I admire skilled labor and the magic of growing food, as much as I love the idea of farms and gardens tucked everywhere, I'm not ready to quit my job and buy a hoop house. I can, however, become more farmer adjacent. Fortunately, Michigan is a good place to connect with farmers. It's easy for me to get eggs and pasture-raised meat directly from Pierre, a small-scale grower, at the farmer's market. I buy blueberries, strawberries, and apples every summer directly from local farms. If we go out to eat, we can easily choose restaurants in our town that feature locally sourced dishes. We tried CSA shares, dropped out for a while, and now we're back. We're moving slowly to reduce our meat consumption, though I make no claim to being super virtuous in that department yet. The more I learn, though, the more I want to join the whole constellation of people and organizations who are helping regenerate our farm- and gardenscapes, cooperating with the death-to-life processes in which we are all embedded.

Homegrown National Park

Since my personal gardening achievements are limited at this point to the most amateur attempts at flowers, tomatoes, and herbs, I was happy to read Douglas Tallamy's book *Nature's Best Hope*, which promotes an alternative form of plant cultivating.[23] Tallamy, a professor of entomology and wildlife ecology at the University of Delaware, argues that while "gardening in the traditional sense is optional, . . . earth stewardship is not."[24] Everyone can participate in earth stewardship, he writes, especially people who own even the smallest bit of land. In the United States, over 80 percent of land is privately owned.[25] And for a variety of cultural reasons, we are obsessed with covering our residential and commercial landscapes with turf lawns, festooned with decorative species of trees, shrubs, and flowers imported from Asia, Europe, and South America. It looks nice, but unfortunately it results in "biologically depauperate" land.[26] In other words, lawns and imported-species plantings do not support biodiversity at nearly the same level that native plant landscapes do. Native plants and insects have evolved together to support a whole community of birds, amphibians, reptiles, and mammals. When we destroy that biological base, we "depauperate" everything above it, reducing the "ecosystem services" our nearby nature provides. Some species don't mind much: robins, white-tailed deer, raccoons, and squirrels— they're fine. Most species, however, have more specialized needs and can't adjust well to our manicured landscaping.

Tallamy has estimated that we are currently mowing, fertilizing, and watering forty million acres of lawn in the United States. His proposal: return half of it to native plants.[27] Nothing is stopping us except custom, notions about status, and—in some cases—neighborhood ordinances that could be changed. "Across the United States," Tallamy writes, "millions of acres now covered in lawn can be quickly restored to viable habitat by untrained citizens with minimal expense and without any costly changes to infrastructures." He calls his vision "Homegrown National Park."[28] Twenty million acres of restored native ecosystem would surpass the combined area of thirteen of our largest national parks. In the world Tallamy envisions, "landscaping will become synonymous with ecological restoration."[29]

We would achieve, with this vision, what we might call patchwork refugia. Tallamy is convinced by his research that insects, birds, and animals will quickly return to areas relandscaped with "keystone" tree species and an understory of native shrubs and plants. For too long, we have imagined that biodiversity and human settlement are incompatible, that "nature" is "out there" in preserves and national parks, and that someone else is responsible for it. It's true that for some species, such as grizzlies and other apex predators, habitat fragmentation is not tolerable; they need large, relatively undisturbed spaces to survive and reproduce. However, many species can happily live near or among humans if they have the particular kinds of food and shelter they need.

Tallamy emphasizes that the benefits of this Homegrown National Park project far outweigh the losses. So we lose a little lawn—so what? We'll be gaining "more pollination services; more free pest control; more carbon safely tucked away in the soil; more rainwater held on and within land for our use in a clean and fresh state; more bluebirds, orioles, and pileated woodpeckers in our yards; more swallowtails and monarchs sipping nectar from our flowers."[30] (He's thinking of his native Pennsylvania with that list; other places would regain other species.) We could gain the delight of living with many more creaturely neighbors, looking after their needs and receiving their ecosystem services—as well as their gifts of beauty and life. Tallamy (of course) quotes Aldo Leopold: "the oldest task in human history" is "to live on a piece of land without spoiling it."[31] Our chief task at this point in human history, we could add, is to live on a piece of land and bring it back to abundant life.

So it turns out that the struggling little refugium in my backyard is one new fragment of Homegrown National Park. Even better, the features of the area that I've thought of as messy and unfinished turn out to be desirable. I knew enough to leave several standing dead trees ("snags"), but Tallamy actually recommends a brush pile or two, some fallen dead trees or small logs, and some messy undergrowth. Check, check, and check. Tallamy also recommends a water feature, which we don't have. Next step!

I already love our little spot, even if it seems ridiculous to restore a mere hundred square yards. Never mind. Tallamy has convinced me that our tiny patch has a vital place and purpose. His book makes a persuasive case for restoration work by citing his research results and by enhancing the book's pages with ravishing photos of moths, birds, and butterflies. While Tallamy satisfyingly answers a number of questions that skeptics might raise, I have to admit that the book makes this restoration work sound simpler than it was for us. Sure, you can go to the recommended websites and look up the most promising native plants for your area. But we couldn't even have begun our project without knowledgeable people, in person, showing us the way. We were lucky to have the expertise of the Plaster Creek Stewards to tell us what buckthorn was, how to remove it, and what to plant instead. I needed Deanna of the Swale right there in my yard to recommend next steps, to supply me with the native plant seedlings, to show up with a crew of hardy under-graduates, and to show us where to plant everything. And it wasn't free either. Our little project has cost—well, several thousand dollars over the last ten years. Not everyone can pull that off.

Tallamy's proposal is aimed at people who already own a little land, who already have some power and agency and interest—that's smart. We can certainly leverage the goodwill of private landowners. But Tallamy is also realistic about the need to create a broader culture of restoration. That will have to include both private landowners and the efforts of communities working together, including those people with less agency and fewer resources. Groups like the Plaster Creek Stewards can help there. They have been doing watershed restoration work since 2004, completing dozens of projects in a variety of public and private spaces with a variety of community partners. To help heal one of the most polluted waterways in the state, they focus on three things: education, research, and restoration projects. They typically use grant money to cover costs, they deploy a lot of volunteer labor, and they focus on areas of the watershed where people have less power to change their surroundings.

I spent a couple happy, muddy hours one October morning planting native seedlings in the Calvin Avenue Basin a few miles from my house, along with about a hundred other volunteers, most of them—once again—intrepid and cheerful undergraduates. An area the size of a small city park, the basin looks like a piece of swampy, undeveloped land surrounded by apartment buildings and starter-home neighborhoods. It's actually an engineered miniecosystem. Plaster Creek emerges from an underground pipe in one corner and meanders through the basin to another corner, where it slips into another pipe to travel beneath the neighborhood. The Stewards have been working on this basin for years, removing invasive species, planting native species, contouring the land to get the creek to meander. When rains come hard and flood the creek, this is one of the areas where the land and the plants manage import-ant work. The rushing floods spread out over the area, the undulating terrain slows the flow, and the plants soak up water and pollutants. The plants don't mind—they're tough natives that can handle it. Filtered and slowed by this restored ecosystem, water resumes its path more safely and cleanly through the watershed.

When I got home from that day of planting and washed off the mud, I went to the Plaster Creek Stewards website and learned some history about my hometown that I never knew. The creek used to be called, by the Ottawa people, Kee-No-Shay, which means "water of the walleye." In the early 1800s, once White settlers started to arrive, Chief Blackbird showed a missionary a particularly beautiful spot where the Ottawa felt especially close to the Creator. Unfortunately for the Ottawa, this spot contained gypsum. The White settlers started mining the gypsum in order to make plaster. Pollutants from the mining process degraded the creek, and it soon became known as Plaster Creek. So much for sacred spots and so much for the walleye. By the early 2000s, the creek carried such high bacterial loads, it was unsafe even to touch the water.[32]

Plaster Creek serves as a metaphor for the interconnections of a whole region. It connects commercial, industrial, residential, and recreation zones. It flows into the Grand River that gives our town its name. The Grand River then flows into Lake Michigan. What happens upstream affects everything and everyone downstream. That's true of degradation, but it's true of restoration too. The Plaster Creek Stewards are helping everyone in this watershed learn to better "love our downstream neighbors." They model and promote what ecophilosopher Glenn Albrecht terms *soliphilia*, the love of working with other people to save loved places at all scales.[33] Caring for place requires fellow feeling, love for neighbor, an abiding concern for the common good, and the stamina to work together over the long term. Soliphilia works against our tendencies to idolize property rights, privacy, and autonomy to the neglect of a wholistic and future-oriented view. Fortunately, we do not need soliphilia to descend magically upon us; we can exercise it, build it, spread it through shared experience.

The Scope of Redemption

Regenerative agriculture and restoration work, for now, are still refugia practices. They happen on smaller scales—dishearteningly small compared to the vast needs across the globe. We can hope that these practices create new capacities and begin to spread more widely and quickly as part of our Great Work toward sustainable ways of life on the

planet. Our human survival depends on it, so there's a practical motivation. It's also a moral imperative, because, by any moral accounting, we
should take responsibility for the damage we've done. More than that,
from a spiritual point of view, regenerative agriculture and restoration
work fulfill the divine purpose given to human beings in the creation
accounts: serve and protect, rejoice and rest. When we ignore or per-
vert those purposes, we participate essentially in uncreation. By fulfilling our healing vocation, on the other hand, we participate in the long
arc of God's redemptive plan, which culminates—we hope and believe,
as best we can—in an ultimate flourishing for the whole community of
creation.

   This long-term thinking raises the question of what's going to happen "in the end." It's a good question, difficult and crucial to answer well,
because bad eschatology can do a world of damage in the present. That
is, if you have the wrong ideas about the end of history—the end point
and ultimate purpose of *all this*, all of existence—then you're likely to be
doing the wrong things now too. The most vulgar version of a Christian
telos is a kind of shrugging disregard and apathy: "Well, God is going to
destroy all this anyway, so what's the point of caring for anything now?"
This attitude is based on hierarchical anthropocentrism, of course—we
humans are the only actors that matter, so why care about the theater
stage? We'll just strike the set after the show. But it's also based in Scripture, or more precisely, in a poor reading of Scripture. Theologian Steve
Bouma-Prediger cites the English translation of a single verse in 2 Peter
as "the most egregious mistranslation in the entire New Testament."
Chapter 3, verse 10 is typically translated something like "the earth and
all that is in it will be burned up to nothing." Bouma-Prediger argues
persuasively that the Greek verb here does not mean "burned up" at all;
it means "found." A more correct translation would be "the earth will be
scrutinized" or "disclosed." The idea, Bouma-Prediger explains, is that
"after a refiner's fire of purification (v. 7), the new earth will be *found*, not
burned up."[34] If you imagine that the earth will simply be tossed aside
in the eschaton, then it follows that "heaven" is all about humans. (And
maybe some beloved pets? Opinions differ.) The current created world,
however magnificent, will disappear, perhaps in a dramatic conflagra-
tion. Moreover, some eschatologies so prize "the spiritual" that what
happens next somehow transcends the biophysical altogether. All creation will evaporate into pure spirit.

This pseudognostic eschatology is only one strain of the tradition though. For Reformers like Luther and Calvin, for example, God is powerfully present in nature—outside and "above" but also within. Thus the more-than-human created world reveals God's glory, poured out in irrepressible abundance by the Holy Spirit's continual creative and sustaining action. Calvin and Luther, like Irenaeus and late Augustine, believed the Bible witnessed to the redemption of all creation, including the creatures. As the Apostles' Creed states, we believe in the resurrection of the body. The telos of all existence is not just blissful human souls floating in ether, then, or even (as Pierre Teilhard de Chardin posits) a culminating "omega point" where everything converts to pure energy. The telos is still earth—biophysical matter—indeed, *this* earth, but renewed and fulfilled.

The most compelling vision of this appears in Revelation 21–22. While it's always wise to tread lightly among the fever dreams in this book, the concluding vision of the new creation comports with God's most lavish and grace-filled promises throughout the Scriptures. John of Patmos sees a vision of "a new heaven and a new earth" (21:1), a garden-city to which all the nations stream, a place of glittering beauty and righteousness, where "death will be no more; mourning and crying and pain will be no more, for the first things have passed away" (21:4). Holiness comes easily in this place, because God is in the midst of it. A tree straddles the river that runs through the center of the city, "and the leaves of the tree are for the healing of the nations" (22:2). The earthly and heavenly realms intertwine in this vision—no more separation in this "new heaven and new earth." Most important, the word "new" in this passage is not the Greek word for "something that didn't exist until now." Instead, it's the word *kainon*, which means "renewed" or, better yet, "fulfilled." The heaven/earth in John's vision is continuous with the former creation, not a replacement.[35] Much will have to "be found" and scrutinized and die about this former creation—all our sins and injustices will have to go on the cosmic compost heap. But God can create new life even out of decay and death. We witness glimpses of this process every day.

Thus the Revelation vision provides a counterwitness to any notion that God intends to end history with some kind of poof in which the material substance of the created world disappears or etherizes into transcendence. H. Paul Santmire proposes that we imagine the telos of the universe as "a commonwealth of creaturely being, where the light of the divine fire unites and permeates all things, *ta panta.*" This commonwealth includes "not just spiritual creatures"—that is, humans—but all creatures, and it expresses a "consummation of all creaturely existence in God."[36] The resurrection of Jesus, then, becomes the "first fruits" of God's intention. It's crucial to note that Christ himself has a body in the Gospel accounts of postresurrection appearances. Jesus's body is not a fresh, new replacement; instead, it's a renewed, fulfilled body, complete with scars. Now multiply Jesus's first-fruit body by all created things, and you have a gloriously renewed biological world. As William P. Brown writes, "Resurrection ultimately cannot be limited to the raising up of individual bodies. Resurrection includes the whole of life in its vast eschatological and ecological sweep."[37]

As I've mentioned before, I have been formed in a Christian tradition that remains appropriately (in my view) shy to spend too much energy trying to nail down the precise nature of the end times or the afterlife. There be plenty of dragons beyond the edges of our theological and scriptural maps. We have God's promises, we have certain images and visions, and we have the beloved world itself. Frankly, I believe that the afterlife is the aspect of salvation we should probably focus on the least—maybe that's my privilege talking. But for those of us with any agency, there's so much resurrection-inspired work to do here and now. When we cooperate with God's death-to-life renewal work here and now, we become better witnesses to God's ultimate purposes. New Testament theologian J. Christiaan Beker discerns in the biblical letters of Paul a vision of the church characterized by this resurrection witness: "Paul's church is not an aggregate of justified sinners or a sacramental institute or a means for private self-sanctification but the avante-garde of the new creation in a hostile world. . . . Because the church is not an elite body separated from a doomed world, but a community placed in the midst of the cosmic community of creation, its task is not merely to win souls but to bear the burdens of creation to which it not only belongs, but to which it must also bear witness."[38] A healthy resurrection theology envisions a community of people who practice healing and restoration in the here and now, bearing burdens for all creation, bearing witness. Or, as William Brown puts it, "Resurrection is God's cosmic victory garden."[39]

Gratitude and Joy

Our first farm share this season from Eighth Day Farm included orca beans, pea shoots, green garlic, lettuces, radishes, and some other odds and ends. What to make with all that? We decided on minestrone soup with salad on the side. It was all so good! And when we sat down to eat it, I felt inspired to give thanks not just out of habit but genuinely from a true feeling of gratitude. I knew where this food grew and who grew it, and I enjoyed concocting something delicious from the ingredients. The impulse to give thanks over a meal runs deep in human cultures around the world and throughout history. If we need to find a place in our lives to cultivate gratitude and joy, mealtime is the place to begin.

Between now and the fulfillment of resurrection hope for all creation comes a long, indefinite meanwhile. How to endure the weariness, discouragements, and suffering in this meanwhile? The great wisdom traditions of the world seem to agree here: the secret to human endurance is to practice gratitude and to practice joy. No one imagines we will always *feel* gratitude and joy. That's why we have to practice. That's why people sing praises to God—not because God demands flattery but because praise helps put sorrow in perspective by holding it up to the light of God's character and work. That's why the poorest people find ways to feast and dance. It's not that they're so happy and content in their poverty; rather, they understand that gratitude and joy are effective tactics for survival.

The Covid-19 pandemic stripped out of my life for a time some key joy-and-gratitude practices I didn't realize I depended on until they were suspended. The practices built into Sunday worship—singing songs of praise, offering prayers of thanks—do not, it turns out, deliver their full power online. Similarly, music has always brought me back into a place of joy, either when I attend concerts or when I play in the community orchestra. During the pandemic, that was all suspended. I felt thrown onto my own private devices, and it turns out my private devices are rather anemic. Joy and gratitude, I came to realize more keenly than ever, are best practiced in community: we need to hold each other up. As the months passed and the pandemic wore on, my household—Ron and I, our son Philip, and his fiancée, Heidi—leaned hard on feasting as our joy practice. We cooked fancy meals and ate together almost every night of the week. After weeks where dinner table conversation devolved too often into deploring things—the pandemic,

American politics, the State of the World—we finally started a practice of saying each night what we were grateful for. And we prayed together. So simple, but it made a difference.

I continue to marvel at those who know far more about spiritual survival in a crisis than I do, and I look for models among those who have lived for generations with grief, limits, and trauma. One of Robin Wall Kimmerer's essays in *Braiding Sweetgrass*, for example, prompted me to rethink Christian gratitude practices in light of Native traditions. In the essay "Allegiance to Gratitude," Kimmerer describes how the people of the Onondaga Nation begin every gathering with what is often called the "Thanksgiving Address." The address, she writes, is "a river of words as old as the people themselves, known more accurately in the Onondaga language as the Words That Come Before All Else."[40] Here's the segment giving thanks for water, as Kimmerer renders it: "We give thanks to all of the waters of the world for quenching our thirst, for providing strength and nurturing life for all beings. We know its power in many forms—waterfalls and rain, mists and streams, rivers and oceans, snow and ice. We are grateful that the waters are still here and meeting their responsibility to the rest of Creation. Can we agree that water is important to our lives and bring our minds together as one to send greetings and thanks to the Water? Now our minds are one."[41] The address goes on for a while, through an inventory of about seventeen or so similar elements of the natural world, covering Mother Earth, waters, fish, plants, food plants, medicine herbs, animals, trees, birds, Four Winds, and so on. The speakers thank each aspect of creation in turn for "fulfilling its Creator-given duty to the others."[42] The address concludes with thanks directly to the Creator: "We now turn our thoughts to the Creator, or Great Spirit, and send greetings and thanks for all the gifts of Creation." Kimmerer observes that the address is not a pledge, a prayer, or a poem, exactly. It serves numerous cultural purposes, forming the scientific, political, and communal worldview of the Onondaga. Above all, the address is a "credo for a culture of gratitude."[43] By repeatedly envisioning the world as a kinship of creatures, all with gifts to share and the responsibility to share them, the Onondaga shape their understanding of human beings as one group among many who are both receivers and givers in the presence of the Creator.

After reading Kimmerer's essay, I wondered about our typical gratitude practices in Christian worship. We sometimes give thanks *for* the creatures in worship, or we note their beauty, or we call them to praise. We raise our song of praise "for the beauty of the earth." We call "all creatures of our God and king" to lift their voices. We declare that "rocks and trees and skies and seas" were wrought by the hand of God. In baptism liturgies, we sometimes acknowledge that water "cleanses, purifies, refreshes, and renews" and cite the ways that God uses water in salvation history. These are all wholesome and biblical liturgical acts. But what if we were to give thanks not just for the creatures but *to* the creatures?

I suppose one could argue that we should only ever thank God, the source of all. Wouldn't thanking the creatures be tantamount to confusing Creator and creation, a slippery slope to panentheism or pantheism? Well, not necessarily. It seems to me that in the address, the creatures are greeted and thanked, not worshipped. One could also argue that in worship we should only address God, or each other, and not be talking at the creatures. But we already do! In the 1674 hymn known as the Doxology, we sing, "Praise God, all creatures here below." Maybe we could use more frequent reminders, as in the address, that the creatures are not just objects, materials, resources. They have *being*. We do not have to surrender human distinctiveness to admit this. We can retain all the Genesis distinctives for humans and still acknowledge that pin oaks and cardinals and Percherons and narwhals have their own kind of being before God, their own gifts and duties. They are beautiful and beloved; they praise God by being themselves. Aren't we glad they do? Can we agree on that?

So what does it hurt to thank the bee for doing its beeish things, pollinating plants and providing wax for the vigil candle and honey for my tea? Why not remind ourselves, gratefully, that bees provide apian services not just to humans but to bluebonnets and bears and the whole matrix of life? I wonder what would happen if we started greeting and thanking the creatures for fulfilling their Creator-given duties to other creatures and to us. Maybe we could create adaptations of the address along these lines: "We thank you, God, for the trees. Thank you for the many families of trees, their shelter and shade, their fruits and beauty, their many useful gifts. The trees help the whole earth breathe and flourish. With one mind we greet and thank the trees of the world. And we thank you, God, for honoring trees in your word from beginning to end as signs of life, healing, and redemption." It wouldn't be so hard to include a little shout-out *to* the creatures in our devotional practices, embedded in appropriate thanks directly to God.

Maybe, as Kimmerer suggests, if we were more deeply formed in this kind of gratitude, we would treat the nonhuman creation with greater respect and protection. Maybe consistently taking a grateful inventory of fellow creatures, acknowledging the abundance the earth provides, would astonish us with how much we have and lead us into radically countercultural contentment. Maybe by establishing that we can at least agree about our gratitude for and to the creatures, we could find some common ground to heal our divisions.

If it seems that adapting an Indigenous tradition is an instance of off-limits cultural appropriation, then I would refer to the end of Kimmerer's essay, where she describes how she asked an Onondaga "Faithkeeper" whether it was permissible for her to write about the Thanksgiving Address and its wise centering of gratitude and communal reciprocity. The Faithkeeper insisted that the address is gift, and the whole point is that gifts must be shared. "If only people would receive it," he said. "We've been waiting five hundred years for people to listen."[44]

Moving from resignation to gratitude, I'm heartened to say, does not require starting with a clean slate. We begin small, where we are. We dig out and repair, we plant seeds, we nurture what we can. We seek joy and give thanks, give thanks and find joy. Everywhere I look, people—and creatures—are doing this resurrection work. Finding them is a matter of lifting up layers of soil, peeking beneath the duff and decay to uncover whole beds of seeds already germinating, already green.

RATTLESNAKE MASTER
ERYNGIUM YUCCIFOLIUM

July
Douglas, Michigan

In 1987, the year before I married my husband, his parents surprised the family and bought a cottage on Lake Michigan near the village of Douglas, Michigan. The place was modest, built in the 1890s. Lakeshore real estate, as one might expect, is extremely expensive, but his mom and dad got this place for a ridiculously low price because the lake levels were dangerously high at the time. They took a chance on the property, believing that since this structure had weathered a hundred years, it was likely stable enough. The cement-block foundation was buried into the base of a steeply sloped, heavily vegetated dune, down a stringer of forty wooden steps from the road above. Lakeward of the house, a shortened foredune sloped down from the deck right to the water's edge. Unlike almost all the owners of neighboring properties, Mom and Dad set out to live on the lake year-round, which required extensive winter-izing of a structure built only for summer dwelling. With new windows and roof, insulation and siding, the cottage was still rustic and simple but now stayed warm in the winter. Mostly.

Thus began for Ron and me and our family decades of regular visits to the lakeshore in all seasons. Happily for us, lake levels receded in the late 1990s, the foredune built back up, beach grass moved in to stabilize, and a good thirty feet of flat, perfect beach—give or take—opened out between the grassy dune and the water's edge. In summers, our kids and dogs romped on the beach all afternoon and into those glorious Michi-gan evenings that linger until almost 10 p.m. In all seasons, we walked the dogs along the road high above the lake, past the newer, posher homes built on the landward side of the road. In winters, we marveled at the snow-covered ice shelf that forms on the lake surface, beginning at the water's edge and accreting outward in fascinating formations, morphing every day as the lake's restless motion sculpts and revises. We learned how very dark winter nights can be. We learned about ferocious winter winds, which offer a convincing explanation why most people abandon the lakeshore in winter. I can say from experience that winter winds off the lake will shake a house to its foundation.

Michiganders love their retreats, out in our woods or along our inland lakes and rivers. We'll find a way—anything from a day spent at a state park, to a tent or trailer set up at a favored campground, to a hand-built cabin in the woods, to a family cottage complete with linoleum floors and bunk beds for the kids. A year-round home right on the big lake is, of course, the ultimate dream, but who can afford that? So when Mom and Dad bought this place, it felt to me like an amazing, unlooked-for gift. I had learned my love of the lakeshore on public beaches and campgrounds and on other people's properties. This place, though, felt like *ours*. We could love it as our own.

During the years Ron and I lived away from Michigan—in New Jersey, Iowa, London, California—I longed to return to our spot on the Michigan lakeshore. Its beauties came to me in dreams: that particular view of the lake, the oaks and maples and sumacs, the curve of the shoreline north and south from our forty-five feet of frontage. I longed for the lake's gentle moods, its roaring moods, its shifting colors and mysteriously spiritual presence. Awe and respect for its wildness, melting affection for its softness and muted colors. This specific place had settled into my muscles and bones and imagination.

When we returned to Michigan in 2006 after living for two years in California, though, something had changed. I couldn't explain it, but it was as if some of this place's bright magic had faded. Mom and Dad were getting older, and family discussions sometimes turned to succession: Could we pass the cottage down to the next generation? We soon realized it's not so easy. How would the four siblings share its management and upkeep, especially when three of them lived hours or plane rides away? How would we pay the taxes? Would Mom and Dad need to cash out the place to supplement their retirement savings? Other families manage the succession process with complicated LLCs and use-sharing agreements among dozens of cousins, but the more we talked, the more likely it seemed that eventually our family would have to let the cottage go. I realized the place was not mine after all, never had been. It was a temporary gift, and someday I would have to say goodbye.

What does it mean to love places that are only yours for a time? Loving a place requires familiarity—repeated, attentive encounter and connection, ideally across generations. But I have been born to an age and a culture that works against such love. Ownership is an easily transferrable piece of paper, an illusion of connection. In this age of crisis, we are called to reconnect with the earth, to dwell more deeply where we live, to naturalize to a place, put down roots. It's hard to trust, though, that this process will be worth the risk and effort when our roots could get pulled up or our places succumb to unwelcome change. Even my connection to West Michigan as a region is only a few generations deep. Who knows where my children will end up settling? How do I manage love for a place knowing my connection could be so tenuous?

We don't know what will happen to our family refuge on the lakeshore in the future. For now, we simply relish each day we spend there. Yesterday we came out to visit Mom and Dad, and it was one of those flawless summer days we never take for granted: eighty-five degrees with water temps in the seventies. Swimming was a religious obligation. The dogs were ecstatic. This morning, Ron and I reluctantly prepare to head into town again. The lake has settled into perfect calm, the water lapping the sand with quiet ripples, almost absentmindedly, like the way you scratch a dog behind the ears when it nudges your hand. The sky is porcelain blue.

I imagine the Ottawa and Potawatomi bands of presettler times who also loved this windy shore. It was theirs through care and attentiveness, through intimate knowledge. Their ancestors were buried near here, generations of Native peoples reaching back thousands of years. White settler illusions of private ownership seemed bizarre to them, a confusion settlers used to their own advantage for centuries. The Native peoples were right all along, though: no one can own a piece of this shoreline, let alone of this big lake. At least not the way we think of ownership today. This place is too wild and free, too full of the wind. It never stays the same. The dunes shift unpredictably every year. The lake roars and churns and storms, then turns utterly gentle. Mighty in its vastness, its implacable indifference to what is small and temporary, to all things gathered up into the rhythms of change.

Chapter 6
From Passivity to Citizenship

The crash of your thunder was in the whirlwind;
your lightnings lit up the world;
the earth trembled and shook.
—PSALM 77:18

ne thing leads to another. That's how I explain to myself how a person like me, with no special biological expertise or outdoorsy credentials, suddenly became passionate about the climate crisis and all things green. Where did it begin? I'm not even sure anymore. Maybe it was reading about food system politics in the 1990s, or hosting Kathleen Dean Moore and Bill McKibben on my university's campus. Or maybe it began long ago, in high school biology class, or among the Queen Anne's lace and milkweed, the "gauzy, furzy" fields covering the half-acre lots around my childhood home, places I loved exploring before people bought those parcels and built modern ranch homes surrounded by well-kept lawns.[1] All I know is that I feel as if something long latent in me has come alive, and I can hardly stop it now. Perhaps this change is not sudden at all but the natural outworking of a long trajectory.

In any case, my bookshelf is now packed with books on ecotheology and the climate movement. My email in-box is cluttered with newsletters from the Land Conservancy of West Michigan, Clean Water Action, the Alliance for Solar Choice, the Yale Forum on Religion and Ecology, Michigan Climate Action Network, and so many more I can't keep track of them all. My podcast app features numerous climate change and sustainability titles. I've joined the Creation Care Team at church, which is part of our denomination's Climate Witness Project. I've attended webinars on everything from trash and recycling handling in my town to plastic waste to the future of Michigan's electrical grid. I've read lengthy online reports and scientific articles. I've made lifestyle changes, gotten involved in local politics—the whole bit. And I venture outdoors a lot more with more knowledge and keener attention.

There's still so much I don't know, and everywhere I turn, there's more to do, more people involved than I had imagined, including here where I live. I did not know that a group called Grand Rapids Whitewater has been working since 2009 to restore the rapids in our namesake river. The rapids were removed after the Civil War so that the logging industry could float logs down the river. Now a group of business, civic, and environmental leaders have a $45 million plan (already 90 percent funded) to remove aging dams on the river and add boulders and rocks to re-create substrate for rapids. The goal is to improve the ecological health of the river, control invasive species like the sea lamprey, and create a thriving recreation culture along the river.[2] Meanwhile, I also did not know that a local group calling itself the Community Collaboration on Climate Change received a grant in 2019 to engage in a planning process with the aim of researching how our community can go carbon neutral by 2030.[3] I attended a webinar (of course) on this project featuring Dr. Missy Stults, one of the architects of Ann Arbor's plan, which is already well on its way. Dr. Stults noted that their guiding words are "equitable, sustainable, transformative." The Grand Rapids organizers are similarly focused on equity, building a leadership structure that centers our urban core and leaders of color.

I page through the book *Drawdown* and learn that people all over the world are developing and analyzing technological processes and tools for mitigating the effects of a changing climate—clean energy, carbon sequestration, sustainable farming.[4] People are doing the hard number crunching to analyze the economics of these solutions too. I marvel at the women interviewed on the *Mothers of Invention* podcast—women in Indonesia, Colombia, Palestine, the South Bronx—who are using their expertise and organizational savvy to save seeds and develop underwater vertical farming and organize youth activists and use political and legal leverage to push their communities and their countries into the future, to build a just transition to a new way of life.[5]

As I admire these people and learn about the work they do, I realize as never before in my life that I must become a better *citizen*. I can't rely, with a wan smile and a shrug—as my mother did—on the assurance that "they'll think of something." "They" is us. "They" is *me*.

The Problem of Scale

I believe the Spirit of God is at work in those people, all over the world, who are committing their intelligence, energy, and love to the Great Work of building climate resilience and reckoning with the injustices of our economies and infrastructures. I also believe that the Spirit of God loves the refugia paradigm. Since refugia are by definition local, particular, relatively small-scale—even temporary or transient—I wonder about the crucial question of scale. Since we need vast, international, and planet-scale transitions, how can a refugia strategy help?

I think the answer is that refugia can be the local- or small-scale particular expressions of global movements. We need the international agreements, but we also need ordinary people doing small-scale work, creating refugia spaces designed to answer needs right where they are.[6] We need to work on both scales at once. The people endeavoring to restore the rapids in the Grand River, creating beautiful public green spaces along a healthier river, are working consciously within the global context of ecosystem restoration. City leaders all over the world are maneuvering through their own local politics, forming community organizations, writing policy statements, and negotiating and persuading, all in order to set carbon-neutral goals and build healthier, more beautiful cities—but they are working consciously alongside others in global alliances.[7]

In ecological contexts, refugia take various forms. Some are in situ, where plants and creatures persist in relatively protected areas of their usual habitat. Some are ex situ, where creatures—if they can—move to a different habitat in order to survive. Some are stepping-stone refugia that migratory birds, for example, visit along their customary routes. Some refugia are ephemeral, lasting only for a short time. In any case, biodiversity persists in refugia because work gets done within them—growth and reproduction, capacity building, adjusting to changing conditions—work that enables refugia to spread outward, across their permeable borders into the areas nearby that need healing. Refugia that spread can link up with other refugia. Thus refugia are meaningful in nature not only because they protect but because they can transform and revive the space around them.

I think in human culture, our refugia take even more varied and complex forms, with even more permeable edges. We find refugia on farms or in gardens, out in wild places, at beloved retreats. We find refugia among people whom we love and trust. We find refugia in worshipping communities, in classrooms, and among friends around the table. We find refugia in meaningful work, alongside others who share our commitments and passions. I think our task is to find and create as many refugia as we can, understanding that we move in and among many kinds of refugia day to day. Some refugia will be stable, literal locations. Others will be more ephemeral—groups that come together for a time, practices that we share with like-minded people. Equipped with the internet and other forms of communication, we humans can create refugia spaces with people on the other side of the globe, and that is how we can work on the local and global scale at once. To thrive, we need a whole mosaic of biological, cultural, and spiritual refugia. The more we find and create refugia, the better chance we have of making connections and expanding to the scale of healing required.

It's been disheartening to me, as I have grown into a clearer understanding of the climate crisis, to learn that when it comes to this crisis Christian groups in North America have not, overall, been acting as the people of refugia. They have not been much of a driving force behind climate activism and, in some contexts, have remained apathetic or resistant. Individual Christians have certainly played, and continue to play, key leadership roles in the climate movement. Many mainline Christian groups have endorsed official statements and launched official central-office initiatives. Pope Francis, of course, has spoken out forcefully in his 2015 encyclical. Ecumenical Patriarch Bartholomew I has been dubbed the "Green Patriarch" for his abiding commitment to environmental activism.[8] Many churches are now "going green" with recycling programs and education hours and closer connection to climate action groups in their denominations or regions.[9] But as a whole, Christians have not exactly been the engine pulling the train.

In 2001, Bill McKibben (a practicing Methodist) summed up his observations about religious leaders and laypeople: "They have faithfully adopted, and then faithfully filed away, any number of right-thinking position papers on toxic waste or global warming (which they deplore) and God's creation (which they cherish). But all in all, it's been a pretty damp squib."[10]

The issue of the journal *Daedalus* in which this essay appeared was dedicated to addressing the question, "Religion and ecology: can the climate change?" Since the mid-1990s, the editors of that journal issue have been working through the Yale Forum on Religion and Ecology to catalyze a worldwide, interfaith movement toward empowering religious people to participate in and lead efforts to heal the earth. Conferences, publications, resources, degree programs, and much more have resulted.[11] But there's much to be done yet before active citizenship in the community of all creation is a given for all faiths. The resources for this commitment are present in all the major world religions, though still, too often, lying latent.

When I interviewed Bill McKibben in the summer of 2020, we lamented together the continued lack of leadership from Christian groups in the climate movement. The situation has improved since 2001, with denominational offices launching climate initiatives and with any number of small groups trying to create refugia-style spaces. Interfaith Power and Light has been working since 1998 to educate and inspire churches to participate in clean-energy transition, for example. The Catholic Climate Covenant, A Rocha International, and Climate Caretakers strive to provide resources and education for churches and model community connection to land. International interfaith groups like GreenFaith help connect Christians to like-minded people of other faiths around the world. Some Christians have formed small, intentional Christian communities that prioritize environmental work, such as EcoFaith Recovery in Portland, Oregon; Faith in Place in Chicago; or the Taos Initiative for Life Together, founded by a Mennonite couple in Taos, New Mexico.[12]

One of the best models of Christian refugia building that I know is the Iona Community. Founded in 1938 as a peace-and-justice ministry to Glasgow's poor, the Iona Community is "a dispersed Christian ecumenical community working for peace and social justice, rebuilding of community and the renewal of worship."[13] Iona folk continue to

prioritize peace, justice, and worship renewal, but environmental concerns have always been enfolded into their work as well. They have a
base in Glasgow as well as a beautiful abbey on the Isle of Iona, where
members gather regularly to worship and welcome the many pilgrims
who visit Iona. Except for summer residencies on the isle, Iona members generally do not live together. They follow a common rule of practice and accountability, but they are dispersed, living in their own home
communities, mostly in the UK. The Iona Community exemplifies the
ripple effect possible with the refugia model. Beyond the members
who have made the more strenuous commitments, the Iona Community
also encompasses associate members, friends, or supporters—about
two thousand around the world.

These Christian refugia groups strive to live in countercultural ways
while remaining engaged with mainstream culture. They are seeking
the resonance between Jesus's teachings and practical climate resilience
on local scales, networking with others who seek the same larger goals.
For the most part, these intentional communities remain refugia-sized,
and appropriately so. They may seed larger movements or maybe not.
Even if not, their work is still meaningful, witnessing to God's work in
the world as salt and leaven. Anyway, scaling up refugia is not a matter
of franchising. Imagine trying to duplicate the same ecosystem everywhere. The point of refugia models is not to promote sameness but
rather to promote dispersal and adaptation to local contexts.

The best of these Christian refugia communities work out of Christian convictions but resist a bunker mentality in which everyone and
everything outside their enclave are hopelessly "secular" or otherwise
benighted.[14] The modern climate movement presents magnificently
convincing evidence that the Spirit of God inspires all kinds of people
to do beautiful things in the world, often enough putting Christians to
shame. "The work of God is happening so much outside the church,"
I blurted out at one point during that interview with Bill McKibben.
Immediately I wondered if I had spoken too harshly. But McKibben, as
an international climate activist well networked across the globe, has
a far more accurate perspective on religious people's participation
than I do, and he sadly confirmed my impression. For those of us who
care about the church's witness, the situation is disappointing, but not
inexplicable. The Spirit of God moves according to divine will—like
the wind, as Jesus observed. If the Christian church is going to drag its

feet in healing the planet, that does not limit the Spirit's work. People of other faiths and no faith will teach Christians what God wants us to learn, despite our resistance.

This is the moment, then, for Christians to be humbled by our own failures; we badly need to learn this humility. Centuries of Christendom seduced the church in the West toward a culpable arrogance, the habit of imagining that Christians are the only ones who get things right. Now is not the time to stay in our exclusively Christian lanes. In the context of the Great Work, we need to surrender our arrogance, recognize and repent of our failures, learn from the wisdom of others, and be content to work in partnership with people who have outstripped us in doing God's work. We need to perceive that the Spirit's inspiration is not confined to our midst.

The Pyramid Problem

Christian passivity in the climate movement may derive in part from some common notions we fall into about God's sovereignty, human authority, and the role of ordinary people—our theology of agency, we might say. Probably this theology of agency operates mostly unconsciously, which is all the more reason to discern and revise it.

After the 2016 US presidential election, American Christians took to bickering over praying for the president. We must pray for our leaders, no matter what, people scolded one another—with people on both sides of our political and religious divide virtue signaling about their prayer lives. Apparently, I am not sanctified enough to pray sincerely for a president who gleefully trampled every day on principles I held as decent and right. So I would pray at our dinner table in vague terms about leaders and justice, but also, as an act of rebellion, I started praying for citizens. Praying only for national political leaders, I reasoned, perpetuates our imagined passivity and helplessness.

I wonder sometimes if Christians are especially prone to the "infantile authority fantasy." From what I can tell, this is not an official term in the psychological community, but Ron learned it years ago during his Clinical Pastoral Education training and we've found that the phrase comes in handy surprisingly often. Infantile authority fantasy describes our common human longing to surrender ourselves to some authority figure who will solve all our problems—some hero—so that we can regress into a comfortable, infantile state of dependency. The infantile authority fantasy arises out of fear: fear of taking responsibility, fear of making difficult choices in a murky moral universe. It's not hard to see how Christian theology can form us into this fantasy. After all, isn't Jesus that very hero who will solve all our problems? Aren't we supposed to be fully dependent on God? God is king, right? It says so in the Bible.

Lutheran theologian Gail Ramshaw, in her study of God and gender, describes the whole metaphor system of God-equals-king as "the myth of the crown."[15] By this phrase, she means, not that the idea is false, but that we have to recognize God's kingship as a metaphor, a meaning-making image system. Certainly, the Bible is full of this imagery, particularly the Old Testament. However, every metaphor for God, Ramshaw observes, must be received with a *yes-no-yes*. Yes, this reveals something true about God. No, some connotations of the metaphor must be rejected. But yes, we use the metaphor, understanding its limitations. Ramshaw explains that the myth of the crown is a residue of an ancient world in which patriarchal, monarchic culture was the rule. The Old Testament establishes God as the one true God in opposition to all the idols of polytheistic religions in the ancient Near East. The God of Israel is God above all false gods and King above all earthly kings. So yes, the myth of the crown reveals something true about God—that God alone is worthy of worship.

The myth of the crown in a contemporary context, however, raises two main problems. First, since a monarchic political system is no longer the norm, this metaphor connects less readily with our everyday reality. More profoundly, though, the image of God as almighty king tends to shove aside, in our minds, all other images. We imagine God as king in a simplistic, cartoonish way, suppressing the radical contradictions that modify this metaphor system in the Old Testament and even more so in the New Testament. Jesus has "made [God] known," according to John 1:18, and Jesus reveals that God's kingship is characterized by paradox. In Jesus, we see that God is not only distant but also with us. God is not only ruler but also servant. God not only saves us but also enters our suffering. In a similarly paradoxical vein, we are not only God's servants but also, as Jesus told his disciples, called friends. So while the myth of the crown rightly signals God's power and sovereign care—the transcendent otherness of God—the gospel witness turns upside down many of our associations with kingship. That's where we activate the *no* part of *yes-no-yes*. Like rust from metal, the gospel scrubs off our associations of kingship with tyranny and ruthlessness, associations derived from the human history of monarchy.

Church life and popular notions about Christianity, sadly, often fail to form people's imaginations with the full biblical witness about God's nature. So we end up stuck on the myth of the crown. We cling to this image for some understandable, pastoral reasons: since we often feel overwhelmed and powerless in the big, wide world, we long for assurance that God is powerful and that all things work together for good in God's vast purposes. However, if kingship is the only image for God in our imaginative diet—if we only sing and pray about bowing down and worshipping a king—then our proper honoring of God's sovereignty can devolve into an improper relinquishing of responsibility. We picture God at the top of some great cosmic pyramid of power, and we are the helpless serfs groveling at the bottom. We imagine that God's sovereignty entails controlling the universe and every detail of our lives in a deterministic way. If that's our view of God, then we have nothing to do except bow down. And it's an easy step to transfer our human leaders onto this pyramid model too. Ramshaw writes, "The triangle is a stable structure, and when society is rocking and pitching, many people willingly take their ancient place at the base of the pyramid and let the crown take over."[16] Sometimes it's easier to bow down before a king, pray for our leaders, and imagine that no one can change the pyramid. Our job is to keep quiet on the bottom and hope for the best.[17]

However, if—as the New Testament witnesses—we are called to be friends of Jesus, brothers and sisters in Christ, then we have responsibilities for God's world. We are called to agency and responsibility, and we may find this calling difficult, costly, and frightening. We might prefer to run back and hide under the pyramid. But God does not seem to want serfs, ultimately. God calls us to imagine ourselves as fellow citizens in a resurrection community. Lutheran pastor Libby Howe recently offered a critique of "Christ the King Sunday," commonly celebrated in more liturgical denominations as the last Sunday of the church year, the Sunday in November before the year resets with Advent. Howe suggests that this recently established liturgical day has not served its intended purpose. Pope Pius XI instituted the day in 1925, intending to signal resistance to the "gods" of consumerism, nationalism, and secularism. Unfortunately, as Howe writes, "At least in the United States, Christ the

King has become a triumphalist and militaristic image of Americanity bearing no resemblance to the ethic of compassion envisioned in Matthew 25." She suggests that we might do better to declare "Christ the Center" Sunday, drawing from the current discourse of "centering" and "de-centering." Howe proposes that a focus on centering Christ would help redirect our attention away from seductive distortions of the king metaphor.[18]

The idea of "Christ the Center" would take us some of the way toward imagining ourselves, not in a pyramid, but in a circle, all looking to Christ at the center. In this community of equality and connection, we depend on the Spirit of God to bind us together and empower our action. Imagining ourselves in a circle creates a profoundly countercultural and liberating calling, especially important for people who truly do find themselves on the bottom of cultural systems of power in which they live.[19]

If we flatten the pyramid, though, do we relinquish our hope in a sovereign God? Do we give up on the assuring idea of God's providence? I would argue that, instead, we deepen and correct our understanding of sovereignty and providence. When awful things happen, Christians sometimes say to each other, "Well, God is in control." Such words are a gesture toward the doctrine of sovereignty and thus an attempt at reassurance. Unfortunately, they often serve to reassure the comforter more than the afflicted person. If God is in control, then the comforter need not take on the sufferer's business—God is on the job. Meanwhile, the sufferer has now run smack into the question of why a God-in-control would cause or allow their suffering.

"Control," in any case, is a poor choice of words to render the doctrine of God's sovereignty. Sovereignty is that attribute of God declaring that God is all-powerful, the king above all kings—hence sovereign. Providence is how that sovereignty gets worked into action, how we experience God's activity in the world. None of this is about deterministic control. Providence is not about puppeteering; it's about provision and meaning. The Calvinist catechism I grew up with, the Heidelberg Catechism, posits as "high" a view of providence as any Christian document. The sovereignty of God is a foundational principle that brooks no compromise in the Calvinist mind. Yet the catechism describes providence as an expression of God's sovereignty ultimately bent on mercy. Providence is God's "almighty and ever present power, whereby, as with his hand, he still upholds heaven and earth and all creatures, and so governs them that leaf and blade, rain and drought, fruitful and barren years, food and drink, health and sickness, riches and poverty, indeed, all things come to us not by chance but by his fatherly hand."[20]

Looking back at these words now, I'm struck by the emphasis on the creatures—an emphasis derived most directly here from Psalm 104. Providence is about God sustaining not just humans but all creation, holding all things together. Providence is also about meaning. The emphasis in that last sentence is on holding chaos at bay. I don't think the catechism is trying to say that God sends drought, poverty, and sickness purposely to torment or test us. It's simply acknowledging that those things are a reality. Sovereignty means that divine will can encompass such things without compromising God's merciful purposes. Even when things look terrible, in other words, we need never despair that all is meaningless or that God has forgotten us. Nothing can separate us, as Romans 8 declares, from the love of God.

Ramshaw writes that when we speak of God's sovereignty—and metaphorically when we invoke the myth of the crown—we should do so in order to speak God's provision and mercy. So instead of saying "God is in control"—as if to say, "This is fine. Apparently God likes this"—perhaps we could say, "This is painful, but God is merciful and will continue to provide." Or "This is painful, but God's Spirit is still at work in this world and in us, and God has not forgotten us." And then we can ask a question that reawakens our calling to agency and responsibility, "How is the Spirit of God empowering us, even now?" As we seek and form refugia spaces for ourselves and others, this call to agency seems fundamental. Refugia faith presumes that there will always be troubles and sorrows, and no earthly hero is going to evaporate them completely. Refugia faith, then, does not look to the top of the pyramid and wait for rescue but looks instead to the nearby places where the Spirit is already at work, joining in that work and drawing strength from others and from the Spirit's power.

The Spirit's work is both mysterious and palpable, more vast than the created universe and as small and specific as that nudge in the back of your mind. We read about the Spirit brooding over the *tohu wabohu*, the "soupy mishmash" in the first few verses of the Bible, stirring the creation into life.[21] We read about the Spirit carrying the Word of the Lord to the prophets, compelling them to speak dry bones into life. In the

Gospels, Jesus tries to explain to the disciples how the Spirit will bind them to God and to one another. The Gospel of John spends five long, central chapters on Jesus's "farewell discourse" to his disciples before he is arrested and crucified. The scene is one of the Scripture's most poignant "circular" moments. Da Vinci's famous painting of the Last Supper may line up the disciples like the bridal party on a wedding dais, but imagine them instead crowded into a small, rented room, preparing to share a Passover meal, anxious about what comes next. Jesus washes his disciples' feet (note: kings do not normally do this), predicts the betrayal and suffering to come, and thoroughly confuses the disciples. But he also offers them comfort. Love one another. Do not let your hearts be troubled. Your grief will turn to joy. Peace I leave with you. I am the vine, you are the branches, he says. And this: "I do not call you servants any longer, because the servant does not know what the master is doing; but I have called you friends, because I have made known to you everything that I have heard from my Father" (John 15:15). Your job, Jesus tells them, is to go and bear fruit.

And how are they supposed to do this, if their teacher is going away into some mysterious mode of existence they cannot currently fathom? Jesus tells them repeatedly: the Father will send a Counselor, the Spirit of truth, the Holy Spirit. The Greek word for counselor here is *paraclete*, which means protector and advocate. The disciples seem to remain muddled in confusion about all this, and one can hardly blame them. Thankfully the next book in the New Testament is Acts, and by chapter 2, we read the story of Pentecost: a dramatic manifestation, complete with special effects, of this Holy Spirit that Jesus had promised. Thus begins, we say, the history of the church. This church becomes the body of Christ, an organism of people empowered by the Spirit to do the work of God in the world. And in this body, the usual hierarchies have been flattened. Each person is marked by baptism as belonging to God, beloved, distinctly gifted and called by the Spirit. Each person is invited into the fellowship of the Trinity, the dynamic life of God that we understand (however dimly) as Father, Son, Holy Spirit in eternal and coequal being. So the pyramid is revealed to be a circle all along, all the way back to the Hebrew prophets, all the way back to the soil creatures tasked with co-sustaining in the garden, all the way back to creation itself, the outpouring of God's fullness into this world's existence.

The Holy Spirit, then, is how we move out of serfdom and into friendship with God. Jesus wanted his disciples to imagine themselves as dependent—yes, as that's only honest—but also empowered, branches in the vine. The Spirit is what imbues the vine, the soil, the air, the water with life. The Spirit creates motion, connection, change: disturbance. That is certainly the witness of the Pentecost story in Acts 2. A roaring wind and flames of fire, a sudden outburst of multilingual skills. Just as disturbance is necessary in the biomes of the earth to stir new life, to urge change and growth, so we need the Spirit's disturbance in our personal lives, our churches, and in the epochs of human history.

The question is whether we dare to "walk by the Spirit" as the Scriptures say, or whether we will attempt to hold hard to the status quo. Much of the destructive disturbance in the earth that we are now experiencing is caused by our own actions, well intended or not. Amid that destruction, the Spirit's disturbance comes alongside. However frightening this disturbance may be, the Spirit's will is to bring about mercy and life. The word for "spirit" in many languages—including Greek and Hebrew—is the same word for "breath" and also for "wind." This Spirit that brooded over chaotic formlessness at the beginning of time still floods all reality with the being of God. I believe the Spirit is breathing into the church right now, but I wonder whether the Spirit will need to bring even more hurricanic disturbance before we fully respond.

Beingness

Another reason for Christian passivity in the Great Work may be that we have gotten lazy with the doctrine that humans are made in the image of God. We use that truth as merely another pious shortcut. For example, I often hear the phrase "made in the image of God" tossed out casually to support an ethic that amounts to "we should all be nice." Or I hear it used to garner a few moral virtue points when majority people (White people, straight people, citizens) note that some perceived other-group (Black people, LGBTQ+ people, immigrants) are made in the image of God and thus not to be reviled. As if that's the end of the matter. Rarely do I hear much reflection on exactly what human faculty constitutes this divine image. Reason? Creativity? Self-consciousness? Tool use? Language? Capacity for religion? A mind? A soul? Moral responsibility? All of the above?

Our status as made in the image of God is a rightly treasured and beautiful truth. The recent renewal of civil rights activism in response to wider awareness of police brutality has prompted Black Christians to claim this truth with even more fervor over against a White supremacist context that denies their dignity. People exhausted from injustice need to remind each other and everyone else that God created them kings and queens—rulers. This declaration becomes a way of countervailing the abuse, oppression, and disregard that they and others have suffered. In the context of humans respecting one another, emphasizing the equality of our image bearing is a powerful theological strategy. In the context of our relationship with the earth, though, that image-bearing language can make us lazy. If we use being made in the image of God as a shortcut warrant for "those who inherently deserve to be valued and respected," then what warrants respect for the more-than-human creation, apparently *not* made in the image of God? Image-of-God theology can drive us right back into hierarchical anthropocentrism. Only we humans matter because only we humans are made in the image of God.

Yet orthodox Christian theology marvels that *everything* in the universe exists only by the sustaining work of the Holy Spirit. In the Genesis creation accounts, not only the *adam* and the woman are given a *nephesh*, a life-spirit. The beasts and birds and creeping things also have a *nephesh*, as Genesis 1:30 indicates. Moreover, God did not merely launch the universe at some alpha point way back when and set it spinning, job done. Rather, the Spirit actively upholds all creation at every moment. This is one place where Christian theology resonates remarkably well with Indigenous worldviews, particularly Native American ways of thinking that find the Great Spirit present in all living things. Have Christians—perhaps in our allergy to anything smelling even vaguely of pantheism—learned to ignore this element of orthodox doctrine? If the Spirit of God upholds and sustains the whole created universe, then all creation is treasured and cared for by God's providence. And if we are made in the image of God, then surely the Spirit is prompting us always to participate with God in that sustaining. In fact, of all the things that being made in the image of God can mean, it seems to me that the most important is *moral responsibility*. We have a choice; we are held accountable. The image of God is therefore both a gift and a burden.

What, then, is the status of other creatures? I recently read Richard Powers's melancholy fantasia of a novel *The Overstory* with a class of undergraduates, many of them science majors. In the first section of the novel, Powers introduces nine human characters. We had to work hard, as a class, to keep track of all their stories, and we had to pay attention to how each character's story was imprinted with significant encounters with particular trees. The students remarked how this novel felt different from other novels they had read, because here the characters' story lines dive and lift, sweeping across years, depicting carefully chosen moments that build our perception of each character's passions and wounds. The novel's pace and perspective, in other words, suggest a long view of time—a tree's-life view, perhaps—in which a particular human life, with all its details, loves, and struggles, passes by in a moment. As the human stories in the novel unfold, Powers prompts us to perceive the subtle, coalescing agency of the trees. Trees seem to be calling to the human characters across the species divide, patiently encroaching with their millennia of wisdom, embodied in a different form of being. Are trees asking humans for help as they face deforestation and climate change?

For many pages, characters ponder this question in ways ranging from mystical conviction to hesitant eco-action to scientific study. One character, Patricia, is a botanist, and through her, Powers delivers most of the wood-wide-web science imbuing the novel. At one point Patricia observes, "It could be the eternal project of mankind, to learn what forests have figured out."[22] Eventually—in a dramatic moment that we had to linger on in class—one of the characters realizes that maybe, rather than asking for help, the trees are somehow *offering* their help to humans. Humans are risking their own survival with their foolish destruction and greed. The trees are trying to warn us and to show us their companionship in the struggle for survival. In this marvelous novel, Powers invites us, through his densely luxuriant writing, to put human scrabbling for survival in the long perspective of life on this planet, a pulsing, irresistible force that will push on with or without us. The novel thus poses, tacitly, a question: Do we choose, still, to join in life's ecstatic dance?

The students seemed quite taken with and even awed by this idea of "beingness." We had a word now to describe what we already knew: humans are not the only creatures on this planet who are *beings*. We are distinctive, of course. But other creatures have beingness too. Any dog or cat or horse lover will tell you that each of their beloved animals has a personality, a little spirit of its own. According to people who know a lot more about animals than I do, the same goes for horses, goats, cockatoos, and even wallabies and lynxes. I imagine it's harder to discern personality for, say, a wasp or termite. But the more we humans learn about our fellow creatures, the more we marvel at their surprising intelligences and abilities. Apes have complex societies and can learn basic language skills. Salmon find their way back to spawning rivers. An octopus can open a jar, escape a holding tank, and express affection or dislike for particular humans.[23] Bees navigate through smell and an internal sun compass, and they communicate locations by dance moves.[24] Even if they are not made in the image of God, these more-than-human creatures have worth and wonder beyond our capacity to calculate.

Biodiversity loss is a grave concern, of course, for human survival: human life depends on the whole web of life on this planet. But should we care in particular about losing, say, the Kirtland's warbler or the right whale or the American chestnut for reasons besides our own survival, convenience, or pleasure? For me, as for most people, it's easier to get worked up about the loss of "charismatic megafauna" like elephants and polar bears. Or megaflora like the hemlock. They're so beautiful and fascinating! Less easy to get worked up when we're talking about some horrid swarming insect. But our feelings of aesthetic delight or disgust are irrelevant to the deeper question: What is the value of other creatures, not only invented by God, but continually upheld by God? What does it mean that they have *beingness*?

I was surprised to discover that thinkers the likes of Paul Tillich and Martin Buber spent serious philosophical effort on the question of whether a person could commune with a tree. These two philosophers reasoned that humans are persons—obviously. God is three-persons-in-one. We know we can connect with other persons, though admittedly it is often difficult. But they wondered, Is a tree a *person*? And is that the required basis for relationship: personhood? Buber famously proposed that we can have I-Thou relationships or I-It relationships. When we have I-It relationships with other people, or with anything else, that opens the door to exploitation of that person or thing. Tillich's solution to what might be called the "it-problem" is "hyperpersonalism." The idea, as I understand it, is that God is the Ground of Being, and all things participate in that being. Therefore, personhood is not the only measure of value. For Tillich, it's not necessary to imagine that every beetle and mushroom is a person, only that "it" has value simply in its unique beingness. Other creatures are not just like us; neither can they be reduced merely "to usefulness or threat," as Richard Bauckham points out. We must regard with respect their "endlessly remarkable quiddity," delighting in the "grace of otherness."[25]

When we speak easily of "creation care" and "stewardship," I wonder how much we are still regarding plants, animals, lakes, or rivers as resources or objects and not as beings. It matters. Because when push comes to ecological shove, on what basis would we consider the needs of anything other than humans? If, as Tillich observes, all things derive their being from God, why would we be surprised if the trees start communicating with us in their treelike ways? Perhaps we are not hearing the actual voices of trees—as the character Olivia seems to do, much to her own surprise, in *The Overstory*. But perhaps we are sensing the Spirit of God translating for us across species divides, reminding us that we are citizens in a whole web of life. All creation groans, says Paul in Romans, and the Spirit groans with us. We should not be surprised if we sense another creature's groaning—or another creature's rejoicing. The Bible is full of passages in the Psalms and in Job where hills and trees and leviathans and mountain goats exult in life itself, and where God rejoices in the creatures entirely apart from human concerns. The Bible is also full of passages like Isaiah 55, where God promises a redemption that includes, in the same divine breath, justice among humans and rejoicing among the hills and trees. Shalom weaves it all together.

Whether more-than-human creatures have souls and can be called persons seem to me distracting and unnecessary questions. They have being, and they are marvelous. God sustains and delights in their being, and they are gathered into the circle of all life. That is enough.

The Countercultural Commons

If our most important human distinctiveness among the creatures is our power and responsibility, then in order to wield that power and responsibility appropriately, we have to work together. That, I'm afraid, definitely requires a miracle. Can the Spirit bring about a miracle of unity and cooperation today—the miracle of the circle, we might call it—at a time when the world desperately needs it?

Everywhere in the context of climate activism is the call for coop-eration and collaboration. Too long we have imagined nations and busi-nesses locked in inevitable competition for power and advantage, say the prophetic voices. Too long we have imagined ourselves as competi-tors or adversaries, but now the earth itself needs us to work together. It seems inevitable that Pope Francis followed up his 2015 encyclical on the climate crisis with 2020's *Fratelli tutti*, a passionate call for comity among all peoples. "Let us dream, then," writes the pope, "as a single human family, as fellow travelers sharing the same flesh, as children of the same earth which is our common home, each of us bringing the richness of his or her beliefs and convictions, each of us with his or her own voice, brothers and sisters all."[26] A breathtakingly beautiful vision, but I wonder if we can muster the capacity. Wise leaders such as the pope and the grand imam Ahmad Al-Tayyeb—whom Pope Francis credits as one of his inspirations for the encyclical—call their people to this vision. And people of faith, theoretically, should expertly model community and collaboration. However, our history of religious con-flict and schism is hardly encouraging. And in the United States, people of faith are typically as deeply formed in the ways of capitalist com-petition and individualism as anything else. Unfortunately, we can-not address a global crisis with only the individualistic tools we have learned to wield.

Our laws and legal philosophies, interestingly, represent one space where individualism and communal spirit battle it out, with conster-nating results for lands and waters. Michigan's governor, Gretchen Whitmer, surprised even the most ardent activists when, in Decem-ber 2020, she revoked a 1953 easement that had allowed Enbridge, the Canadian oil and gas company, to run a pipeline under the Straits of Mackinac. She gave a deadline of May 2021 to shut the thing down.[27] The pipeline is old, damaged, and ripe for bursting. In 2018, a tugboat accidentally dragged anchor for miles, bumping right over the creaking pipeline, further denting and gouging it. Any number of other incidents and vulnerabilities could have resulted in disaster, as an oil spill into the straits would devastate the waters and nearby shorelines for seven hundred miles.[28] For seven years leading up to the shutdown, dozens of citizen groups, businesses, and tribal governments had been working together to expose Enbridge's many breaches of trust, easement vio-lations, cover-ups, and shoddy safety procedures. Flurries of lawsuits had inundated Michigan's courts. Finally, Gov. Whitmer invoked public trust law to revoke the easement.

Public trust law is based on the idea that a government's job is to protect what is held in public trust, including air, water, and—most pertinent here—the "bottomlands" of lakes and rivers. Enbridge had proven itself an irresponsible and careless "tenant" of the land they were leasing, greatly increasing the chances of an oil spill and thus endangering the creatures who live in and around the water as well as the livelihood of people who fish and work in the businesses along the shoreline. Until this moment, Enbridge's corporate interests had long prevailed over Michigan's public interests.[29] Even after this action, Enbridge contests the ruling and continues to attempt to push through its plan to build a tunnel under the straits and run a new pipeline through. Activists—now having built an effective organizational infrastructure—continue to insist on a full environmental analysis of the proposed tunnel, an analysis that takes into account not only the effects of constructing the tunnel but also the effects of burning the liquids that would flow through it.

Private property rights are so deeply enshrined in the American psyche that to question them in the slightest invites cries of economic blasphemy. This reverence for private property helps explain American reluctance to place limits on privately owned or stockholder-owned businesses in their use of land, air, and water. As long as businesses provide jobs, they can poison the land they own or send toxic waste down a river or spew pollution into the air, and we have only weak laws to challenge them. Regulations are declared to be nonsensical, onerous burdens on corporate prosperity. In this land of freedom and independence, we have found it difficult to imagine a "commons." Private ownership is the norm; public ownership and trust, the reluctant exception. This is, of course, not merely an American problem. Thomas Berry wrote in 1999 that transnational corporations "own or control the natural resources of the entire planet directly or indirectly" and overall create the economies of the world. "Yet they have no proportionate responsibility for the public welfare. Indeed they insist on being recipients of government grants and exemptions—'corporate welfare,' as it is now called."[30] Note that Berry is writing long before the 2010 *Citizens United* ruling in the United States, which further extended corporate influence over those who make and enforce laws.

Recently, in the United States and in other nations, activist groups have succeeded in launching an innovative legal strategy: declaring natural entities "persons" in order to endow them with rights. In 2019, the Lake Erie Bill of Rights, drawn up by Toledo residents, passed in a public referendum.[31] Lake Erie was legally declared to be an ecosystem with legal personhood and thus the right "to exist, flourish, and naturally evolve." This was, admittedly, a desperate measure. The idea was to create some leverage so residents and government could demand mitigation and repair the lake's many woes. Lake Erie's troubles date back to the mid to late 1800s, when White settlers decided to drain the Great Black Swamp that covered most of northeastern Ohio. Draining the swamp, it was thought, would not only make passage from the East into the Midwest a lot easier but also create excellent farmland. The settlers were right on both counts. What they didn't realize was that this vast system of wetlands served as the lake's kidneys. Draining it deprived the lake of watershed purifying services, resulting in two hundred years of pollution buildup in the lake, mostly from storm and agricultural runoff. The lake's natural filtration and drainage systems simply couldn't keep up with the pollution load. The federal Clean Water Act in 1972 helped temporarily, but in recent decades, algal blooms large enough to be visible from space have devastated the lake's ecology, made recreation on the lake life-threatening, and poisoned water sources for Toledo and surrounding areas.[32] Hundreds of thousands of farms and businesses were responsible for creating this situation over many decades. But who is responsible for healing it? As Aldo Leopold wrote in the 1940s, "There is a clear tendency in American conservation to relegate to government all necessary jobs that private landowners fail to perform."[33] And then we resent government for its "overreach."

The rights-of-nature movement now has proponents all over the world. Ecuador, most famously, enshrined the rights of "Pachamama" (Mother Earth) into its constitution in 2008. Bolivia's Legislative Assembly passed the "Law of Mother Earth" in 2010. As Robert Macfarlane writes, though, the rights-of-nature movement is not an ideal solution in the long run. Legal analysts note that calling a natural entity a person is a category error that makes these laws vulnerable to judicial challenge. And the whole approach capitulates to an anthropocentric and post-Enlightenment insistence that only a person can have rights, and only legal rights oblige us to care for something. Because modern legal philosophies have so little regard for the value of more-than-human life, we are trying to fit the desperate cries of the more-than-human world into our small, clumsy boxes of human individualistic legal philosophy.[34]

So what will we do with this blasphemous observation that the tools of individualism and free markets, while they have an essential role, are insufficient to address a global climate crisis? As with the Line 5 battle, we are going to have to strengthen our capacities to imagine a commons. The health of air, water, and land—even land under private or corporate ownership—is a matter of public trust. Enforcing laws that already acknowledge private responsibility to protect the public trust will help. Enhancing those laws will help. But ultimately we need a conversion of the heart. In the next decades, citizens will need to push against inertia in governments, institutions, businesses, and one another to preserve the benefits of private ownership and individual rights while also creating rules for everyone that protect the commons. In the industrial West, we haven't much bothered to consider the more-than-human world as anything but the inert game board for our prosperity games. Now we have to remember what we have forgotten: everything is interrelated, the game board is alive. The more-than-human world has its own value, its own being, apart from our economic valuations. And none of our games matter in the long run if we don't honor that whole web of life.

Activism as Refugial Practice

Becoming citizens requires working together. This is the part that scares me most. *Community* is a fraught word for me. Thankfully, I have experienced good community in healthy church congregations and in Christian institutions. Even so, when I imagine community, my first impulse is self-protection: I want some distance from other people, just in case. I want my own space, some latitude for autonomy. We all know how fragile community can be. When the Covid-19 pandemic hit, we all wondered whether a shared global crisis could bring us together. The answer was yes and no. On the one hand, people did help one another, urging one another toward communal sacrifice and care. Many people sacrificed heroically. On the other hand, the pandemic revealed, like a black light, the neon-bright divisions in the United States in our views of government, common life, even reality itself. The United States remains severely divided, with the fault lines running right down the middle of neighborhood streets—including mine. Not a great moment for trust in the power of community.

This capacity to see ourselves as fellow citizens of the planet, working side by side—at least enough to cooperate despite our disagreements—this is the capacity we most need to exercise. The scale is daunting. Refugia spaces can help, as we practice communal care on small scales and seek, with the guidance of the Spirit, the wisdom and resources our faith traditions provide. In building this capacity, the first step may be simply to act, simply to do something. Change of heart will follow from action. As McKibben writes in that *Daedalus* essay mentioned earlier, "The deepest religious insights on the relation between God, nature, and humans may not emerge until religious people, acting on the terms indicated by their traditions, join these movements. The act of engagement will itself spur new thinking, new understanding."[35] If we begin with action, we may well uncover those latent theological resources, repairing the distortions that have buried them in the first place.

Fortunately, young people are leading the way. Young people are, as we might say in biology, "sensitive populations." They sense a threat before the rest of us do because they have not developed the denial and cynicism we oldsters depend on to protect ourselves. Younger generations also tend to understand and presume global citizenship in ways their elders, steeped in national loyalties and scarred by historical conflicts, seem to find elusive. The massive global youth protests to promote climate action, the thousands of youth-led organizations all over the world—these suggest that the young have much to teach the old. They realize they are more vulnerable because, chances are, they have more years to go on the planet. They sense the crisis, so they seek refugia where they can build the capacities needed to survive—and often those refugia are activist groups.

The organization 350.org, for example, now a "planet-wide collaboration of organizers, community groups and regular people," was started by Bill McKibben and a handful of college students at Middlebury College in Vermont in 2008 with zero budget.[36] They wanted to do something, they didn't even know what. They recognized immediately that all the many localized activist groups needed somehow to be stitched together in order to have the leverage they needed. So these students used social media to organize "global days of action" and send the message to world leaders that the planet needs to stay below 350 parts per million of carbon dioxide. (We're already at 419 now.)[37] The results were astonishing: people all over the world were already poised to work together, learn from one another, and support each other. They just needed a way to connect. Today, after only a decade of marches, global days of action, divestment campaigns, and many other initiatives, 350.org serves to empower, connect, and support thousands of climate action groups all over the world.[38] The Sunrise Movement is one of those partner groups. A youth organization only a few years old, it was formed to influence the 2018 midterm elections in the United States. It has now succeeded in influencing President Biden's climate policy and cabinet picks as well as inspiring other youth-led organizations across the world. The Sunrise Movement is one of many groups influencing continued work on a Green New Deal, whatever actions that ambitious legislative initiative may finally impel.[39] Activist groups exemplify how dogged, collaborative efforts can leverage the refugia model to address the problem of scale. Local groups, connected to their own place and suited to the people within them, can connect with other local groups. When those connections start to form, refugia seed other refugia, and the refugia begin to merge together and cover a whole ecosystem—or a whole globe—with possibility.

Even in more conservative Christian spaces, young people are seeking and forming refugia through activism. Kyle Meyaard-Schaap, until recently the national organizer and spokesperson for the organization Young Evangelicals for Climate Action, told me that many of his young leaders "feel like exiles in our faith communities." Parents and elders who taught them the faith refuse to listen to their concerns about the future of the planet. The youngers perceive an obvious connection between faith and the call to address the climate crisis, but the elders—having succumbed to the politicizing of all things climate—at worst dismiss their concerns as "fake news" and at best exhort them to keep such matters out of the church. Feeling betrayed, this young generation of Christians, says Kyle, is "looking for spaces that can bring life out of that pain, out of that hurt." As they learn, write letters to editors, lobby representatives, organize events, and study policy together, they find refugia among other young activists.[40]

I recently spoke with two alumnae of my university: Katerina Parsons, in graduate school for international development, and Kathryn Mae Post, a religion journalist and graduate of divinity school.

Both Katerina and Kathryn described, with pain but also joy, how they have had to reconstruct their faith as young adults. While grateful for much about their religious upbringing, they also recognized that their churches did not prepare them well for life in a global, diverse world facing multiple urgent crises. Both of them, in different ways, have sought a more embodied and wholistic faith, one that fully responds to the Bible's emphasis on justice and mercy. Both of them described activism as one of their new spiritual disciplines. Activism, faith-based and otherwise, is where they found community, where they found the Spirit of God at work.[41]

Intercessory Forests

In the effort to move toward a Spirit-breathed refugia model, reconnected to the Spirit's work in healing all creation, we might find an inspiringly literal exemplar in the church forests of Ethiopia. A hundred years ago, the highlands of Ethiopia were covered with forest. Today, only about 3 percent of that forest remains, the rest having been sacrificed to cattle grazing, agriculture, and human habitat. What's left are twenty thousand tiny patches of forest, about eight or ten hectares each, dotting the barren landscape every three kilometers or so. These forest islands persist because at the center of each one is a simple, circular building like a button on a round, green circle—a church. Writer Fred Bahnson describes how Ethiopian Orthodox churches, protecting the small bits of forest around them, create a "mystical geography": the church building forms the central node in concentric circles of holy space, the outer circle being the forest remnant itself.[42] This church-in-the-forest arrangement, modeled on Jewish sacred architecture, creates an experience of moving from the outside world deeper into sacred space, a journey toward a holy of holies that enacts "the soul's journey to God." For these churches, the forests symbolize paradise, the garden of Eden, and tending these forests is equivalent to curating holy space. The forests shelter creatures and provide "habitat" for the mysterious holy hermits who live solitary lives of prayer hidden within them.

Ethiopian ecologist Dr. Alemayehu Wassie, along with an American collaborator, ecologist Dr. Margaret Lowman, has been working with Ethiopian Orthodox priests to help them understand on a biological level the treasures of life they have been preserving. The forests are, as

Fred Bahnson observes, "living arks of biodiversity," floating the region's distinctive African junipers and vervet monkeys and hammerkops through a time of severe threat. Drs. Wassie and Lowman have identified forty of these "arks," the ones that appear richest in biodiversity, to prioritize for preservation. The churches, to enhance their role as keepers of these forests, are now building simple, dry-stack walls around the perimeters to keep out cattle and help protect the vulnerable forest edges. These outer walls echo the inner walls that separate the trees from the courtyard areas directly surrounding the church buildings, thus emphasizing that circular pattern of holy space. Only fourteen forests are protected so far, the first wall having been built at Zhara in 2010.

Bahnson sees these forests as potent models of the kind of arks— literal and figurative—that we must build to get us through this time of severe threat to a livable planet. He writes, "As we sail into the Anthropocene bottleneck, a constriction of our own making, places like Ethiopia's church forests offer a vision of a future that we are making even now. We will need many more arks like them, tens of thousands of arks: cultural, biological, spiritual. Only then will we survive the storms that are surely coming, that have already arrived."[43] The metaphor of the ark works beautifully here to signal the desperation prompting human action. Arks are hardly ideal ecosystems; they are last-ditch measures, vessels of survival one hopes are only temporary. At the same time, biologically speaking, the church forests of Ethiopia are literally refugia. They are, precisely, places where biodiversity persists in a crisis. Humans did not create the forests, but humans have been protecting them as remnants. How wonderful that this protection has come from Christian churches that understand their caretaking as an essential element of their role in the world: they embrace this echo of Eden, considering the more-than-human forest an essential holder of holy space for healing and prayer. Also fitting to the biological definition of refugia is the potential for expansion and renewal. Dr. Massie, working with nongovernmental organizations, hopes to help the churches expand these refugial forests by moving the walls slowly outward as the forest edges stabilize. He hopes to plant trees along the rivers that connect the forests. His ultimate goal is to restore 40 percent of Ethiopia's highlands back to forested land.

While the Ethiopian church forests date back to the fourth century CE, the church's modern involvement in conscious ecosystem protection makes it a participant in a broader movement linking churches and restoration of land.[44] Prompted by seventy nations, the United Nations has now declared 2021–30 as the "Decade on Ecosystem Restoration." The website explains that "the UN Decade on Ecosystem Restoration is a rallying call for the protection and revival of ecosystems all around the world, for the benefit of people and nature. It aims to halt the degradation of ecosystems, and restore them to achieve global goals. Only with healthy ecosystems can we enhance people's livelihoods, counteract climate change, and stop the collapse of biodiversity."[45] The UN is aware that this initiative needs the support of faith-based organizations in order to succeed. Thus getting faith-based organizations all over the world involved is one key plank of the whole program. One of the goals of this effort is "to promote the mainstreaming of ecosystem restoration as a core activity amongst religious communities."[46] Clearly the UN recognizes that co-sustaining with God is not currently "mainstream" or "core" for world religions.

Some people use the term *rewilding* to suggest that the earth would do better if humans retreated from taking up so much space, retreated from our high-tech ways and became fewer and more primitive. However, rewilding does not have to mean we all become anarcho-primitivist hunter-gatherers. In the context of restoration ecology, rewilding is a more technical process that restores core wilderness areas and corridors among them. In a broader sense, rewilding is coming to mean a deepening of ordinary people's knowledge, so we might be better partners with the more-than-human world—better citizens. I wonder if *rewilding* could also be a word to describe listening better to where the Holy Spirit is moving in the world. The Spirit cannot be controlled or contained by the church. The Spirit moves through people and through all creation, connecting us all. When the Spirit creates disturbance—through teenage activists, through upheavals in our ways of life that we don't necessarily welcome, through the winds in the tops of trees—will we resist or respond?

As Ferris Jabr points out in his essay on the mycorrhizal network, we now have a rudimentary scientific account of a marvel many cultures have long affirmed in their mythologies: everything is connected. Jabr notes, for example, "In Mesoamerican mythology, an immense tree grows at the center of the universe, stretching its roots into the underworld and cradling earth and heaven in its trunk and branches."[47]

Numerous cultures honor trees as symbols of life's interconnectedness. What if we reflected more deeply on the importance of trees in the Old and New Testaments? Significant trees frame the whole arc of biblical narrative, after all. The Genesis creation stories feature two significant trees, the Tree of Knowledge of Good and Evil and the Tree of Life. In Genesis 3, Adam and Eve fail to observe their limits; their overreach sends them out of the garden, lest they also eat of the Tree of Life and live forever in a state of exile. That Tree of Life goes underground, as it were, for all of Scripture, but it isn't gone. It appears again in Revelation 22 as the central feature in John of Patmos's vision of the renewed Jerusalem. Here, no angel-flame sword guards the tree. It stands in the middle of the garden-city, its roots straddling a river—the "river of the water of life" flowing from "the throne of God and of the Lamb" (Rev 22:1). This tree generously serves the garden-city, bearing fruit in all seasons. And its leaves, says the Scripture, "are for the healing of the nations" (22:2).

Of all the strange images in Revelation, some of them seem more potentially literal than others. What if the leaves of actual trees can heal the nations? Perhaps, as in *The Overstory*, trees are groaning with us in their own treeish ways. As Fred Bahnson writes, perhaps we are now called to "notice the intercessory work of forests, breathing their invisible sighs from every copse, stand, and canopy."[48] The Spirit of God may be revealing anew our interconnections with all living things and prompting us into a new unity with each other. What if the whole creation strains not just *with* us but by God's grace *for* us?

Operation What-Is-That?

Two months after planting native seedlings in our backyard refugium, it's time to assess. Some of the babies are doing well. The Culver's root seems to have languished in one spot but thrived in another. The delightfully quirky rattlesnake master looks as if it wants to be a cactus when it grows up, with spiny points trimming its long leaf edges. The swamp milkweed shot up and popped out airy pink blooms. The marsh blazing stars are not far behind, with a starlike lavender cluster ready to bloom at the top of each spiky-leafed sprout. As for the other species, I'm not entirely sure what's what. I think I can recognize the black-eyed Susan babies, still close-to-the-ground spreads of dark leaves.

However, there are clearly some unwelcome interlopers. What is *this* thing? Some kind of grass? I'm not sure, but it's all over, so I text Deanna of the Swale with a photo. Her unceremonious reply: "That's a weed! Pull it!" I spend a good hour shoveling out at least a dozen of these stinkers, some of them already four feet tall. I'm a little worried now. How am I supposed to tell "good" native grasses from "bad" ones? I can recognize heavy metal switchgrass, Karl Foerster grass, big bluestem, a couple others. But what are all these other things?

I download photos from the web, trying to get representative profile photos of all twelve species we planted. My plan is to identify all the baby plants we planted and then pull out most everything else. Well, it's not quite that simple. My baby plants do not look like the photos of mature, flowering versions I found on the web. So I call in reinforcements, requesting that Deanna stop by sometime and take me on a guided tour of friends and foes. A few days later, she walks through, easily naming the purple loosestrife and willow herb. Turns out willow herb looks rather different before and after flowering, so that's a not-so-fun challenge. I try to keep up, taking photos on my phone to remind me what needs to come out.

The next Saturday, I don my gloves and stoke my determination. It's time to yank! I pull the purple loosestrife out easily by the roots and then get to work on the willow herb, discovering baby rattlesnake master underneath. Careful not to uproot that! It takes a while to clear the infested areas, but the steady progress feels satisfying. Meanwhile, I do know buckthorn when I see it, and I yank quite a lot of little buckthorn nasties too. The larger stems I clip and spray with the "buckthorn-B-gone" solution I mixed up according to the Plaster Creek Stewards' recipe, adding blue dye so I can see where I've squirted. I tear out the wild grapevines tangling their way around the fallen box elder. After a while, Ron and Linda come out to help. Working together, we tidy the place nicely in a couple hours, ending up with impressive heaps of weeds that we stuff into our composting service bin to be sent away. Don't worry—they use enough heat in their composting process that the invasive species seeds will not survive.

This is unglamorous, imprecise work. I think we avoided ripping out any good seedlings, but we certainly did not catch every last baddie. We're just helping as best we can, trying to give the little ones a chance to establish without too much competition. We have to be patient, as the new native seedlings take three years to establish well, put down a secure root system, find their esprit de corps, and spread. As gardeners say: first year sleep, second year creep, third year leap.

In the scheme of things, our little refugium is pitifully tiny, but I suppose it's a fair-enough symbol of what it means to be a citizen: You do your part, along with your neighbors, in the space under your care, however large or small. You take into account the needs of the larger community, and you do your best, risking both the satisfactions and the bereavements that come with caring.

A few weeks after our cleanup operations, the bunnies decide that swamp milkweed is yummy. In a matter of days, they strip every last leaf from the two-foot stems, leaving nothing but bare upright stalks behind. What can we do but hope the roots will hold anyway, saving their strength for next spring?

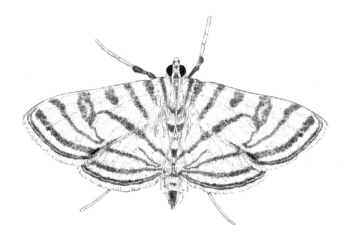

Zebra Conchylodes Moth
Conchylodes Ovulalis

September
Douglas, Michigan

We stole one last day of summer that Sunday afternoon, all of us hip-deep in the calm, silky lake, throwing a Frisbee to each other around a wide circle. Ron and I and Mia and Josh and Philip and John and Michelle—and Maizey, of course. She paddled eagerly among us, grinning her Labrador grin, swirling in circles trying to chase that crisscrossing Frisbee. She caught it only when we threw it to her on purpose.

Heaps of fluffy white clouds, rays of sunlight shooting from behind them, floated above the warm water, the happy family, the delirious dog. Later we all sat on the beach talking together for a long time. The sun eased down the sky till it was five thirty and time to shake out towels and fold beach chairs and step carefully through the beach grass onto the path back up to the cottage. Monday called, and it was time to head back to town.

That day we missed evening on the beach, my favorite time. The waves tend to ease in the evening, the wind gentles. I love to bask in the lingering heat, listening to the shushing of the waves as the sinking sun's light angles onto the water and dazzles the surface all the way to the horizon with diamond-light.

But our weekend visit was over, and within an hour we had stripped and remade the beds, extracted all our gear, removed the extra leaves from the dining-room table, tidied, and left everything back in place for Mom and Dad. Then we all evacuated the premises. Gone. I wonder how Mom and Dad feel after the whirlwind comes and goes, leaving only tufts of dog hair on the carpeting and a stray sock in an upstairs bedroom. Exhausted, probably. Relieved but, I hope, pleased.

I wonder now if those long days of beach play and evening reveries are over. They have been a beautiful gift, but now the grandchildren are teenagers and young adults, launched into their lives. The beach is gone. We watched the lake and its winds build that beach and a substantial foredune over decades, patiently depositing sand, carving, smoothing. Grasses and shrubs established, leaf litter dissolved into soil, saplings shot up, birds and squirrels set up housekeeping, deer stepped through evening shadows. Now the lake reclaims it all, devouring the dune and ripping down even the oldest trees. Seagulls go right on with their lives, of course, gliding along the wind currents on crooked wings, unperturbed by the tossing waves.

We were uncommonly privileged to enjoy this lovely spot on earth for a time. If we are given more days like this, we will cherish them. If not, well, we will give thanks for the days we had. Changes come. Always. Our little aches of ecomemory amount to a feather in a world of so much grief and change.

I remember one night, deep in the Michigan winter, when I stayed at the cottage alone: Mom and Dad were in Arizona and Ron was on a research trip. After an evening by the fire with a book, I went to bed at midnight. A full moon hovered at the top of the curtainless bedroom window, still high in a violet sky. At the horizon, moonlight pooled on the lake's soothed, sable surface, setting shards of water glittering near the shore.

I slept for a couple hours and woke again. Then the moon was lower, larger, laying down a long path of light on the water like a tunnel in time.

I slept again and dreamed of the moon. Was I still dreaming when I watched the moon sink silently into the lake? Or was that real?

Lingering summer evenings, moonshine on black winter nights, always I see light on water. I carry that light with me wherever I go, along with the feel of warm sand and the freedom song of a long horizon. The lakeshore is where my conscious love of place began. I know there are other beautiful places in the world, far more spectacular places than this stretch of shore with its undulating dunes and flowing beach grass, sumac and wild grapevines, towering cottonwoods, generous oaks, and shaggy pines. I've seen a small sampling of the earth's other more magnificent wonders. But a freshwater sea and sugar-sand dunes awakened my heart, and so I carry that awakened heart back into town, past the cornfields and suburban housing developments, into the neighborhoods and parks and school campuses and commercial strips and highway overpasses and downtown office buildings and bridges over the river—into all the ordinary contours of this place where I live. I let this awakened heart carry me back into the memory of the beech-maple and oak-hickory forests and oak savannahs that covered this place, now long gone. I let my awakened heart carry me into an imagined future, a future this generation can dream into being, where people everywhere awaken again to the loveliness and possibility of this world.

Chapter 7

From Indifference to Attention

I will give thanks to the Lord with my whole heart;
I will tell of all your wonderful deeds.
—PSALM 9:1

A ct 2 of Shakespeare's *As You like It* opens with the exiled Duke Senior in the Forest of Arden, gathered with a few faithful courtiers. The audience already knows that Duke Senior's brother, for reasons not explained, has usurped the duke's place and sent him packing. When Duke Senior appears on stage, though, he seems rather cheerful. The forest, he observes, turns out to provide a nice change from court. He and his men can be "co-mates and brothers in exile" here, and their rustic life is "more sweet / Than that of painted pomp." Free of the intrigues and envies of court, they encounter what's *real*. Even the cold weather, says the duke, has its benefits. Here he can feel

the icy fang
And churlish chiding of the winter's wind,
Which when it bites and blows upon my body
Even till I shrink with cold, I smile and say
"This is no flattery; these are counselors
That feelingly persuade me what I am." (2.1.1–3, 6–11)[1]

This life, he continues, has much to teach. The very trees and brooks and stones instruct them.

A number of Shakespeare's plays begin with sharp civil conflict and then spin some of the characters into an alternative space, a contrasting setting where the usual rules don't apply. There may be fairies dancing about, or remote islands and sorcery, or cross-dressing and disguise, or maybe—as with *As You like It*—deer and a working sheep croft. In Shakespeare scholarship, we refer to these spaces as "green worlds." They create opportunity for the characters to engage in playful or perhaps risky experimentation, making way for forgiveness, falling in love, refreshed identity, a change of heart. And then, one way or another, the characters return to the civic space, their conflicts more or less repaired. On a meta level, the green worlds mirror the magic of the theater itself.

When I teach Shakespeare, I notice that students love the idea of the green world. By the time we get to *Hamlet*, in fact, students are convinced that if only poor Hamlet knew a nice forest nearby, he could grab Ophelia by the hand and retreat from Elsinore for a while, and the whole play would turn out differently. I suppose we intuitively understand the power of retreat, perhaps because we recognize the weary inevitability of trouble in civic life. Political division and institutional inertia, pettiness and cruelty in our organizations and communities, "Th'oppressors wrong, the proud man's contumely"—we know these miseries well, along with all the other standard evils that Hamlet lists as he inventories his own reasons for needing escape.[2] We are plagued, always and fundamentally, by the primal sin of brother-crime, the sin that the Genesis stories place immediately after the flaming-sword angel exiles Adam and Eve from the garden. Even now, we long to get back to the garden, hoping we will find there the means to undo what we have done. Hence a long tradition in literature of the pastoral escape, the wilderness escape, the idyll or adventurous pilgrimage. In our imaginative life, we are always yearning for some green space where we can untangle the knots and start anew. We are always lighting out for the territories.

Literary green worlds might fit the definition of ex situ refugia: they are places to which characters flee in order to "persist" and gain strength for surviving the crisis at hand. If we also consider the typical green-world pattern of fleeing and then returning, we could call literary green worlds "pilgrimage refugia." In our real lives, that pattern of out and return promises healing, so we seek green worlds on scales small and large. Sometimes, our pilgrimage places are literally green. They are summer camps and woodland walks, family cabins and camping trips, hikes and kayak runs, garden and farmwork, travels to new places. Sometimes, we find our green spaces in less literal ways, with trusted friends or in churches where we feel safe and loved, maybe while making music together or working side by side on some worthy project. I suppose the trick is to build a life in which the green world is not a matter of escape at all but a pattern built into daily life, into civic life, so that everyone has access.

Fictional green worlds, though, remind us that refugia are not always entirely pleasant places. Duke Senior and his men feel the "icy fang" of the wind. The four lovers in *A Midsummer Night's Dream* flee to the wood of Athens, but they experience this magical, fairy-infested wood as confusing and fearful. The green world provides shelter but also challenges, and those challenges are precisely what prepares the characters to face a return to civic life, their various transformations fitting together like puzzle pieces to form a more harmonious civic space.

Unlike in fiction, real-world conflicts and troubles cannot be confined to the narrow outlines of a single dramatic arc. The challenges we face right now are globally scaled, layered, and infinitely complex. Each of us may need different kinds of refugia, because we have different kinds of wilderness work to do and different needs for relief and shelter. No single refugium will suffice to sustain us, humans and more-than-human, even temporarily. Instead, we need a whole network of refugia, a "portfolio strategy," as the biologists say. What Fred Bahnson says about arks, I would echo about refugia spaces: we need tens of thousands of them, cultural, biological, spiritual.[3] Find and create enough refugia, connect them, and eventually you may have a new habitat, a "coarse" one more varied and resilient to withstand the crises ahead.

In the context of the climate crisis, we will especially need attention to located, embodied refugia—like gardens and restored ecosystems and green city spaces—refugia that reorient our imaginations and habits to the thriving of the land and water where we live. We will need practical refuge for people who lose their homes. And we will need plenty of spiritual refugia as people adjust to a changing world. For some, like me, refugia reorientation means a steep learning curve and new habits of attentiveness and involvement. It requires putting indifference aside and carrying a piece of this age's grief, shouldering my share of the challenge and finding a new kind of courage for an unknown future.

Every habitat is dynamic, of course. Disturbance comes and goes. We will never reach the perfect steady state—until, I suppose, such time as God fulfills the promised vision for which the whole creation yearns. In the meantime, I take the yearning itself as a sign of the promise. I take heart, too, from what Randy Woodley, the founder of Eloheh Farm and Indigenous Center for Earth Justice, told me in an interview. He was expanding on that concept of *eloheh*, the Cherokee word that describes balance or harmony, and he compared *eloheh* to the Hebrew word *shalom*, that rich concept of flourishing and peace. Like shalom, he explained, *eloheh* does not mean perfect utopia but is more like a dynamic state of harmony embracing both consonance and dissonance. And he added, we are always moving in and out of shalom.[4] We find it, we lose it, and we find it again.

What would it take to build refugia patterns into so many cultural, biological, and spiritual spaces that no one has to flee far to find one? How can Christians commit to becoming people of refugia? Rather than walling ourselves off in enclaves of superior holiness, we would tend a variety of hospitable, sheltering spaces for people on their pilgrim way. Rather than seeking cultural dominance, we would model spaces that seek restoration of human relationships with each other and the whole community of creation, trusting that God loves to work from the hidden and humble.

The ecumenical church has long understood that to sustain this discipline over the long haul, we need patterns—patterns that give shape and meaning to our days, weeks, and years. Those patterns, thoughtfully arranged, give us something steady to uphold us, sturdy fence posts to grab on to when wilder winds blow. So the early church learned from its Jewish roots how to lay over the cycles of earth-seasons another cycle, a cycle of stories and teachings meant to imprint on our experience of time the fundamentals of the faith, meant to awaken us to the holiness of time itself. The Christian church year from Advent to Pentecost—roughly December to June—focuses on the life of Christ and the birth of the church. After Pentecost, though, we face a long stretch of Ordinary Time, Sunday after Sunday of nothing special, at least not in terms of church festivals.

While churches have experimented with creative ways to break up the long stretch between Pentecost and Advent, there's wisdom, too, in simply living into a long stretch of ordinary. Most of our lives are ordinary—at least we hope so. It's precisely in those ordinary times, ideally, that we can focus on building habits that hold us up when times are harder, much like a good exercise routine and a good diet make you more resistant to illness and injury. Refugia faith draws from this wisdom. If each of us chooses to become a person of refugia, reshaping our ordinary habits toward that goal, then the Great Work of this age will seem less overwhelming and impossible.

Is There Hope?

As anyone who writes or speaks about the climate crisis will report, audiences always ask about hope. People want to know, with a catch in their voice, *Is there hope?* We can address that question in a number of ways, but the first step is to recalibrate our definition of hope.

In the context of the climate crisis, we want to think of hope as the promise that things will get better. We can fix all this, right? Maybe if we all hold hands and get along, install solar panels and raise wind turbines and drive electric cars, then there will come a day when we no longer have to worry about the climate crisis. If that's what constitutes hope, then we need to temper our expectations. The planet has changed, and even if we do everything "right" in the next twenty years, we will not return the planet to patterns of equilibrium from two hundred or fifty or even twenty years ago. No matter what, our great-grandchildren will be dealing with a more volatile planet.[5]

Is there hope, then, that we can mitigate the effects? Perhaps. The next ten years can make a substantial difference if enough people respond to the call and if businesses and governments at all levels fully participate. Every tenth of a degree of warming we prevent will help calm the rocking.[6] We may be surprised by how readily the ocean starts to heal, some endangered species rebound, some forests regrow. We may take deep breaths of fresher air and wonder why we didn't retire polluting coal plants sooner. We may conclude that this new way of life is in some ways harder, but in many ways better. No more fossil-fuel smells or exhaust or polluting refineries. Improved public health. Less garbage and waste and more zero-waste communities. Long overdue cleanups and restorations in regions and neighborhoods where the poorest have suffered from asthma and waterborne illness. Fresher, better food, less junk, more local foodways. A slower pace. Better local knowledge of landforms, biomes, animals. Maybe—and this is the ardent hope of many climate leaders and organizations—working together to transform our ways of life will move us closer to full inclusion and fairer leadership structures. Maybe we can take good strides forward on equality and justice. Maybe we'll experience less loneliness and more community pride.

Prediction is a tricky business, though. As Katharine Hayhoe explained in an interview, we are performing an "unprecedented experiment with the only home we have."[7] As sophisticated as our climate prediction models may be, we can't know for sure what the next decades will bring. We could face unforeseen tipping points and cascading effects.[8] Strains on our resources and forced migration will threaten to incite or worsen conflicts, locally and internationally. At least in some aspects of human life, we will probably be managing decline.

The future is always uncertain. Likely what each of us truly wants to know when we wonder about hope is, Will I, and my loved ones, be OK? That depends, as it always does, on who you are, where you are, and what you mean by OK.

What shall we mean by hope, then? I have learned much from listening to people who have long grieved and worked, not in the climate fight, but in a related one though distinct struggle: racial injustice. These are people who understand that hope can feel like a thin euphemism. The writer Ta-Nehisi Coates has been criticized for his bracing and beautiful memoir, *Between the World and Me*, because, readers complained, it lacked hope. But Coates does not see his job as the provision of hope. He has explained in interviews that he sees himself as a journalist, and therefore his job is to perceive clearly.[9] Based on his keen perception of America's entrenched racism, he does not expect a sunshiny new day anytime soon, certainly not in terms of equity and justice. He expects struggle, and that is what he commends to his son, to whom *Between the World and Me* is addressed. He writes, "I have always wanted you to attack every day of your brief bright life in struggle. . . . I would have you be a conscious citizen of this terrible and beautiful world."[10]

It would be easy—and a mistake—to chalk up Coates's wariness of hope to his atheism. But Austin Channing Brown, a Christian, offers a similar critique of easy hope. In her book *I'm Still Here*, she recounts her experiences living daily with the traumas, small and great, of being a

Black woman in America. In the White, Christian spaces where she has lived and worked, her hopes for respect and equality have been constantly disappointed. "And so," she writes, "hope for me has died one thousand deaths. . . . I have learned not to fear the death of hope. In order for me to stay in this work, hope must die."[11] But beyond hope, she continues, something else emerges: "The death of hope gives way to a sadness that heals, to anger that inspires, to a wisdom that empowers me the next time I get to work, pick up my pen, join a march, tell my story." She reaches, she explains, a new clarity, a realignment. She has learned "to rest in the shadow of hope." And in that shadow, she finds new resolve: "Knowing that we may never see the realization of our dreams, and yet still showing up."[12]

Coates and Channing Brown quarrel with the word *hope*, I think, because they understand how easily people (particularly "those who believe they are White," in their analysis) hide apathy and fear behind that word. What Coates and Channing Brown describe in the context of race in America parallels the words of those who write about the climate crisis. In *Great Tide Rising*, Kathleen Dean Moore considers the dangers of both lazy hope and lazy cynicism. She reasons that neither is a morally acceptable response to our present crisis. Naïve hope is a failure of vision and courage, but cynicism is almost worse. To say, out loud or in one's heart, "Why bother? We can't fix this. We're doomed"—that is a posture based on the idea that we should only do what is right if we are assured sufficiently satisfactory consequences. From the standpoint of ethical philosophy, this is a lousy way to live. It's a "consequentialist" position, which Moore argues is inadequate. We would do better, she insists, to rely on virtue ethics, which call us to do what is right, not because our actions always produce the desired consequences, but because we strive to be the kind of people who do what is right: "If hope fails us, the moral abdication of despair is not an alternative. Beyond hope we can inhabit the wide moral ground of personal integrity, matching our actions to our moral convictions."[13] As antidotes to looming despair, Moore recommends grieving, working, and practicing gratitude. She recommends, in other words, what Joanna Macy describes as "Active Hope," a hope that leads to renewed engagement. Moore writes, "And here's the paradox of hope: that as we move beyond empty optimism and choose to live the lives we believe in, hope becomes transformed into something else entirely. It becomes stubborn, defiant courage. It becomes principled clarity."[14] Beyond our naïve conceptions of hope, Moore arrives precisely where Coates and Channing Brown arrive: clarity, courage, the struggle. Maybe one reason so many leaders in the climate movement are Black, Indigenous, and people of color is that they have long hiked the rugged trail where hope refracts into clarity, courage, the struggle.

We use the word *hope* all the time in Christian contexts. Faith, hope, and love abide, says Paul in 1 Corinthians, establishing what came to be called the three theological virtues (as distinct from the classical cardinal virtues: temperance, prudence, justice, and fortitude). When I ask myself what I think Christian hope means, I admit that part of me imagines hope as the notion that God will make everything all right *for me*. My shallow hope is essentially selfish: if I pray hard enough and stay faithful, well then, God will see to it that I escape any real hardship. Obviously, the evidence that God operates this way is spotty at best. Even if I personally have managed to elude disaster in my own life (so far), the history of the faithful provides ample evidence that even God's most saintly followers suffer plenty. My Calvinist ancestors, with stern conviction, would point out that God cannot be manipulated like some ancient pagan deity who responds when you get the incantations just right. God is sovereign and faithful, God shows mercy and favor, but God is not our personal happiness dispenser. If Christian hope is not about fixating on personal prosperity and safety, then must we fasten our hope only on life beyond this life? Does Christian hope amount only to one's personal union with God after this life and, beyond that, toward the Great Consummation at the end of all history?

I do believe in the next life and in the healing of history. The promise that God will "wipe every tear from their eyes" (Rev 21:4) and renew all things—that promise offers deep and blessed assurance, especially to those in the midst of great suffering here and now. God will not forget us forever. But what about right now? The promise of a sweet by-and-by maybe precious, but it can also become pernicious. Rewards in the afterlife have sometimes been used to quiet rebellion against injustice in this world—a common strategy for the White enslavers of Black Americans, for example.[15] Too exclusive a focus on *someday* is an effective strategy to keep the oppressed quiet. *Someday* can also keep the privileged complacent. I needn't bother myself about what's going on here, however unjust, because this world is not my home. I'm just passing through.

To review what the Bible might say about hope, I did an online word search through an English Bible translation. Obviously this is no way to do real biblical scholarship on a major Christian virtue; however, the process was revealing.[16] I noticed many instances of the word *hope* in Job, the Psalms, and the Major and Minor Prophets. Often, the context is a dearth of hope, a voice crying out in pain, or an exhortation to wait in hope. My little word-search survey revealed that the Bible can be seen, from one angle, as a long struggle to cling to hope in the midst of the world's many desperations. Hope is often lost, and God's people fight to hold on to it.

Eventually I zeroed in on the famous passages in Romans. First, Romans 5, in which Paul audaciously suggests that we "boast in our sufferings, knowing that suffering produces endurance, and endurance produces character, and character produces hope, and hope does not disappoint us, because God's love has been poured into our hearts through the Holy Spirit that has been given to us" (Rom 5:3–5). Hope in this passage draws from the source of God's love, secured in our experience by the Spirit's work. Hope amounts to trust-filled resilience. Then in Romans 8, the word appears again in the context of suffering, this time the suffering of all creation. Here, remarkably, it is God who hopes. God has "subjected" the creation "to futility" in the hope

> that the creation itself will be set free from its bondage to decay and will obtain the freedom of the glory of the children of God. We know that the whole creation has been groaning in labor pains until now; and not only the creation, but we ourselves, who have the first fruits of the Spirit, groan inwardly while we wait for adoption, the redemption of our bodies. For in hope we were saved. Now hope that is seen is not hope. For who hopes for what is seen? But if we hope for what we do not see, we wait for it with patience. (Rom 8:21–25)

Hope arises amid suffering and looks beyond what one can currently see.

I want very much to believe that things will get better, soon, on the ground, in the here and now. I look around at all the amazing people rising up in this moment—young and old, of every race and ethnicity, from around the globe. I read the words of visionary women leaders in the climate movement—lawyers, artists, policy wonks, teachers—bundling their determination together in the book *All We Can Save*.[17] And I think, Why would God be inspiring all these people to rise up in this moment if God did not intend for us, somehow, to navigate through the crisis? So many people of extraordinary courage and talent are already forming and nurturing that refugia network—so many "awakened souls," "able vessels in the water," as Clarissa Pinkola Estés describes them in her famous encouragement that, whatever their terror and promise, "we were made for these times."[18]

Even so, hope finally is not about believing that God will make things better in the next moment but about God's faithfulness, always, whatever the facts on the ground. Hope is the conviction that even when things look bleak, God means us well—means the whole creation well. We wait and watch for the actions of that faithful, beneficent God, trying to rest in the conviction, as Paul soaringly declares in the next few verses of Romans 8 that nothing can separate us from the love of God. Our waiting and watching, in order to be faith filled, must also be active. The poet T. S. Eliot, in his meditative *Four Quartets*, warns against letting the future distract us from our present work: "For us, there is only the trying," he writes. "The rest is not our business."[19] We are called not only to thought and concern but also to showing up and doing the work, to what Eliot calls the "life of significant soil."[20] We do what is right because, through our actions, we become witnesses—witnesses to God's desires for our lives and for this world.

This active hope, it must be said, does not always feel wonderful; courage, clarity, and struggle often feel like groaning. This is why theologian Willie James Jennings describes hope as a discipline, a pattern we commit to over the long haul. Hope, he says, is a discipline to which God calls us.[21] It's the discipline of our ordinary days.

A Refugia Summary

My goal in these pages has not been to outline a ten-step procedure for creating refugia. That would hardly fit the nature of refugia. My goal has been to spark imagination, ask the what-if questions, propose a somewhat different paradigm for what it means to be people of faith. Gathering together some observations from the previous chapters, I would suggest that as we imagine the habits and disciplines we need as we seek and create refugia, we can look for some essential characteristics.

Humility. Resisting arrogance and anthropocentrism, we see ourselves as members of the whole community of creation. We seek—especially in those contexts where we have the most power—to abide by house rules that allow all people and indeed all life to flourish.

Inclusivity. Refugia spaces provide shelter in crisis. They are hospitable. Their purpose is to support diversity and therefore resilience. In human contexts, refugia spaces model just structures, giving agency and voice to those who have experienced disempowerment. Refugia provide opportunity for thriving and growth to people and more-than-human creatures that are threatened or suppressed elsewhere.

Lament. In refugia, we can express our grief and fear honestly. We can ask why. Where fitting, lament leads to repentance and commitment to change.

Challenge. Refugia prompt change toward greater resilience, and this change requires deconstruction or relinquishment as well as capacity-building work. In refugia, we respond to crisis by sharing in meaningful work, both individual and communal action. Even if the action seems insufficient, we focus on mitigation and doing what is right for its own sake.

Healing. Refugia are places to heal. We seek to create healing contexts for people and the earth. We recognize healing as redemptive work.

Reorientation. Refugia faith entails reexamination of received traditions and ideas, including theological ones. We unwrap the treasures but also repair what is broken. We seek the Holy Spirit's guidance as we do so.

I have focused in this book on ideas rather than on specific religious practices. How a refugia paradigm might renew worship practices or church structures—those are topics for another book. Here, though, I will at least point to the potential in Sabbath rest, worship, and the sacraments. These gifts of the church, practiced well, can provide regular reorientation, forming us over time as people of refugia. The Sabbath, as a refugium in time, becomes a slow lane where we can take stock and gain strength, even amid crisis and rapid change. Drawing from the biblical Sabbath themes of rest, delight, and liberation, Sabbath practices mark our resistance to all that enslaves, securing our identity as God's beloved. Rest becomes a countercultural act, and we welcome others into this rest and this true identity. Similarly, worship and the sacraments serve as reorientation, opening us to experiences of transcendence, providing grace and consolation. The sacraments transform the ordinary stuff of the physical world—water, wine, bread—fundamentals of survival. Through human art and the blessing of the Spirit, the simplest things become special means of grace so that we might see grace in the simplest of things.[22]

Joy. Finally, refugia are incomplete without joy. We learn joy through practices of gratitude, marking God's gifts and practicing reciprocity with each other and the more-than-human creation. We learn joy in community. We learn joy by practicing attention and wonder.

The Virtue of Wonder

On the topic of wonder, we need to talk about moths. I had never given much thought to moths. They are drab little things that congregate in annoying flutters around electric lights on summer nights. But then someone on my Facebook feed shared a link to an astonishing web page with photos of all the moths native to Michigan.[23] I could not stop staring. Michigan is not the Amazon Rainforest; we are not known for our extraordinary biodiversity. Yet hundreds of species of moths are native to this state, all the way from the Abbott's sphinx moth to the zebra conchylodes moth. I kept the web page open in my browser for days, repeatedly going back to marvel at these little creatures. The white-lined sphinx moth looks like an art deco brooch. The green pug moth could be made of jade. The spun glass slug moth looks like a miniature plushie puppy, flopped on its belly; in its caterpillar stage, it does indeed seem made of spun glass. But don't touch—the shard-like barbs sting and cause "raging dermatitis."[24] There's a fuzzy, greenish thing called "the joker" and a frothy pink-and-yellow confection called the rosy maple moth. Who would have thought I could find myself agape over moths? Yet they are astonishing, exquisitely designed creatures. They have water-resistant wings.[25] They are each adapted to particular plants. They go about their mothy business while all but the most entomologically inclined remain utterly oblivious.

Writers are forever commending the practice of wonder. *Pay attention!* they are always saying, and through their writing they strive to seduce readers into paying attention to all kinds of things: the stories all around us, the expressiveness of human faces, the emotional contours of our lives. Nature writers, of course, invite us into attention especially to the more-than-human creation so that we might wonder at everything from swirling galaxies and star nurseries to microbes and quarks. Wonder is a gift we receive at birth as part of our human nature, but this gift needs cultivation. So John Muir writes *The Yosemite* to rhapsodize about Half Dome, Rachel Carson writes *A Sense of Wonder* to encourage us to practice wonder with small children, Annie Dillard writes *Pilgrim at Tinker Creek* to demonstrate that an ordinary acreage in Virginia is full of marvels, and Mary Oliver pours her own wonder into poem after poem about the Cape Cod coast.[26] These writers and many others use their art to model the virtue of wonder, a virtue modeled equally well by people who aren't writers at all but silently cast their fishing line in a creek at sunrise or catch with their camera an ibis in flight. Wonder is a wonderfully flexible and portable virtue. Anyone can practice it anywhere, just by attending to our senses. As theologian Steve Bouma-Prediger notes, wonder and humility are partner virtues.[27] Wonder requires a humble posture toward the world: I'm laying aside my self-obsession and paying attention to *you* now, world, and I am ready to perceive your beauty.

In the context of the climate crisis, wonder takes on renewed urgency and moral significance. Kathleen Dean Moore considers whether "joyous attention"—her descriptive phrase for wonder—can help repair our disregard, our insensitivities, our prideful and destructive inattention. Maybe. It depends on a chain of "ifs": "If attentiveness can lead to wonder, and wonder can lead to love, and love can lead to protective action, then maybe being aware of the beautiful complexity of lives on Earth is at least a first step toward saving the great systems our lives depend on."[28] Wonder, in other words, can motivate us to act. Meanwhile, Robin Wall Kimmerer, who combines the attentiveness of

the writer with the equally potent attentiveness of the scientist, writes
that "paying attention is a form of reciprocity with the living world,
receiving the gifts with open eyes and open heart."[29] Wonder becomes a
form of gratitude. Wonder is a religious disposition too. While anyone
can practice wonder, people of faith ought to have lifelong training in
it and extra motivation for it. If we seek after God, why would we not
seek the revelation of God hidden within every wonder of this world?
Mary Evelyn Tucker, in her book *Worldly Wonder*, calls on all the great
religions to lean into those dispositions most applicable to addressing
the climate crisis: "Along with gratitude, and reverence, wonder may be
a key to release the flourishing potential of our species and our planet."[30]

It seems to me that, ideally, any religious faith should cultivate, at
the very center of its reflection and practice, a profound wonder—for the
divine reality that in our various ways we call God. In Christianity, we
speak of Christ as that divine reality intimately stitched into the world,
eternally incarnate and present by the Spirit. Deeper love for this exqui-
site world draws us then, naturally, into deeper love for God. It works
the other way around too: to deepen our love for God, we can deepen our
love for the world through the practice of wonder.

As I look back on my own life, I understand now that for me, my
deepest motivations and passions all started with beauty. I came alive
to my inner life in the music and poetry of worship, so that words,
music, and worship weave together into the whole fabric of my life's
work. I found beauty, too, in weedy fields and along a windy shore.
Beauty awakened longing, and longing drew me into wonder, entan-
gling me in the net of God. I'm beginning to understand that for me,
as is true of many others, beauty remains at the heart of my own "little
work" in response to the climate crisis and to this moment in history.
I lament the beauty of what has been lost; I feel a fierce loyalty to
the beauty that remains. I imagine with longing a beautiful vision of
renewal. I seek God's purposes, hoping that they are as beautiful as I
want to believe.

When I feel discouraged and my hope withers, wonder often revives
me. Moths, maybe, or birdsong, or the big lake. Or the marvels of human
creativity. Music. Clever humor. While I know we must be cautious
about "hope" that things will get better, I derive dangerous hope from
all that is wonderful. While I marvel, gratefully, at the brilliant people who engineer solar inverters, design distributed generation grids,

manage mathematical climate models, write policy, lobby lawmakers, and organize citizens, I have a special appreciation for the artists who help us cultivate wonder. Among my favorites are Robert Macfarlane and Jackie Morris, who together created a project called *The Lost Words*.[31] When Macfarlane—a linguist, poet, philosopher, and writer—noticed that words like *acorn* and *kingfisher* had been removed from the 2007 *Oxford Junior Dictionary* to be replaced by words like *voice mail* and *broadband*, he worried about what we are teaching our children to notice and know and care about. If we lose the words for ordinary birds and trees, how easy it is to lose the things themselves through our disregard. So Macfarlane worked with artist Jackie Morris in that nexus where artistic beauty and natural beauty converge, creating a lavishly illustrated book of "spells"—playful, delightful poems that capture the essence of willows, bluebells, herons, and more, "summoning" them back into our consciousness through words and art.

The book has indeed turned out to have a kind of healing magic. It has "begun a grass-roots movement to re-wild childhood across Britain, Europe, and North America," according to the book's Amazon page description. *The Lost Words* soon prompted the companion album and book *Spell Songs*.[32] The songs are inspired by *The Lost Words* and collaboratively composed by a group of mostly British folk artists. The final song in the *Spell Songs* cycle, "The Lost Words Blessing," is a heartbreaking lullaby calling us to "walk through the world with care, my love / And sing the things you see." Those words serve as a blessing and a summons, fully resonant with religious devotion. They are words we most need to heed. Humans are ill equipped for so much in our relationship with the earth, but we are given the capacity for wonder, awe, and gratitude. We can love, we can bear witness.

Hairy Beardtongue Triumphant

At some point in the writing of this book, I decided I wanted to end it with singing pines. I've never heard a pine sing, exactly, but apparently they have been singing since the classical period at least. Theocritus wrote about singing pines.[33] So did some of the novelists and poets of Michigan's cutover period, according to scholar John Knott. Longfellow put singing pines in *Hiawatha*.[34] I thought it would be poetic to plant a pine in my own backyard refugium and describe it singing.

Never happened. It turns out that even a native eastern white pine would probably struggle in the soggy clay in our backyard refugium—pines appreciate drier, sandier conditions. So no singing pines. Unfortunately, no Tammy the Tamarack either. During her first winter in the refugium, she was savagely attacked by marauding bunnies. Bunnies chewed off her lower branches and chewed off the bark all the way around her base: Tammy got girdled. I wish I'd known about this danger. I would have protected her. This spring, she's bravely sending out a carpet of soft, green sprigs at her base, but the rest is a snag—still standing, but dead. I cut the dead parts and I'll give her some time to see if she can recover, but I worry she won't make it.

For a while, I wondered if anything much would sprout this spring. In April, the area still looked relatively bare. Whatever was popping up I couldn't identify. Then rather suddenly, the refugium leapt to life. I recognized rattlesnake master, of course, and goldenrod, coneflower, marsh blazing star, and a number of other things I couldn't name though I recognized them as larger, stronger versions of last year's babies. Even the swamp milkweed, chomped late last summer by the bunnies, sprung up much taller this year. The hairy beardtongue won the prize for first to flower: a drift of long stalks pushed up tall and bloomed beautifully by early June. I saw bees slipping past the ruffled lip of the trumpet-shaped white flowers and popping out again, satisfied; I saw a hummingbird visit too. The plants did their work. They put down roots and prepared for the future.

Weeds are coming up too, of course. I've got more willow herb and purple loosestrife. I've also got a shovel. We'll do some clearing out of the ambitious invasives so that the native plants can develop a second year's growth of roots and seeds. There are some bare spots here and there, where nothing much managed to take. And buckthorn lurks around the edges. Still! I'm amazed at the resilience of our humble native wildflowers.

Meanwhile, I started tomatoes from seed this year, and Ron and I built a small raised bed—complete with deer- and bunny-preventive fencing, of course. I learned the Florida weave to trellis the tomatoes and some pruning techniques to keep them in line, but they're doing so well I can hardly keep up. When I go out to check on the tomatoes, I also visit the mama robin who has made her nest under the eaves on the curve of the downspout. I noticed her when I was walking past the big spruce and sent her into fits. Since she was clearly not happy with me being around, I figured she was nesting in the spruce, but later I saw her flying up under the eave, and sure enough, a nest. I checked in on her daily as she sat on the eggs, then tended to four wobbly, open-beaked fluff balls, then fledged them all successfully.

Lake Michigan water levels have receded somewhat, leaving a narrow strip of walkable beach. The washed-out foredune still means a long drop from the deck to the beach. To prevent even more erosion, Mom and Dad had to arrange, at considerable expense, for a pile of boulders to be laid against the seawall. Up and down the beach, cottage owners had to order rocks shipped in, a messy and expensive business involving barges and power shovels. The rocks break the force of the waves and create a substrate. If the lake decides to rebuild the foredune, whatever sand it offers, the rocks will receive and hold. For now, we still have to scramble clumsily down the exposed rocks, at least until the county rebuilds the ruined public beach steps next door. Our aging Maizey can't make it down to the beach anymore. Even good, solid steps are too hard for her weak hips and legs.

Out at the lake one day, Ron and I brave the rocks and walk the narrow strip of beach. The wind has lured the lake into full motion, flying over the wrinkled surface as if pushing long folds of water toward the shore. The water near shore is sage green, full of churned-up sand. Good. Maybe some will deposit on the beach again. Beyond that a strip of radiant Caribbean green, then a deep royal blue to the horizon.

The last years have brought us so much challenge, so much change. I feel stretched and weary. I've learned so much, carried my own and other people's anxieties, grieved and wondered, and tried, at least, to trust the promises and faithfulness of God. What will come next?

In a recent essay, climate writer Mary Annaïse Heglar describes how she responds to people, newly alert to the climate crisis, who ask her, pleadingly, What can I do?[35] The answer, she writes, is actually quite simple: "Do what you're good at. And do your best." Some people are worried they don't have the right kind of skills to be useful in this time, but she assures them this is not the case: "The artists I spoke to ... lamented the fact that they weren't engineers or scientists or some other type of 'expert.' But as I told them, it is not their job to design the policy plans for rapid decarbonization, to decide which coal plants to shut down first, and what exactly to replace them with. We have people on that. As the writer Toni Cade Bambara once put it, the role of the artist is to 'make revolution irresistible.'" In all these pages, I have tried to do what I'm good at. I know how to read books. I find it more possible than most people to string together a million sentences. I've spent a whole life in the texts and communities and mysteries of the Christian faith. So this is what I've done. Whether I've written about revolution, I don't know. I think I've simply told my story and tried to put a name on what I perceive God is inviting us to become: people of refugia.

I still feel overwhelmed by all there is to learn and adjust to. But as my friend Josh reminded me, feeling overwhelmed can be good. It's much healthier than apathy and numbness. And maybe, Josh suggested, overwhelmed feelings form a threshold to wonder and hope. "Wonder in waiting," he called this state.

In the years ahead, I will probably have to thin out my email in-box and narrow down my involvements to a few manageable activist groups. I still have dozens of books I want to read. On the other hand, maybe I have already read too many. I think my work now is to put the books aside—at least for a while—and slip out the back door, listen for tamaracks, hickories, cottonwoods, and pines. Listen for the robins and nuthatches, for the waves and wind. Listen alongside all the other people who are transforming their fear and love into the active discipline of hope. Listen, as long as I can, while the whole world sings.

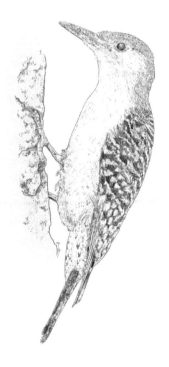

RED-BELLIED WOODPECKER
MELANERPES CAROLINUS

Acknowledgments

I begin with two extraordinary people, Kathleen Dean Moore and Bill McKibben. The extent of my debt to you both is only partly obvious in these pages. Bill, your book *Eaarth* stopped me in my tracks. Then your appearance at the Festival of Faith and Writing in 2018 not only was a good time but also propelled me down a new path, one full of seriousness but also community and joy. Kathleen, during your visit to Calvin University in 2019—also a good time—you modeled the courage to do the work. Your visit, plus four key pages in *Great Tide Rising*, planted the seeds for this book. I admire both of you not only as prolific writers and activists but as generous and beautiful human beings. Thank you for changing the world.

To all the authors, scholars, theologians, podcasters, activists, filmmakers, artists, number crunchers, scientists, report writers, journalists, and others whose work I studied for this book: thank you. Thank for you pushing through anxiety, grief, weariness, and opposition to do your work. Thank you for showing us what's possible.

My colleagues and friends Dave Koetje and Tim Van Deelen convinced me early on that stealing an idea from biology and trampling all over it with metaphorical applications was not necessarily a crime. I've learned so much from you both, not only about science, but also about stories that need to be told and grief that needs to be shared.

A great deal of material in this book appeared in earlier versions on the *Reformed Journal*'s blog, *The Twelve*. I'm grateful to the readers of *The Twelve* for letting me write about all kinds of things, from silly to serious, over ten years, and for cheering me on as I have leaned into eco-theology and nature writing.

Calvin University (formerly Calvin College) has supported this book in numerous ways. The Beyond Stewardship project, funded by the Calvin Center for Christian Scholarship, gathered a delightful cadre of colleagues during the summer of 2018. Project directors and editors David Warners and Matt Heun: thank you for welcoming me into the group at the very last minute. I'm also grateful to all the contributors for our rich conversations and fellowship: Aminah Al-Attas Bradford, Mark Bjelland, Dietrich Bouma, Steve Bouma-Prediger, Bill Deutsch, Susan Felch, Kathi Groenendyk, Gail Gunst Heffner, Matt Halteman, Becky Haney, Clarence Joldersma, Michelle Loyd-Paige, Kyle Meyaard-Schaap, Jamie Skillen, and Randy Van Dragt.

During the summer of 2019, grants from the McGregor Fellows program and several Calvin Centers and Institutes allowed a few of us Calvin faculty to experiment with making our scholarly work more available to wider audiences. John Hwang was the mover and shaker behind the whole endeavor. John, you were the firecracker who startled us out of our scholarly bunkers. Thank you again for the innumerable hours of professional expertise and labor you contributed to us, simply because you believe in what we do and believe we can do more. Thanks to Kristin Du Mez and Kevin Timpe, my partners in crime that summer, for your example and inspiration. I also thank my student partners—Lauren Cole, Garrett Strpko, and Kayla Cooper—who jumped into the deep end without a life jacket and made it possible for a clueless professor to pull off the first season of a podcast.

A Calvin sabbatical leave during the spring semester of 2020 allowed me to spend the first months of the pandemic buried in books and notes and drafts rather than trying to learn how to teach online. I'm grateful to our wonderful Calvin librarians for the collection they've built: I was able to access a number of key books in electronic form even during quarantine. In 2021, the Calvin Center for Christian Scholarship provided funds for research assistance that allowed me to finish the book on time. They also provided funds for the original interior art. David Wunder, you were the guiding hand that made a lot of this funding possible. Thank you.

Eighteen gracious people agreed to serve as guests on the *Refugia Podcast*, and to all of you: I'm so grateful for what you shared, honestly and expertly, with listeners and with me. Your wisdom weaves through this book in ways both obvious and subtle. I'm especially grateful to

David Koetje for serving as a generative conversation partner in the opening and closing episodes of each season. Many thanks to Fred Bahnson, Steve Bouma-Prediger, Jeff Chu, Christina Edmondson, Ruth Harvey, David Jellema, Kate Kooyman, Bill McKibben, Kyle Meyaard-Schaap, Katerina Parsons, Kathryn Mae Post, Hillary Scholten, Jamie Skillen, Tim Van Deelen, Jo-Ann Van Reeuwyk, John Witvliet, and Randy Woodley. For the second season of the podcast, Josh Parks and Philip Rienstra saved the day. Thanks to Josh for publicity support and transcript editing and to Philip for audio and transcript editing.

My science division colleagues have proven remarkably hospitable to an English professor who inexplicably turns up on their side of campus asking questions and butting in. I'm especially grateful to Deanna van Dijk (Deanna of the Dunes) for allowing me to sit in on her remarkable Geo 181 course. Deanna, you are intrepid and wonderful and a master teacher. You deserve that teaching award you won, and then some.

Thanks also to the Plaster Creek Stewards folks, especially Deanna Geelhoed (Deanna of the Swale), who designed our backyard refugium and who never laughs at me when I ask dumb questions. And thanks to David Warners and Gail Gunst Heffner. The more I worked on this book, the more I realized that you are the heroes at Calvin who figured out refugia long ago. Your behind-the-scenes watershed restoration work is the kind of refugia work every community needs. Thanks also to Henry Kingma and Michael Ryskamp, who taught me about buckthorn and also did not laugh when I asked dumb questions.

I'm grateful to several classes of students who shared their honest responses to reading assignments on environmental topics that I squeezed into creative nonfiction, written rhetoric, Brit lit, and that one course where I made you all read *The Overstory* in three weeks in January. You have helped me see the world as you see it, at least a little, and I'm honored to work beside you to "think deeply, act justly, and live wholeheartedly as Christ's agents of renewal." It's a great mission statement, and I'm glad we can try living it together.

Andy Rozendaal of Eighth Day Farm and Nurya Love Parish and Emily Ulmer of Plainsong Farm shared with me their joys and struggles with faith-based farming. Nurya, you taught me the prayer I needed at just the right time. Thank you.

A dozen people read terrible drafts of this book and gave indispensable feedback. I'm especially grateful to Suzanne McDonald for reading the entire manuscript and also for enticing some of her students at Western Theological Seminary to read it. Suzanne, your enthusiasm buoyed me from beginning to end in this process. I am grateful for all your comments but especially for your "theological nervousness moments." I hope I've addressed them successfully. Be it known that if I've written something heretical, it is not Suzanne's fault. Deep gratitude to Suzanne's students at Western Theological Seminary: Elliot Weidenaar, Katherine Newendorp, Emily Anderson, Miranda Craig, and Tom Oord. Each of you shared your heart and offered critique that changed this book for the better. Kate Kooyman and Abby Zwart read good chunks of the early manuscript and represented different kinds of readers in very helpful ways. Dave Koetje and Tim Van Deelen went through looking for any egregious science errors. Thank you.

My editor, Beth Gaede, believed in this project when it was little more than an amorphous blob. Thank you, Beth, for advocating for this book and putting up with my authorly neuroses. Your editing work disciplined my writing, which too often resembles an untrellised, indeterminate tomato plant. My thanks to the whole team at Fortress, with a special shout-out to Elvis Ramirez for production coordination and to Kristin Miller for taking special care with the book design. Thanks, Kristin, for welcoming interior art into the book and for your patience with my authorly meddling.

I'm especially thrilled to feature in this book the work of artist Gabrielle Eisma. Readers should realize that Gabrielle was still an undergraduate when she did the interior art for these pages. Gabrielle, you're a rock star.

Speaking of rock stars: Josh Parks. Josh was essential to this project. Besides helping me with the second season of the *Refugia Podcast*, Josh read the entire manuscript of this book—more than once—wrangled all the endnotes, and chased down some of the thornier research questions. Josh, I'm grateful for your skill and patience with scholarly labors but equally for your perceptive comments and suggestions. A lot of places in this book are sharper and more generous because of your ideas. It's been wonderful to move from those "hesitating but sane Hamlet" days in Shakespeare class to collaborating as colleagues and friends. Someday you can hire me to do the wrangling work on *your* book's endnotes, OK?

Trevor and Linda Rubingh turn up in all my books, with good reason. Your friendship has been a lifelong treasure. Thank you for gamely going along with the refugium experiment in our—well, mostly your—backyard. Thank you for your pandemic companionship. And your prayers.

Gayle Boss prayed. Gayle, you have sustained me with your encouragement and prayers. Thank you. As a fellow writer, you understand all the struggles of spirit we encounter along the way.

Mom and Dad Rienstra, thank you for encouraging us to feel welcome, always, at the cottage. You had a moment of real estate genius in 1987, but more importantly, your abiding love and hospitality have made so much possible. Thank you for enabling the whole family to deepen our love for the big lake by barging in on your home. You have flooded countless people's lives with blessing, including mine.

Finally, I'm grateful to Philip Rienstra and Heidi Keswick Rienstra for their companionship throughout the pandemic. We agonized together, feasted together, and tried to create a refugium in our home during uncommonly trying times. I'm so glad you were with us.

For my husband, Ron, I need to quote Robert Macfarlane. Macfarlane writes in his book *Underland* about a story from Ovid's *Metamorphoses*, the story of Baucis and Philemon.[1] These two are "transformed into an intertwining oak and linden, each supporting the other in terms of both structure and sustenance, drawing strength for each other from the ground through their roots—and tenderly sharing that strength through their en-kissing."

Ron, that's you and me. We have grown our roots together for a long time. You have been part of this book from the earliest speculations years ago, right through to the final manuscript. Everything I do is intertwined with your love, intelligence, humor, and strength. I'm so grateful to share the soil and sky with you.

Notes

October—Douglas, Michigan

1 Rev 21:5.

Introduction

1 Kathleen Dean Moore, *Great Tide Rising: Towards Clarity and Moral Courage in a Time of Planetary Change* (Berkeley, CA: Counterpoint, 2017), 139–42.

2 The separation impulse gained expression recently in Rod Dreher, *The Benedict Option: A Strategy for Christians in a Post-Christian Nation* (New York: Sentinel/Penguin, 2017). The refugia model is distinct from any us-versus-them culture-war separation.

3 Mary Evelyn Tucker, *Worldly Wonder: Religions Enter Their Ecological Phase* (Chicago: Open Court, 2003), 8–10.

4 Pope Francis, *Laudato si': On Care for Our Common Home*, Vatican Publishing House, May 24, 2015, http://www.vatican.va/content/francesco/en/encyclicals/documents/papa-francesco_20150524_enciclica-laudato-si.html, sec. 63. See also sec. 14.

5 IPCC, *Special Report: Global Warming of 1.5 °C: Summary for Policymakers*, October 8, 2018, https://www.ipcc.ch/sr15/chapter/spm/, sec. B.

6 Brad Plumer, "Humans Are Speeding Extinction and Altering the Natural World at an 'Unprecedented' Pace," *New York Times*, May 6, 2019, https://www.nytimes.com/2019/05/06/climate/biodiversity-extinction-united-nations.html. The report is Eduardo Brondizio, Sandra Diaz, and Josef Settele, eds., *Global Assessment Report on Biodiversity and Ecosystem Services of the Intergovernmental Science-Policy Platform on Biodiversity and Ecosystem Services* (Bonn, Germany: IPBES Secretariat, 2019), https://doi.org/10.5281/zenodo.3831673.

7 William J. Ripple et al., "World Scientists' Warning of a Climate Emergency," *BioScience* 70, no. 1 (2020): 8–12, https://academic.oup.com/bioscience/article/70/1/8/5610806.

8 IPCC, "Summary for Policymakers," in *Climate Change 2021: The Physical Science Basis; Contribution of Working Group I to the Sixth Assessment Report of the Intergovernmental Panel on Climate Change*, ed. V. Masson-Delmotte et al. (Cambridge: Cambridge University Press, 2021), https://www.ipcc.ch/report/ar6/wg1/.

9 In March 2020, 60 percent of Americans considered global climate change a "major threat." That's up from 44 percent in 2009 (Brian Kennedy, "U.S. Concern about Climate Change Is Rising, but Mainly among Democrats," FactTank, Pew Research Center, April 16, 2020, https://www.pewresearch.org/fact-tank/2020/04/16/u-s-concern-about-climate-change-is-rising-but-mainly-among-democrats/). Another poll from April of 2020 found that 73 percent believe climate change is happening and 62 percent attribute it to human activity (John Schwartz, "Americans See Climate as a Concern, Even amid Coronavirus Crisis," *New York Times*, May 19, 2020, https://www.nytimes.com/2020/05/19/climate/coronavirus-climate-change-survey.html). A survey of Americans conducted in December 2020 by the Yale Program on Climate Change Communication and George Mason University's Center for Climate Change Communication found that 72 percent of respondents believe climate change is happening, as opposed to 13 percent who do not. Also, 58 percent of Americans believe that climate change is "mostly human caused" (Anthony Leiserowitz et al., "Climate wChange in the American Mind: December 2020," Yale Program on Climate Change Communication, February 10, 2020, https://climatecommunication.yale.edu/publications/climate-change-in-the-american-mind-december-2020/).

10 David Carlin, "The Case for Fossil Fuel Divestment," *Forbes*, February 20, 2021, https://www.forbes.com/sites/davidcarlin/2021/02/20/the-case-for-fossil-fuel-divestment/?sh=1816388576d2.

11 Annie White, "Here Are All the Promises Automakers Have Made about Electric Cars," *Car and Driver*, February 20, 2021, https://www.caranddriver.com/news/g35562831/ev-plans-automakers-timeline/.

12 While Kristin Kobes Du Mez does not use the phrase "church of empire," she carefully accounts for the White American evangelicalism's long-term love affair with militant masculinity and other forms of domination. See *Jesus and John Wayne: How White Evangelicals Corrupted a Faith and Fractured a Nation* (New York: Liveright, 2020).

13 Caitlin Gent, "An Apostate's Epistle," *the post calvin*, February 4, 2018, https://thepostcalvin.com/an-apostates-epistle/. Caitlin's essay is also available in Josh deLacy et al., eds., *the post calvin: Essays 2016–2019* (Grand Rapids, MI: Josh deLacy, 2019), 140–43.

14 Gent, "Apostate's Epistle."

15 Matthew Schneider-Mayerson and Kit Ling Leong, "Eco-reproductive Concerns in the Age of Climate Change," *Climatic Change* 163 (2020): 1007–23, https://doi.org/10.1007/s10584-020-02923-y.

16 Amitav Ghosh, *The Great Derangement: Climate Change and the Unthinkable* (Chicago: University of Chicago Press, 2017).

17 Brad Plumer, "Carbon Dioxide in Atmosphere Hits Record High despite Pandemic Dip," *New York Times*, June 7, 2021, https://www.nytimes.com/2021/06/07/climate/climate-change-emissions.html. For more on why 350 ppm is considered safe, see James Hansen et al., "Target Atmospheric CO_2: Where Should

Humanity Aim?," *Open Atmospheric Scientific Journal* 2 (2008): 217–31, https://arxiv.org/abs/0804.1126. For a useful summary from 2017 on the science of CO_2 level tracking, see Nikola Jones, "How the World Passed a Carbon Threshold and Why It Matters," *E360*, Yale School of the Environment, January 26, 2017, https://e360.yale.edu/features/how-the-world-passed-a-carbon-threshold-400ppm-and-why-it-matters. You can track the earth's current atmospheric CO_2 level at https://www.co2.earth/.

18 Bob Berwyn, "Paying for Extreme Weather: Wildlife, Hurricanes, Floods and Droughts Quadrupled in Cost since 1980," *Inside Climate News*, August 25, 2020, https://insideclimatenews.org/news/25082020/extreme-weather-costs-wildfire-climate-change/.

19 This is true in the United States as well as globally. Environmental racism is the subject of extensive literature. For one brief introductory account of environmental racism in the United States, see Hiroko Tabuchi and Nadja Popovich, "People of Color Breathe More Hazardous Air. The Sources Are Everywhere," *New York Times*, April 28, 2021, https://www.nytimes.com/2021/04/28/climate/air-pollution-minorities.html. For more on environmental racism worldwide, see Álvaro Fernández-Llamazares et al., "A State-of-the-Art Review of Indigenous Peoples and Environmental Pollution," *Integrated Environmental Assessment and Management* 16, no. 3 (2020): 324–41, https://www.ncbi.nlm.nih.gov/pmc/articles/PMC7187223/.

20 Thomas Berry, *The Great Work: Our Way into the Future* (New York: Bell Tower, 1999), 7–8.

21 Joanna Macy, *Coming Back to Life* (Gabriola Island, BC: New Society, 1998), 6, 17.

22 Berry, *Great Work*, 10.

23 Fred Bahnson and Norman Wirzba, *Making Peace with the Land: God's Call to Reconcile with Creation* (Downers Grove, IL: InterVarsity, 2012), 28.

24 Wendell Berry, "It All Turns on Affection," in *It All Turns on Affection: The Jefferson Lecture and Other Essays* (Berkeley, CA: Counterpoint, 2012), 9–40.

25 Berry, *Great Work*, 12.

26 IPCC, "Summary for Policymakers," A.I., p. SPM-5.

27 John Milton, *Paradise Lost*, bk. 12, lines 566–68, 581–82.

28 Moore, *Great Tide Rising*, 311–19.

29 Larry Rasmussen, *Earth-Honoring Faith: Religious Ethics in a New Key* (Oxford: Oxford University Press, 2013), 7.

January—Douglas, Michigan

1 "Great Lakes Water Level Observations," NOAA Great Lakes Environmental Research Laboratory, January 21, 2021, https://www.glerl.noaa.gov/data/wlevels/levels.html#observations. Also, since 2014, lake levels in Michigan-Huron have never before risen so quickly (Environmental Law & Policy Center, "Preparing for Great Lakes Flooding an ELPC Thinks Webinar," YouTube video, April 8, 2020, https://www.youtube.com/watch?v=7gDBVnoMWqQ).

2 "An Assessment of the Impacts of Climate Change on the Great Lakes," Environmental Law & Policy Center, 2019, http://elpc.org/glclimatechange/.

Chapter 1

1   Bill Bryson, *The Life and Times of the Thunderbolt Kid: A Memoir* (New York: Broadway Books, 2006), chap. 4.

2   Robert N. Watson, *Back to Nature: The Green and the Real in the Late Renaissance* (Philadelphia: University of Pennsylvania Press, 2006), 72.

3   Macy, *Coming Back to Life*, 16.

4   Bill McKibben, *Eaarth: Making a Life on a Tough New Planet* (New York: St. Martin's Griffin, 2011).

5   Berry, *Great Work*, 167.

6   Charlotte McDonald, "How Many Earths Do We Need?," BBC News, June 16, 2015, https://www.bbc.com/news/magazine-33133712.

7   These charts are helpfully gathered in Rasmussen, *Earth-Honoring Faith*, 56–57.

8   Will Steffan et al., "The Trajectory of the Anthropocene: The Great Acceleration," *Anthropocene Review* 2, no. 1 (2015): 81–98, https://journals.sagepub.com/doi/10.1177/2053019614564785. Steffan first coined the term in 2004.

9   Rasmussen, *Earth-Honoring Faith*, 58. Rasmussen cites Fareed Zakaria, "Fueling the Future," *New York Times Book Review*, September 25, 2011, 5. Zakaria is reviewing Daniel Yergin, *The Quest: Energy, Security, and the Remaking of the Modern World* (New York: Penguin, 2011). Zakaria's column is also available at https://fareedzakaria.com/columns/2011/09/23/how-will-we-fuel-the-future.

10 Rasmussen, *Earth-Honoring Faith*, 54. Rasmussen cites Alan T. Durning, *How Much Is Enough?* (London: Earthscan, 1992), 38.

11 Bill McKibben, *The End of Nature* (New York: Random House, 2006).

12 Will Steffan, Paul J. Curtzen, and John R. McNeill, "The Anthropocene: Are Humans Now Overwhelming the Great Forces of Nature?," *Ambio* 36, no. 8 (2007): 614–21, https://www.jstor.org/stable/25547826.

13 IPCC, *Special Report*, sec. A.2. See also Timothy M. Lenton et al., "Climate Tipping Points—Too Risky to Bet Against," *Nature*, November 27, 2019, https://www.nature.com/articles/d41586-019-03595-0; and John Branch and Brad Plumer, "Climate Disruption Is Now Locked In. The Next Moves Will Be Crucial," *New York Times*, September 22, 2020, https://www.nytimes.com/2020/09/22/climate/climate-change-future.html.

14 Masson-Delmotte et al., *Climate Change 2021*, B.5.4, p. SPM-28.

15 Mary Annaïse Heglar, "I Work in the Environmental Movement. I Don't Care If You Recycle," Vox, June 4, 2019, https://www.vox.com/the-highlight/2019/5/28/18629833/climate-change-2019-green-new-deal.

16 The phrase is from "Oh Holy Night," lyrics by Placide Cappeau, translated by John S. Dwight.

17 Covid is a zoonotic disease resulting in part from environmental degradation and climate change. For an explanation of the connection between Covid and climate change, see C. Manore, C. Xu, and J. M. Fair, "Climate Change Is Driving the Expansion of Zoonotic Diseases," Research Outreach, 2020, https://researchoutreach.org/articles/climate-change-driving-expansion-zoonotic-diseases/.

18 H. Paul Santmire, *Nature Reborn: The Ecological and Cosmic Promise of Christian Theology* (Minneapolis, MN: Fortress, 2000), 13.

19 Henry David Thoreau, "Walking," *Atlantic*, June 1862, https://www.theatlantic
    .com/magazine/archive/1862/06/walking/304674/. Thoreau's full sentence is
    "In wildness is the preservation of the world."
20 For one examination of how we conceptualize wilderness, see William Cronon,
    "The Trouble with Wilderness: Or, Getting Back to the Wrong Nature," *Envi-
    ronmental History* 1, no. 1 (1996): 7–28, https://faculty.washington.edu/timbillo/
    Readings%20and%20documents/Wilderness/Cronon%20The%20trouble
    %20with%20Wilderness.pdf.
21 John Knott, *Imagining the Forest: Narratives of Michigan and the Upper Midwest* (Ann
    Arbor: University of Michigan Press, 2012), 18.
22 Knott, 63.
23 Camden Burd, "Imagining a Pure Michigan Landscape: Advertisers, Tourists,
    and the Making of Michigan's Northern Vacationlands," *Michigan Historical
    Review* 42, no. 2 (2016): 35, https://doi.org/10.5342/michhistrevi.42.2.0031.
24 Knott, *Imagining the Forest*, 64.
25 Thanks to Jim Johnson, interpreter at the Hartwick Pines Logging Museum, and
    Hillary Pines, Northern Lower Peninsula historian for the Michigan Depart-
    ment of Natural Resources, for assistance in verifying these facts through per-
    sonal interviews on May 31 and June 4, 2021.
26 Ferris Jabr, "The Social Life of Forests," *New York Times Magazine*, December 2,
    2020, https://www.nytimes.com/interactive/2020/12/02/magazine/tree
    -communication-mycorrhiza.html. The figures are derived from "US Forest
    Facts and Historical Trends," US Department of Agriculture Forest Service, 2001,
    https://www.fia.fs.fed.us/library/brochures/docs/2000/ForestFactsMetric.pdf.
27 Knott, *Imagining the Forest*, 27.
28 Knott, 33.
29 Knott, 35.
30 The song "Michigan-I-O" and nine others have been arranged and recorded,
    based on Alan Lomax's archived recordings, by Michigan musicians as part of
    the Michigan-I-O project. Recordings and information available at https://www
    .michiganio.com.
31 Stewart Edward White, *The Riverman* (New York: Doubleday, 1909), 113, qtd. in
    Knott, *Imagining the Forest*, 109.
32 Knott, *Imagining the Forest*, 109.
33 "MI Vegetation circa 1800 Viewer," Michigan Natural Features Inventory, accessed
    May 24, 2021, https://mnfi.maps.arcgis.com/apps/StorytellingSwipe/index.html
    ?appid=c285e9eab9774c77a36d8726474fa408.
34 This scheme is based on Raymond Williams, "Dominant, Residual, and Emer-
    gent," in *Marxism and Literature* (Oxford: Oxford University Press, 1978), chap. 8.
35 The most up-to-date statistics on public opinion on climate change are
    available at the Yale Program on Climate Change Communication website,
    https://climatecommunication.yale.edu/.
36 Richard Rohr, *The Universal Christ: How a Forgotten Reality Can Change Everything
    We See, Hope for, and Believe* (New York: Convergent, 2019), 247.
37 Barbara Brown Taylor, "Evolving Faith and the Wilderness," Evolving Faith
    Conference, Denver, CO, October 4, 2019.

38 Ellen Davis points out that the Hebrews did not likely enjoy meat themselves, since meat was reserved for the wealthy. Thus the Hebrews' complaints to Moses seem especially foolish. Ellen F. Davis, *Scripture, Culture, Agriculture: An Agrarian Reading of the Bible* (New York: Cambridge, 2009), 70.

39 Belden Lane, *The Solace of Fierce Landscapes: Exploring Desert and Mountain Spirituality* (Oxford: Oxford University Press, 1998), 67.

40 For an account of the "deep adaptation" approach, which proposes that disaster is inevitable and we must simply prepare for the end of civilization, see Jonah E. Bromwich, "The Darkest Timeline," *New York Times*, December 26, 2020, https://www.nytimes.com/2020/12/26/style/climate-change-deep-adaptation.html.

41 Chuck DeGroat, *Leaving Egypt: Finding God in the Wilderness Places* (Grand Rapids, MI: Square Inch, 2011), 129.

42 Tom Boogaart, professor emeritus, Western Theological Seminary, "Lecture on the Tabernacle," provided through personal correspondence.

43 There are many sources and translations for the O Antiphons. This is adapted from a version used at Western Theological Seminary in Holland, Michigan.

Chapter 2

1 Amy Leach, "God," in *Things That Are: Essays* (Minneapolis, MN: Milkweed Editions, 2012), 99–101. For a performance in which Amy Leach reads the essay and plays background music on the violin, see Milkweed Editions, "'God' by Amy Leach | Book Video for Things That Are," YouTube video, June 7, 2012, https://www.youtube.com/watch?v=8AxEnPNS7jk.

2 Gunnar Keppel et al., "Refugia: Identifying and Understanding Safe Havens for Biodiversity under Climate Change," *Global Ecology and Biogeography* 21, no. 4 (2012): 394. This article is foundational for the modern study of refugia science.

3 William Allen, "Plant Blindness," *BioScience* 53, no. 10 (2003): 926.

4 Richard Louv, *Last Child in the Woods: Saving Our Children from Nature-Deficit Disorder* (Chapel Hill, NC: Algonquin Books, 2003).

5 A recent report on environmental justice in my city notes, among many other factors, the lack of green space in stressed urban neighborhoods as a matter of environmental justice. The conclusion of the report also lists the "Principles of Environmental Justice" drafted in 1991 during the First National People of Color Environmental Leadership Summit (LINC UP / Detroiters Working for Environmental Justice, *Neighborhood Environmental Action Report: Health, Environment and Race in Grand Rapids*, April 2019).

6 The Covid-19 pandemic helped raise awareness of the ways in which lower-income people and people of color have long been exposed disproportionately to toxic waste and industrialized landscapes. See, for example, Hiroko Tabuchi, "In the Shadows of America's Smokestacks, Virus Is One More Deadly Risk," *New York Times*, May 17, 2020, https://www.nytimes.com/2020/05/17/climate/pollution-poverty-coronavirus.html.

7 For a history of the environmental justice movement, see Dorceta E. Taylor, *Toxic Communities: Environmental Racism, Industrial Pollution, and Residential Mobility* (New York: New York University Press, 2014); and Robert D. Bullard, *Unequal*

Protection: Environmental Justice and Communities of Color (San Francisco: Sierra Club Books, 1994); as well as other works by these authors.

8 Marguerite L. Spencer, "Environmental Racism and Black Theology: James H. Cone Instructs Us on Whiteness," *University of St. Thomas Law Journal* 5, no. 1 (2008): 288–311.

9 Edward O. Wilson, *Biophilia* (Cambridge, MA: Harvard University Press, 1984), 1.

10 Lynn White Jr., "The Historical Roots of Our Ecological Crisis," *Science* 155, no. 3767 (1967): 1203–7, https://science.sciencemag.org/content/155/3767/1203. Also available as a PDF here: https://www.cmu.ca/faculty/gmatties/lynnwhiterootsofcrisis.pdf.

11 White, 1206.

12 White, 1206.

13 H. Paul Santmire, *The Travail of Nature: The Ambiguous Ecological Promise of Christian Theology* (Minneapolis, MN: Fortress, 1985).

14 Steven Bouma-Prediger makes a similar point in *For the Beauty of the Earth: A Christian Vision for Creation Care* (Grand Rapids, MI: Baker Academic, 2001), 124.

15 Keppel et al., "Refugia," 394.

16 These principles are explained in David D. Ackerly, "Topoclimates, Refugia, and Biotic Responses to Climate Change," *Frontiers in Ecology and the Environment* 18, no. 5 (2020): 288–97, https://esajournals.onlinelibrary.wiley.com/doi/10.1002/fee.2204.

17 Santmire, *Travail of Nature*, 9, 13–29.

18 Dante Alighieri, *The Divine Comedy, Paradiso*, canto 33, lines 85–93, in *The Portable Dante*, trans. and ed. Mark Musa (New York: Penguin, 1995), 583.

19 Huston Smith, *Forgotten Truth: The Common Vision of the World's Religions* (New York: HarperOne, 1997), esp. chaps. 2 and 3.

20 Santmire, *Travail of Nature*, 8–10.

21 This phrase is from Watson, *Back to Nature*, 48. Watson describes Gnosticism as a "dyspeptic version of deep ecology."

22 The phrase is from Calvin's commentary on the book of Hebrews, chap. 11, v. 3. Calvin speaks of the glory of God revealed in creation in *Institutes* I.v and throughout his writings, also referring to the world as a "shining theater," "glittering theater," and "most beautiful theater" (Calvin, *Institutes of the Christian Religion*, I.i.1, I.v.8, I.vi.2, I.xiv.20). He also uses metaphors of a palace, mansion, and mirror, among others. For a useful summary of Calvin's view of creation, as well as an argument against a view of Calvin as antimaterialist, see David O. Taylor, *The Theater of God's Glory: Calvin, Creation, and the Liturgical Arts* (Grand Rapids, MI: Eerdmans, 2017), esp. chap. 2. For a more extended treatment of Calvin's creation theology, see Susan E. Schreiner, *The Theater of His Glory: Nature and the Natural Order in the Thought of John Calvin* (Grand Rapids, MI: Baker, 2001).

23 Willie James Jennings, *The Christian Imagination: Theology and the Origins of Race* (New Haven, CT: Yale University Press, 2010). Liberation theology has, of course, an extensive and varied literature. For one of the founding texts, see Gustavo Gutiérrez, *A Theology of Liberation: History, Politics, and Salvation*, trans. and ed. Caridad Inda and John Eagleson (Maryknoll, NY: Orbis, 1988). For an example of how liberation theology continues to be debated in the United States, see Raphael G. Warnock, *The Divided Mind of the Black Church: Theology, Piety, and Public Witness* (New York: New York University Press, 2013).

24   Milton, *Paradise Lost*, bk. 3, line 99.

25   Milton, bk. 2, line 1052.

26   Rohr, *Universal Christ*, 62.

27   Tucker, *Worldly Wonder*, 45.

28   Rohr, *Universal Christ*, 50.

29   Godfrey Goodman, *The Creatures Praysing God: or The Religion of Dumbe Creatures* (1622), qtd. in David Glimp, "Figuring Belief: George Herbert's Devotional Creatures," in *Go Figure: Energies, Forms, and Institutions in the Early Modern World*, ed. Judith A. Anderson and Joan Pong Linton (New York: Fordham University Press, 2011), 120.

30   Suzanne W. Simard et al., "Net Transfer of Carbon between Ectomycorrhizal Tree Species in the Field," *Nature* 388 (1997): 579–82. The term *wood wide web* appears to have been coined in T. Helgason et al., "Ploughing Up the Wood-Wide Web?," *Nature* 394 (1998): 431, which cites Simard et al.'s work.

31   For a brief introduction, see Robert Macfarlane, "The Secrets of the Wood Wide Web," *New Yorker*, August 7, 2016, https://www.newyorker.com/tech/annals-of -technology/the-secrets-of-the-wood-wide-web. A more extensive account of the science is presented in Jabr, "Social Life of Forests." Macfarlane offers another helpful description of the wood wide web in "Understorey," a chapter in *Underland: A Deep Time Journey* (New York: W. W. Norton, 2019), 87–116. Suzanne Simard provides a detailed account of her scientific work over decades in her memoir, *Finding the Mother Tree: Discovering the Wisdom of the Forest* (New York: Alfred A. Knopf, 2021).

32   Claire Marshall, "Wood Wide Web: Trees' Social Networks Are Mapped," BBC News, May 15, 2019, https://www.bbc.com/news/science-environment -48257315.

33   The term was coined by botanist Lynn Margulis in Lynn R. Margulis and Rene Fester, eds., *Symbiosis as a Source of Evolutionary Innovation: Speciation and Morphgenesis* (Boston: MIT Press, 1991).

34   For one example of how recent scientific work has verified quantum entanglement, see Jennifer Chu, "Light from Ancient Quasars Helps Confirm Quantum Entanglement," *MIT News*, Massachusetts Institute of Technology, August 19, 2018, https://news.mit.edu/2018/light-ancient-quasars-helps-confirm-quantum -entanglement-0820. For an accessible explanation of entanglement, see Frank Wilczek, "Entanglement Made Simple," *Quanta Magazine*, April 28, 2016, https:// www.quantamagazine.org/entanglement-made-simple-20160428.

35   David Abram, "Creaturely Migrations on a Breathing Planet," in *Living Earth Community: Multiple Ways of Being and Knowing*, ed. Sam Mickey, Mary Evelyn Tucker, and John Grim (Cambridge: Open Book, 2020), 16–17.

36   Santmire, *Travail of Nature*, 130.

37   Qtd. in Rasmussen, *Earth-Honoring Faith*, 291.

38   H. Paul Santmire introduces the metaphor of a magnet in his discussion of Pierre Teilhard de Chardin. See Santmire, *Nature Reborn*, 52.

Chapter 3

1 "Maritime Museum," Sleeping Bear Dunes, National Park Service, accessed August 31, 2021, https://www.nps.gov/slbe/planyourvisit/maritimemusem.htm.

2 Sallie McFague, "New House Rules: Christianity, Economics, and Planetary Living," in "Religion and Ecology: Can the Climate Change?," ed. Mary Evelyn Tucker and John A. Grim, special issue, *Daedalus* 130, no. 4 (Fall 2001): 125–40.

3 The fossil fuel industry in particular has coordinated with conservative religious leaders to promote the idea that any curtailment of the free market will hurt the poor and that God will not let fossil fuels hurt the earth, and to police legislators who resist this view. See Brendan O'Connor, "How Fossil Fuel Money Made Climate Denial the Word of God," *Splinter*, August 8, 2017, https://splinternews.com/how-fossil-fuel-money-made-climate-denial-the-word-of-g-1797466298.

4 McFague, "New House Rules," 126.

5 New York Times Events, "Climate Change | Supporting Net Zero through a Circular Economy," *New York Times* Climate Hub, YouTube video, May 20, 2021, 47:00, https://www.youtube.com/watch?v=kVuobyENqoE. The expert cited is Martijn Lopes Cardozo, CEO of Circle Economy. For a brief and insightful analysis of how businesses are adjusting to a zero-carbon economy, see Robinson Meyer, "How the U.S. Made Progress on Climate Change without Ever Passing a Bill," *Atlantic*, June 16, 2021, https://www.theatlantic.com/science/archive/2021/06/climate-change-green-vortex-america/619228/.

6 Randy Woodley, *Shalom and the Community of Creation: An Indigenous Vision* (Grand Rapids, MI: Eerdmans, 2012), 40.

7 Steve Bouma-Prediger, "From Stewardship to Earthkeeping: Why We Should Move beyond Stewardship," in *Beyond Stewardship: New Approaches to Creation Care*, ed. David Paul Warners and Matthew Kuperus Heun (Grand Rapids, MI: Calvin, 2019), 81–91. See also Bouma-Prediger, *For the Beauty of the Earth*.

8 Tarvarious Haywood, "Battle over Saugatuck Dunes Development Still Heated after a Two-Year Fight," News Channel 3, August 8, 2019, https://wwmt.com/news/local/battle-over-saugatuck-dunes-development-still-heated-after-a-two-year-fight. The group striving to protect the area is the Saugatuck Dunes Coastal Alliance, https://saugatuckdunescoastalalliance.com/northshore-development/.

9 O'Connor, "Fossil Fuel Money."

10 Walter Brueggemann, *Genesis: Interpretation: A Bible Commentary for Teaching and Preaching* (Louisville, KY: Westminster John Knox, 1982), 16. The following paragraphs draw from pp. 1–54.

11 Some of the parallels between the Genesis stories and the Anishinaabe origin stories are remarkable, including the way names create relationship between Nanabozho and the creatures, for example. For one version of these stories, see Robin Wall Kimmerer, *Braiding Sweetgrass: Indigenous Wisdom, Scientific Knowledge, and the Teachings of Plants* (Minneapolis, MN: Milkweed Editions, 2013), 208.

12 John L. Thompson, ed., *Old Testament I: Genesis 1–11*, Reformation Commentary on Scripture (Downers Grove, IL: InterVarsity, 2012), 97–99.

13 For some examples of both ravished praises and fears, see Santmire, *Travail of Nature*.

14 Theodore Hiebert, *The Yahwist's Landscape: Nature and Religion in Early Israel* (Oxford: Oxford University Press, 1996), 60. Randy Woodley offers a similar reading of this passage and based his reading on Cree theologian Ray Aldred (Woodley, *Shalom*, 51).

15 Alexander Schmemann, *For the Life of the World: Sacraments and Orthodoxy* (Crestwood, NY: St. Vladimir's Seminary Press, 1988), 15.

16 Brueggemann, *Genesis*, 8.

17 Kimmerer, *Braiding Sweetgrass*, 341–47.

18 Kimmerer, 346.

19 Kimmerer, 346.

20 Kimmerer, 368.

21 Kimmerer, 48.

22 Kimmerer, 124.

23 Hildegard of Bingen, *Causae et curae*, in *Hildegard of Bingen on Natural Philosophy and Medicine*, trans. Margret Berger (Cambridge: D. S. Brewer, 1999), 25.

24 Kimmerer, *Braiding Sweetgrass*, 189.

25 For a presettlement history of Michigan, see Charles E. Cleland, *Rites of Conquest: The History and Culture of Michigan's Native Americans* (Ann Arbor: University of Michigan Press, 1992).

26 Diane Stalberg et al., "Climate-Change Refugia in Boreal North America: What, Where, and for How Long?," *Frontiers in Ecology and the Environment* 18, no. 5 (2020): 261.

27 The issue is available with open access at https://esajournals.onlinelibrary.wiley .com/toc/15409309/2020/18/5.

28 Joseph L. Ebersole et al., "Managing Climate Refugia for Freshwater Fishes under an Expanding Human Footprint," *Frontiers in Ecology and the Environment* 18, no. 5 (2020): 274.

29 James H. Thorne et al., "Vegetation Refugia Can Inform Climate-Adaptive Land Management under Global Warming," *Frontiers in Ecology and the Environment* 18, no. 5 (2020): 281–87.

30 Richard Bauckham, *Living with Other Creatures: Green Exegesis and Theology* (Waco, TX: Baylor University Press, 2011), 62. Bauckham offers a helpful history of how both dominion and stewardship have been understood in the West.

31 Emma Marris, "To Keep the Planet Flourishing, 30% of Earth Needs Protection by 2030," *National Geographic*, January 31, 2019, https://www.nationalgeographic .com/environment/2019/01/conservation-groups-call-for-protecting-30 -percent-earth-2030/.

32 Emma Marris, "This Map Shows Where on Earth Humans Aren't," *National Geographic*, June 5, 2020, https://www.nationalgeographic.com/science/article/ where-people-arent.

33 Marris, "To Keep the Planet Flourishing."

34 Marris, "This Map Shows." For a book-length treatment of why these ambitious protection goals are needed and how they can be achieved in North America in particular, see Tony Hiss, *Rescuing the Planet: Protecting Half the Land to Heal the Earth* (New York: Alfred A. Knopf, 2021).

35 For a brief account of the Curtis Prairie project, see "Curtis Prairie: 75-Year-Old Restoration Research Site," Arboretum Leaflets, University of Wisconsin–Madison,

August 2008, https://arboretum.wisc.edu/content/uploads/2015/04/16_ArbLeaflet
.pdf; "Embattled Curtis Prairie a Test Bed for New Restoration Techniques,"
University of Wisconsin–Madison News, July 6, 2005, https://news.wisc.edu/
embattled-curtis-prairie-a-test-bed-for-new-restoration-techniques/; and Corey
Ritterbusch, "Curtis Prairie: First Prairie Restoration Is Going Strong," *Journal Stan-*
dard, March 15, 2013, https://www.journalstandard.com/article/20130315/NEWS/
303159922.

36 Aldo Leopold, "Conservation," in *Round River: From the Journals of Aldo Leopold*, ed.
Luna B. Leopold (Oxford: Oxford University Press, 1993), 147.

37 Aldo Leopold, "The Land Ethic," in *A Sand County Almanac: And Sketches Here and*
There (Oxford: Oxford University Press, 1987), 224–25.

38 Leopold, *Sand County Almanac*, 90.

39 Marie Orttenburger, "From Turf Grass to Tallgrass," Land Conservancy of
West Michigan, July 15, 2019, https://naturenearby.org/from-turf-grass-to
-tallgrass/.

August—Sleeping Bear Point, Michigan

1 P. J. Higman and M. R. Penskar, "*Cirsium pitcheri*," Michigan Natural Features
Inventory, 2004, https://mnfi.anr.msu.edu/abstracts/botany/Cirsium_pitcheri
.pdf.

Chapter 4

1 While it's possible that others devised this term simultaneously, the originator
I am aware of is Benjamin D. Crosby.

2 Robin Barnes, "Stirring, Shaking, and Flooding: Apocalyptic Visions and the
Reformation Explosion," in *Stirring the World: German Printmaking in the Age of*
Luther, ed. Henry Luttikhuizen (Grand Rapids, MI: Calvin College Center Art
Gallery, 2017), 14–15.

3 Annie Dillard, *Pilgrim at Tinker Creek* (New York: Harper Perennial, 2007), 232.

4 Dillard, 245.

5 Thor Arthur Hansen, "Cretaceous Period," *Encyclopaedia Britannica*, accessed
June 8, 2021, https://www.britannica.com/science/Cretaceous-Period. See also
"Why the Dinosaurs' Extinction Is an Ongoing Puzzle," *National Geographic*, July 3,
2020, https://video.nationalgeographic.com/video/science/nat-geo-explores/
00000173-11a4-de99-ad7b-1ba5eba00000.

6 Elizabeth Kolbert, *The Sixth Extinction: An Unnatural History* (New York: Picador,
2015), 4–8. The paper Kolbert cites is David B. Wake and Vance T. Vredenburg,
"Are We in the Midst of the Sixth Mass Extinction? A View from the World
of Amphibians," *PNAS* 105, suppl. 1 (2008): 11466–73, https://www.pnas.org/
content/105/Supplement_1/11466.

7 Kolbert, *Sixth Extinction*, 17.

8 "Summary Statistics," IUCN Red List, International Union for Conservation of
Nature, accessed June 8, 2021, https://www.iucnredlist.org/resources/summary
-statistics.

9　For a brief explanation of background extinction rate and how it is calculated, see Kolbert, *Sixth Extinction*, 15–18.

10　"Extinct Species, Explained," *National Geographic*, February 5, 2019, https://www .nationalgeographic.com/animals/reference/extinct-species/.

11　The phrase is from Alfred, Lord Tennyson's 1850 poem, "In Memoriam, A. H. H.," canto 56.

12　For a simple introduction to the "Great Pacific Garbage Patch," see "What Is the Great Pacific Garbage Patch?," National Ocean Service, February 2, 2021, https://oceanservice.noaa.gov/facts/garbagepatch.html. The United States is a particularly large contributor to plastic waste in the ocean (Kara Lavender Law et al., "The United States' Contribution of Plastic Waste to Land and Ocean," *Science Advances* 6, no. 44 [2020], https://advances.sciencemag.org/content/6/ 44/eabd0288). On plastics in our bodies, see Roman Lehner et al., "Emergence of Nanoplastic in the Environment and Possible Impact on Human Health," *Environmental Science and Technology* 53, no. 4 (2019): 1748–65, https://pubs.acs .org/doi/pdf/10.1021/acs.est.8b05512.

13　Kolbert, *Sixth Extinction*, 114. For a fuller account of ocean acidification, see Ove Hoegh-Guldberg et al., "The Ocean," in *Climate Change 2014: Impacts, Adaptation, and Vulnerability. Part B: Regional Aspects*, IPCC (Cambridge: Cambridge University Press, 2014), 1655–731, https://www.ipcc.ch/site/assets/uploads/2018/02/ WGIIAR5-Chap30_FINAL.pdf.

14　This summary appeared in Marris, "To Keep the Planet Flourishing." Marris cites Yinon M. Bar-On, Rob Phillips, and Ron Milo, "The Biomass Distribution on Earth," *PNAS* 115, no. 25 (2018): 6506–11, https://www.pnas.org/content/115/ 25/6506.

15　Robert P. Harrison, "Toward a Philosophy of Nature," in *Uncommon Ground: Rethinking the Human Place in Nature*, ed. William Cronon (New York: Norton, 1996), 486. This term is sometimes credited to Michael Vincent McGinnis, who cites Harrison and provides an expanded definition in a chapter coauthored with Freeman House and William Jordan III, "Bioregional Restoration: Re-establishing an Ecology of Shared Identity," in *Bioregionalism*, ed. Michael Vincent McGinnis (New York: Routledge, 1999).

16　Robert Macfarlane, Twitter post, September 4, 2018, 2:00 a.m., https://twitter .com/RobGMacfarlane/status/1036856458044948480.

17　Leopold, *Round River*, 165.

18　Kimmerer, *Braiding Sweetgrass*, 346.

19　Frederica Perera, "Pollution from Fossil-Fuel Combustion Is the Leading Environmental Threat to Global Pediatric Health and Equity: Solutions Exist," *International Journal of Environmental Research and Public Health* 15, no. 1 (2018): 16, https://www.ncbi.nlm.nih.gov/pmc/articles/PMC5800116/.

20　*The Flint Water Crisis: Systemic Racism Through the Lens of Flint*, Michigan Civil Rights Commission, February 17, 2012, https://www.michigan.gov/documents/ mdcr/VFlintCrisisRep-F-Edited3-13-17_554317_7.pdf.

21　Somini Sengupta, "Even amid a Pandemic, More Than 40 Million People Fled Their Homes," *New York Times*, May 20, 2021, https://www.nytimes.com/2021/ 05/20/climate/storms-floods-wildfires-displacement.html.

22 Oli Brown, "Migration and Climate Change," International Organization for Migra-
    tion, 2008, https://olibrown.org/wp-content/uploads/2019/01/2008-Migration
    -and-Climate-Change-IOM.pdf.

23 Nenad Jarić Dauenhauer, "On Front Line of Climate Change as Maldives Fights
    Rising Seas," *New Scientist*, March 20, 2017, https://www.newscientist.com/article/
    2125198-on-front-line-of-climate-change-as-maldives-fights-rising-seas/. For a
    comprehensive report on climate mitigation in the Maldives, see *National Adap-
    tation: Program of Action*, Ministry of Environment, Energy and Water, Republic
    of Maldives, 2007, https://unfccc.int/resource/docs/napa/mdv01.pdf.

24 Elizabeth Rush, *Rising: Dispatches from the New American Shore* (Minneapolis, MN:
    Milkweed Editions, 2018), 19–41.

25 "2019 State of U.S. High Tide Flooding with a 2020 Outlook," National Oceanic
    and Atmospheric Administration, July 2020, https://tidesandcurrents.noaa
    .gov/publications/Techrpt_092_2019_State_of_US_High_Tide_Flooding_with
    _a_2020_Outlook_30June2020.pdf.

26 Somini Sengupta, "'The City I Love' and Climate Change: A Miami Story," inter-
    view with Mario Alejandro Aliza, Climate Forward Newsletter, *New York Times*,
    July 15, 2020.

27 Glenn A. Albrecht, *Earth Emotions: New Words for a New World* (Ithaca, NY: Cor-
    nell University Press, 2019), 27–61.

28 Wendell Berry, "Christianity and the Survival of Creation," in *Sex, Economy, Free-
    dom, and Community* (New York: Pantheon, 1993), 98.

29 Francis, *Laudato si'*, sec. 21.

30 Francis, sec. 161.

31 Francis, sec. 33.

32 Francis, sec. 217.

33 Moore, *Great Tide Rising*, 9.

34 Moore, 285.

35 Moore, 161–62.

36 For more, see https://earthcharter.org.

37 Bill McKibben, "Dartmouth Baccalaureate Address," June 11, 2011, http://www
    .dartmouth.edu/~commence/news/speeches/2011/mckibben.html.

38 Josh Parks, "Bird Listening," *the postcalvin*, September 8, 2018, https://thepostcalvin
    .com/bird-listening/. Josh's essay is also available in deLacy et al., *post calvin*, 103.

39 William P. Brown, *Sacred Sense: Discovering the Wonder of God's Word and World*
    (Grand Rapids, MI: Eerdmans, 2015), 70, 77.

40 Moore, *Great Tide Rising*, 305.

41 Both Matthew Fox's and Pierre Teilhard de Chardin's views are conveniently
    summarized in Santmire, *Nature Reborn*, 53.

42 Santmire, 58–59.

43 Mary Annaïse Heglar, "Climate Change Isn't the First Existential Threat," *Zora*,
    February 19, 2019, https://zora.medium.com/sorry-yall-but-climate-change-ain
    -t-the-first-existential-threat-b3c999267aa0.

44 Wendell Berry, "No, No, There Is No Going Back," in *A Timbered Choir: The Sabbath
    Poems 1979–1997* (Washington, DC: Counterpoint, 1998), 167.

45 Cameron W. Barrows et al., "Validating Climate-Change Refugia: Empirical
    Bottom-Up Approaches to Support Management Actions," *Frontiers in Ecology*

and the Environment 18, no. 5 (2020): 298–306, https://esajournals.onlinelibrary .wiley.com/doi/10.1002/fee.2205.

46 McKibben, *End of Nature*, 182.

47 McKibben, *Eaarth*, 204.

48 Carl Safina makes a similar point in "The Moral Climate," in *Moral Ground: Ethical Action for a Planet in Peril*, ed. Kathleen Dean Moore and Michael P. Nelson (San Antonio, TX: Trinity University Press, 2010), 324–26.

49 J. R. R. Tolkien, *The Fellowship of the Ring* (New York: Houghton Mifflin, 1999), 348.

February—Grand Haven, Michigan

1 One explanation of ecomemory in an ecowomanist context is Melanie L. Harris, *Ecowomanism: African American Women and Earth-Honoring Faiths* (Maryknoll, NY: Orbis, 2017), loc. 555 of 2846, Kindle edition.

2 Wallace K. Ewing, *Destination: The Haven* (self-pub., 2019), PDF.

Chapter 5

1 Victoria Emily Jones, "She Mistook Him for the Gardener," *Art and Theology*, April 5, 2016, https://artandtheology.org/2016/04/05/she-mistook-him-for-the -gardener/.

2 Franco Mormando, "Christ in the Garden: An Easter Reflection on Fontana's 'Noli Me Tangere,'" *America*, April 20, 2009, https://www.americamagazine.org/ issue/694/fine-arts/christ-garden.

3 William P. Brown offers a lovely meditation on Jesus as gardener in *Sacred Sense*, 132–36.

4 Gordon D. Fee, *The First Epistle to the Corinthians* (Grand Rapids, MI: Eerdmans, 1987), 786. The section on 1 Cor 15 is 775–809.

5 Jones, "She Mistook Him for the Gardener."

6 Woodley, *Shalom*, 26.

7 Nurya Love Parish and Emily Ulmer, personal interview with the author, September 11, 2020. All quotations from Nurya and Emily in the following pages are from this interview.

8 Fred Bahnson, *Soil and Sacrament: A Spiritual Memoir of Food and Faith* (New York: Simon & Schuster, 2013).

9 Michael Pollan, *The Omnivore's Dilemma: A Natural History of Four Meals* (New York: Penguin, 2006).

10 "Climate Change and Land: Summary for Policymakers," IPCC, January 2020, https://www.ipcc.ch/srccl/chapter/summary-for-policymakers/, A.3.

11 "Managed Grazing," in *Drawdown: The Most Comprehensive Plan Ever Proposed to Reverse Global Warming*, ed. Paul Hawken (New York: Penguin, 2017), 72–74. See also "Managed Grazing: Technical Summary," Project Drawdown, accessed June 10, 2021, https://www.drawdown.org/solutions/managed-grazing/technical -summary.

12 This complex history is helpfully summarized in Pollan, *Omnivore's Dilemma*, 32–56.

13 One excellent source of examples is the *Mothers of Invention* podcast, esp. episodes 3.4 and 1.5. Available online at https://www.mothersofinvention.online/.

14 "2019 Organic Survey," National Agriculture Statistics Service, United States Department of Agriculture, https://www.nass.usda.gov/Publications/AgCensus/2017/Online_Resources/Organics/index.php, table 1. The 2011 figure can be found in the comparable report at https://downloads.usda.library.cornell.edu/usda-esmis/files/zg64tk92g/8623j1717/rb68xf642/OrganicProduction-10-04-2012.pdf.

15 "Managed Grazing: Technical Summary."

16 "About Eloheh," Eloheh Indigenous Center for Earth Justice, accessed June 10, 2021, https://www.eloheh.org/about.

17 For more on Eloheh Farm and Indigenous Center for Earth Justice, see https://www.eloheh.org. A little more of the Woodleys' story is summarized on Eloheh's Patreon page: https://www.patreon.com/posts/eloheh-story-25402627.

18 "Apocalypse Survival Skill #4: Braiding Seeds," *How to Survive the End of the World* podcast, April 23, 2020, https://www.endoftheworldshow.org. For more on Soul Fire Farm, see https://www.soulfirefarm.org.

19 Wendell Berry, "Manifesto: The Mad Farmer Liberation Front," in *New Collected Poems* (Berkeley, CA: Counterpoint, 2013), 173.

20 For a brief introduction to Hillside Paradise gardens, see KingCountyTV, "Transforming Parking Lots to Fight Water Pollution | King County Climate Action," YouTube video, August 26, 2020, https://www.youtube.com/watch?v=353k-yL5YTA.

21 Andy Rozendaal, personal interview with the author, March 4, 2021. An edited version of the interview is available at https://blog.reformedjournal.com/2021/03/27/farming-where-the-sidewalk-ends-andy-rozendaal-and-eighth-day-farm/.

22 "The Theology of Compost with Jeff Chu," *Evolving Faith* podcast, ep. 3, July 8, 2020, https://evolvingfaith.com/all-podcast-episodes/episode-3. The episode features a recording of the talk Jeff gave called "Some Thoughts on Compost and Worms," Evolving Faith Conference, Montreat, NC, October 26, 2018.

23 Douglas W. Tallamy, *Nature's Best Hope: A New Approach to Conservation That Starts in Your Yard* (Portland, OR: Timber Press, 2020).

24 Tallamy, 11.

25 Tallamy, 25.

26 Tallamy, 10.

27 Tallamy, 40.

28 Tallamy, 62.

29 Tallamy, 12.

30 Tallamy, 12–13.

31 Aldo Leopold, "Engineering and Conservation," in *The River of the Mother of God and Other Essays by Aldo Leopold*, ed. Susan L. Flader and J. Baird Callicott (Madison: University of Wisconsin Press, 1991), 254, qtd. in Tallamy, *Nature's Best Hope*, 26.

32 "History," Plaster Creek Stewards, Calvin University, accessed June 10, 2021, https://calvin.edu/plaster-creek-stewards/about/history/.

33 Albrecht, *Earth Emotions*, 121–24.

34 Bouma-Prediger, *For the Beauty of the Earth*, 76–77.

35 Bouma-Prediger provides a helpful summary of scholarship on this point (110–16).

36 Santmire, *Travail of Nature*, 72.

37 Brown, *Sacred Sense*, 136.

38 J. Christiaan Beker, *Paul the Apostle: The Triumph of God in Life and Thought* (Minneapolis, MN: Fortress, 1980), 33, 364, qtd. in Santmire, *Travail of Nature*, 210.

39 Brown, *Sacred Sense*, 136.

40 Kimmerer, *Braiding Sweetgrass*, 107.

41 Kimmerer, 108.

42 Kimmerer, 111.

43 Kimmerer, 115.

44 Kimmerer, 116. There is not a set, word-for-word version of the Thanksgiving Address, since every speaker or group improvises based on their ability and style. One version is available at https://americanindian.si.edu/environment/pdf/01_02_Thanksgiving_Address.pdf.

Chapter 6

1 The terms *gauzy* and *furzy* are the best words I've ever heard to describe a good, weedy lot. The words come from a poem by Mary Oliver, "The Best I Could Do," in *Why I Wake Early: New Poems* (Boston: Beacon Press, 2004), 54.

2 Grand Rapids WhiteWater, accessed June 16, 2021, http://www.grandrapids whitewater.org.

3 Kendra McNeil, "Meaningful Involvement: Local Grassroots Organizations Collaborate around Environmental Justice," Rapid Growth Media, March 19, 2020, https://www.rapidgrowthmedia.com/innovationnews/climate%20change _environmental%20justice.aspx. Another example of city-level climate action in Michigan is Ann Arbor's A2 Climate Partnership, which works to cut the city's carbon emissions, promote climate education, and improve public transit. For more, see "About," A2 Climate Project, accessed June 16, 2021, https://www.a2cp.org/ann-arbor-climate-partnership.

4 Hawken, *Drawdown*.

5 *Mothers of Invention* podcast, accessed June 16, 2021, https://www.mothersof invention.online.

6 For my discussion of this question with Bill McKibben, see "Momentum into the Next Thing: Bill McKibben on Fighting Overwhelming Odds and Praying through Mental Static," *Refugia Podcast*, ep. 15, October 3, 2020, https://debrarienstra .com/episode-15-momentum-into-the-next-thing-bill-mckibben-on-fighting -overwhelming-odds-and-praying-through-mental-static/.

7 See the Carbon Neutral Cities Alliance, accessed June 16, 2021, https://carbon neutralcities.org/cities/.

8 Marlise Simons, "Orthodox Leader Deepens Progressive Stance on Environment," *New York Times*, December 3, 2012, https://www.nytimes.com/2012/12/04/science/bartholomew-i-of-constantinoples-bold-green-stance.html.

9 Joan Huyser-Honig, "Green Congregations Become Centers of Creation Care and Renewal," Calvin Institute of Christian Worship, October 9, 2013, https://worship.calvin.edu/resources/resource-library/green-congregations-become -centers-of-creation-care-and-renewal.

10   Bill McKibben, "Where Do We Go from Here?," in Tucker and Grim, "Religion and Ecology," 302.

11   "History," Yale Forum on Religion and Ecology, accessed June 16, 2021, https:// fore.yale.edu/About-Us/What-We-Do/History.

12   These examples are from Lisa Wells, *Believers: Making a Life at the End of the World* (New York: Farrar, Straus & Giroux, 2021). An excerpt from the book appears as "Promised Lands" in *Orion*, Summer 2021, 66–73. The Mennonite couple is Todd Wynward and Peg Bartlett. Todd Wynward's book is *Rewilding the Way: Breaking Free to Follow an Untamed God* (Harrisonburg, VA: Herald Press, 2015). The New Monastic movement is related to these communities, though with less of an emphasis on environmental goals. For a brief summary of the New Monastic movement, see Jason Byassee, "The New Monastics: Alternative Christian Communities," *Christian Century*, October 18, 2005, https://www.christiancentury.org/article/2005-10/ new-monastics.

13   Iona Community, accessed June 16, 2021, https://iona.org.uk. For more on the Iona Community, see "Kites and Kingfishers: Ruth Harvey on the Iona Community and Emerging Patterns," *Refugia Podcast*, ep. 16, October 10, 2020, https://debrarienstra .com/episode-16-kites-and-kingfishers-ruth-harvey-on-the-iona-community -and-emerging-patterns/.

14   This is the temptation, in my view, to which the so-called Benedict Option succumbs. See Dreher, *Benedict Option*.

15   Gail Ramshaw, *God beyond Gender: Feminist Christian God-Language* (Minneapolis, MN: Fortress, 1995), 59–74.

16   Ramshaw, 65–66.

17   The previous paragraphs are adapted from Debra Rienstra and Ron Rienstra, *Worship Words: Discipling Language for Faithful Ministry* (Grand Rapids, MI: Baker Academic, 2009), 150–52.

18   Libby Howe, "Reflections on the Lectionary, November 22, Reign of Christ," *Christian Century*, November 4, 2020, 23.

19   I am not qualified to write about this tradition, but Barbara Holmes describes the powerful symbolism and experience of the "ring shout" in the Black American church. See Barbara A. Holmes, *Joy Unspeakable: Contemplative Practices and the Black Church* (Minneapolis, MN: Augsburg Fortress, 2004), 60–69.

20   Heidelberg Catechism, Lord's Day 10, question 27.

21   The phrase is from the delightful description of Gen 1:1 in Brown, *Sacred Sense*, 17–18.

22   Richard Powers, *The Overstory* (New York: Norton, 2018), 285.

23   Sy Montgomery, "Deep Intellect: Inside the Mind of an Octopus," *Orion*, November/December 2011. For a beautiful story of one man's relationship with a single wild octopus, see Pippa Ehrlich and James Reed, dirs., *My Octopus Teacher* (Netflix, 2020).

24   C. Evangelista et al., "Honeybee Navigation: Critically Examining the Role of the Polarization Compass," *Philosophical Transactions of the Royal Society B* 369, no. 1636 (February 19, 2014), https://doi.org/10.1098/rstb.2013.0037.

25   Bauckham, *Living with Other Creatures*, 154 and 132.

26   Pope Francis, *Fratelli tutti*, Vatican Publishing House, October 3, 2020, sec. 8, http://www.vatican.va/content/francesco/en/encyclicals/documents/papa -francesco_20201003_enciclica-fratelli-tutti.html.

27 "Line 5 Easement Revoked," *Speaking of Resilience* podcast, Groundwork Center for Resilient Communities, ep. 15, November 13, 2020, https://www.ground workcenter.org/podcast/.

28 David J. Schwab, "Statistical Analysis of Straits of Mackinac Line 5: Worst Case Spill Scenarios," University of Michigan Water Center, March 2016, http://graham .umich.edu/media/pubs/Mackinac-Line-5-Worst-Case-Spill-Scenarios.pdf.

29 The basic facts are gathered with links to official documents at "Gov. Whitmer and DNR Revoke Line 5 Easement," Oil & Water Don't Mix, November 13, 2020, https://www.oilandwaterdontmix.org/gov_whitmer_and_dnr_revoke_line_5 _easement. For an account of how Michigan does and does not benefit from the liquids passing through the pipeline, see Beth LeBlanc, "What a Line 5 Shutdown Would Mean for Michigan's Energy," *Detroit News*, December 19, 2019, https:// www.detroitnews.com/story/news/politics/2019/12/19/what-line-5-shutdown -means-michigan-energy-enbridge/4334264002/.

30 Berry, *Great Work*, 121.

31 Robert Macfarlane, "Should This Tree Have the Same Rights as You?," *Guardian*, November 2, 2019, https://www.theguardian.com/books/2019/nov/02/trees -have-rights-too-robert-macfarlane-on-the-new-laws-of-nature.

32 Dan Egan, *The Death and Life of the Great Lakes* (New York: Norton, 2017), 212–44.

33 Aldo Leopold, "The Land Ethic," in *A Sand County Almanac* (Oxford: Oxford University Press, 1949), 213.

34 Macfarlane, "Should This Tree Have the Same Rights?"

35 McKibben, "Where Do We Go from Here?," 302.

36 "About 350," 350.org, accessed June 17, 2021, https://350.org/about/. McKibben recounts 350.org's origin story in *Oil and Honey: The Education of an Unlikely Activist* (New York: Times Books, 2013).

37 Plumer, "Carbon Dioxide."

38 "The Next 10," 350.org, accessed June 17, 2021, https://350.org/10-years/.

39 To read numerous influential figures making a persuasive case for the Green New Deal, see Varshini Prakash and Guido Girgenti, eds., *Winning the Green New Deal: Why We Must, How We Can* (New York: Simon & Schuster, 2020). Also see "Recognizing the Duty of the Federal Government to Create a Green New Deal," Congressional Resolution, H.R. 109, 116th Cong., 1st Session (2019), https:// congress.gov/116/bills/hres109/BILLS-116hres109ih.pdf.

40 "New Generation Rising: Kyle Meyaard-Schaap on Young Evangelicals and the Climate Crisis," *Refugia Podcast*, ep. 5, October 11, 2019, https://debrarienstra.com/ episode-5-new-generation-rising-kyle-meyaard-schaap-on-young-evangelicals -and-the-climate-crisis/.

41 "Where Beauty Is Happening: Katerina Parsons on International Development, Ripple Effects, and Hunger for Deep Roots" and "Imaginative and Messy: Kathryn Mae Post on Religion Journalism and Reconstructing Faith," *Refugia Podcast*, ep. 18, October 24, 2020, and ep. 20, November 7, 2020, https://debrarienstra.com/ episode-18-where-beauty-is-happening-katerina-parsons-on-international -development-ripple-effects-and-hunger-for-deep-roots/, https://debrarienstra .com/episode-20-imaginative-and-messy-kathryn-mae-post-on-religion -journalism-and-reconstructing-faith/.

42 Fred Bahnson, "The Church Forests of Ethiopia: A Mystical Geography," *Emergence Magazine*, February 2020, https://emergencemagazine.org/story/the-church-forests-of-ethiopia/. For another account of Ethiopia's church forests, see Maheder Haileselassie Tadese, "Ethiopians Make Progress Restoring Precious Church Forests," *Mongabay*, October 31, 2018, https://news.mongabay.com/2018/10/land-restoration-makes-progress-in-ethiopia/.

43 Bahnson, "Church Forests of Ethiopia."

44 Alejandra Borunda, "Ethiopia's 'Church Forests' Are Incredible Oases of Green," *National Geographic*, January 18, 2019, https://www.nationalgeographic.com/environment/2019/01/ethiopian-church-forest-conservation-biodiversity/.

45 "About the UN Decade," UN Decade on Ecosystem Restoration, accessed June 17, 2021, https://www.decadeonrestoration.org/about-un-decade.

46 "The Role of Faith-Based Organizations in Ecosystem Restoration," UN Environment Programme, December 2, 2020, https://www.unep.org/events/webinar/role-faith-based-organizations-ecosystem-restoration.

47 Jabr, "Social Life of Forests."

48 Bahnson, "Church Forests of Ethiopia."

Chapter 7

1 William Shakespeare, *As You like It*, in *The Complete Works of Shakespeare*, ed. David Bevington, 4th ed. (London: Longman, 1997), 299.

2 William Shakespeare, *Hamlet*, in Bevington, *Complete Works of Shakespeare*, 3.1.72.

3 Bahnson, "Church Forests of Ethiopia."

4 "Dreaming of Eloheh: Randy Woodley on Following the Harmony Way," *Refugia Podcast*, ep. 17, October 17, 2020, https://debrarienstra.com/episode-17-dreaming-of-eloheh-randy-woodley-on-following-the-harmony-way/.

5 The most recent IPCC report specifies what we can expect in the next century and beyond based on five climate models, depending on how much we are able to reduce greenhouse gas emissions. See IPCC, "Summary for Policymakers."

6 For a helpful discussion of what climate models predict on this level of specificity, see "Apocalyptic Narratives, Climate Date, and Hope, with Zeke Hausfather and Diego Arguedas Ortis," *Warm Regards* podcast, December 28, 2020, https://warmregardspodcast.com/episodes/apocalyptic-narratives-climate-data-and-hope-with-s1!f8331.

7 Qtd. in Kevin O'Sullivan, "Climate Crisis May Trigger Recessions like One Caused by Covid, Scientist Predicts," *Irish Times*, May 19, 2021, https://www.irishtimes.com/news/environment/climate-crisis-may-trigger-recessions-like-one-caused-by-covid-scientist-predicts-1.4569345.

8 "Weathering the Storms with Dr. Katherine Hayhoe," *No Place like Home* podcast, ep. 16, September 9, 2017, https://soundcloud.com/noplacelikehome/16-weathering-the-storms.

9 Krista Tippett, "Ta-Nehisi Coates: Imagining a New America," *On Being* podcast, ep. 762, November 16, 2017, https://onbeing.org/programs/ta-nehisi-coates-imagining-a-new-america/, 15:00–20:00.

10 Ta-Nehisi Coates, *Between the World and Me* (New York: Spiegel & Grau, 2015), 108.

11 Austin Channing Brown, *I'm Still Here: Black Dignity in a World Made for Whiteness* (New York: Convergent, 2018), 178.

12 Brown, 178–80.

13 Moore, *Great Tide Rising*, 114.

14 Moore, 318.

15 Jemar Tisby gives an account of the White church's strategic use of the Bible to perpetuate slavery in *The Color of Compromise: The Truth about the American Church's Complicity in Racism* (Grand Rapids, MI: Zondervan, 2019), esp. chap. 5.

16 For real Christian scholarship on this major Christian virtue in an ecological context, see Steve Bouma-Prediger, *Earthkeeping and Character: Exploring a Christian Biblical Virtue Ethic* (Grand Rapids, MI: Baker Academic, 2019), chap. 5.

17 Ayana Elizabeth Johnson and Katharine K. Wilkinson, eds., *All We Can Save: Truth, Courage, and Solutions for the Climate Crisis* (New York: Penguin Random House, 2020).

18 Christina Pinkola Estés, "Letter to a Young Activist during Troubled Times," Maven Productions, accessed June 18, 2021, https://www.mavenproductions .com/letter-to-a-young-activist.

19 T. S. Eliot, "East Coker," in *Four Quartets* (San Diego, CA: Harvest/HBJ, 1971), 31.

20 T. S. Eliot, "Dry Salvages," in *Four Quartets*, 45.

21 Willie James Jennings, "Building Life beyond Whiteness," talk for Reimagining Black History Month, Calvin University, February 4, 2020.

22 Debra Rienstra, *So Much More: An Invitation to Christian Spirituality* (Hoboken, NJ: Wiley, 2003), 175.

23 "Butterflies and Moths of Michigan," Insect Identification, accessed June 18, 2021, https://www.insectidentification.org/insects-by-type-and-region.php?thisState =michigan&thisType=Butterfly%20or%20Moth.

24 Amanda Ellis, "Dazzling and Deadly—Meet the Spun Glass Caterpillar," Roaring Earth, accessed June 18, 2021, https://roaring.earth/dazzling-and-deadly -the-spun-glass-caterpillar/.

25 Krishna Ramanujan, "Armor on Butterfly Wings Protects against Heavy Rain," *Cornell Chronicle*, June 8, 2020, https://news.cornell.edu/stories/2020/06/armor -butterfly-wings-protects-against-heavy-rain.

26 John Muir, *The Yosemite* (New York: Century, 1912); Rachel Carson, *The Sense of Wonder: A Celebration of Nature for Parents and Children* (New York: Harper & Row, 1965); Annie Dillard, *Pilgrim at Tinker Creek* (New York: Harper & Row, 1974). Mary Oliver published dozens of poetry collections, including *Why I Wake Early* and *Thirst* (Boston: Beacon Press, 2006).

27 Bouma-Prediger, *Earthkeeping and Character*, 29–50.

28 Moore, *Great Tide Rising*, 79. The phrase "joyous attention" is the title of the chapter beginning on p. 75.

29 Kimmerer, *Braiding Sweetgrass*, 222.

30 Tucker, *Worldly Wonder*, 11–12.

31 Robert Macfarlane and Jackie Morris, *The Lost Words: A Spell Book* (New York: Penguin, 2017). For more information on the Lost Words project, see https:// www.thelostwords.org/lostwordsbook/.

32 Robert Macfarlane and Jackie Morris, *Spell Songs* (n.p.: Folk by the Oak, 2019).

33 Watson, *Back to Nature*, 68.

34   Knott, *Imagining the Forest*, 90.
35   Mary Annaïse Heglar, "We Can't Tackle Climate Change without You," *Wired*, April 1, 2020, https://www.wired.com/story/what-you-can-do-solve-climate-change/.

Acknowledgments

1   Macfarlane, *Underland*, 92.

Suggested Resources

ere are a few books and other resources that have been espe-cially helpful to me. This list is not meant to be comprehen-sive, as the number of available resources is already huge and constantly growing. Obviously, I do not personally endorse every idea or action represented in the resources below. The list is meant to be an informative beginning that inspires further exploration.

For a more up-to-date and expanded list, including a list of Michigan-specific resources, please visit my website at debrarienstra.com.

Where to Start

Kimmerer, Robin Wall. *Braiding Sweetgrass: Indigenous Wisdom, Scientific Knowledge, and the Teachings of Plants*. Minneapolis, MN: Milkweed Editions, 2013.

This work features literary essays on the themes of reciprocity and gratitude, blending Indigenous and scientific wisdom. A best seller for good reason.

McKibben, Bill. *Eaarth: Making a Life on a Tough New Planet*. New York: St. Martin's Griffin, 2011.

Although this book is over ten years old, it still serves as a bracing and compre-hensive introduction to the climate crisis.

Moore, Kathleen Dean. *Great Tide Rising: Towards Clarity and Moral Courage in a Time of Planetary Change*. Berkeley, CA: Counterpoint, 2016.

This book makes a persuasive case for the moral imperative to act in response to the climate crisis. Moore's beautiful nature writing is a bonus.

New York Times. "A Crash Course on Climate Change." April 2020. https://www .nytimes.com/interactive/2020/04/19/climate/climate-crash-course-1.html.

The *New York Times* does excellent reporting on climate change. Their handy crash course website is organized and accessible, providing recent statistics and informa-tion and answering common questions.

Project Drawdown, https://drawdown.org.

Project Drawdown is an international collaborative focused on solutions to the climate crisis. This group researches what each solution will cost and what it will save. It is a great site to explore when you wonder how the transition can possibly happen.

Robinson, Mary, Maeve Higgins, and Thimali Kodikara. *Mothers of Invention*. Podcast. https://www.mothersofinvention.online.

Hosted by Mary Robinson, Maeve Higgins, and Thimali Kodikara, each episode features remarkable women doing inspiring and practical work in addressing the climate crisis.

Climate Facts and News

A weekly newsletter from the *New Yorker*
https://www.newyorker.com/newsletter/the-climate-crisis

Climate Change 2021: The Physical Science Basis, IPCC, 2021
https://www.ipcc.ch/report/ar6/wg1/

Climate Forward: the *New York Times'* weekly newsletter
https://www.nytimes.com/newsletters/climate-change

Fourth National Climate Assessment, US Global Change Research Program, 2018
https://nca2018.globalchange.gov

"Global Weirding with Katharine Hayhoe": YouTube channel
https://www.youtube.com/channel/UCi6RkdaEqgRVKi3AzidF4ow

National Oceanic and Atmospheric Administration Climate Dashboard
https://www.climate.gov

Project Drawdown
https://drawdown.org

Special Report: Global Warming of 1.5 °C, IPCC, 2018
https://www.ipcc.ch/sr15/

Yale Program on Climate Change Communication
https://climatecommunication.yale.edu

Theology, Philosophy, Journalism

Bahnson, Fred. *Soil and Sacrament: A Spiritual Memoir of Food and Faith*. New York: Simon & Schuster, 2013.

Bauckham, Richard. *Living with Other Creatures: Green Exegesis and Theology*. Waco, TX: Baylor University Press, 2011.

Berry, Thomas. *The Great Work: Our Way into the Future.* New York: Bell Tower, 1999.

Boss, Gayle. *All Creation Waits: The Advent Mystery of New Beginnings.* Brewster, MA: Paraclete, 2016.

———. *Wild Hope: Stories for Lent from the Vanishing.* Brewster, MA: Paraclete, 2020.

Bouma-Prediger, Steven. *For the Beauty of the Earth: A Christian Vision for Creation Care.* Grand Rapids, MI: Baker Academic, 2010.

Francis (pope). *Laudato si': On Care for Our Common Home.* Vatican Publishing House, May 24, 2015. http://www.vatican.va/content/francesco/en/encyclicals/documents/papa-francesco_20150524_enciclica-laudato-si.html.

Jennings, Willie James. *The Christian Imagination: Theology and the Origins of Race.* New Haven, CT: Yale University Press, 2010.

Johnson, Ayana Elizabeth, and Katharine K. Wilkinson, eds. *All We Can Save: Truth, Courage, and Solutions for the Climate Crisis.* New York: Penguin Random House, 2020.

Kolbert, Elizabeth. *The Sixth Extinction: An Unnatural History.* New York: Picador, 2015.

McKibben, Bill. *Eaarth: Making a Life on a Tough New Planet.* New York: Times Books, 2010.

Moore, Kathleen Dean. *Great Tide Rising: Towards Clarity and Moral Courage in a Time of Planetary Change.* Berkeley, CA: Counterpoint, 2016.

Moore, Kathleen Dean, and Michael P. Nelson, eds. *Moral Ground: Ethical Action for a Planet in Peril.* San Antonio, TX: Trinity University Press, 2011.

Myers, Ched, ed. *Watershed Discipleship: Reinhabiting Bioregional Faith and Practice.* Eugene, OR: Cascade Books, 2016.

Santmire, H. Paul. *The Travail of Nature: The Ambiguous Ecological Promise of Christian Theology.* Minneapolis, MN: Fortress, 1985.

Warners, David Paul, and Matthew Kuperus Heun, eds. *Beyond Stewardship: New Approaches to Creation Care.* Grand Rapids, MI: Calvin, 2019.

Woodley, Randy. *Shalom and the Community of Creation: An Indigenous Vision.* Grand Rapids, MI: Eerdmans, 2012.

Yale Forum on Religion and Ecology (a hub for educational resources, news, events, and inspiration for people of faith concerned about the climate crisis), https://fore.yale.edu.

Literature

Accounting for all the marvelous fiction, poetry, and nonfiction connected to the climate crisis would require far more space than I can give here. Below are just a few recent favorites.

Kimmerer, Robin Wall. *Braiding Sweetgrass: Indigenous Wisdom, Scientific Knowledge, and the Teachings of Plants*. Minneapolis, MN: Milkweed Editions, 2013.

Macfarlane, Robert. *Underland: A Deep Time Journey*. New York: W. W. Norton, 2019.

Macfarlane, Robert, and Jackie Morris. *The Lost Spells*. New York: Penguin, 2020.

———. *The Lost Words: A Spell Book*. New York: Penguin, 2017.

———. *Spell Songs*. N.p.: Folk by the Oak, 2019 (includes audio CD).

Oliver, Mary. *Why I Wake Early: New Poems*. Boston: Beacon Press, 2004.

Orion magazine, https://orionmagazine.org.

Powers, Richard. *The Overstory*. New York: Norton, 2018.

Robinson, Kim Stanley. *The Ministry for the Future*. New York: Orbit, 2020.

For a book list compiled by the *New York Times*, see "The Year You Finally Read about Climate Change," April 19, 2020, https://www.nytimes.com/interactive/2020/climate/climate-change-books.html.

Activism and Legislation

Some organizations below are faith based and some are not. These are larger national and international organizations. I recommend connecting with local groups in one's own city, region, denomination, or interest area as well as with local chapters of national groups.

Climate Justice Alliance

Creation Justice Ministries

Evangelical Environmental Network / Young Evangelicals for Climate Action

Extinction Rebellion

GreenFaith

Interfaith Power and Light

Sunrise Movement

350.org

Films and Videos

Casciato, Tom, Martha Jeffries, Drew Magratten, Ivy Meeropol, Jon Meyersohn, Jonathan Schienberg, Sydney Trattner, and David Gelber, dirs. *Years of Living Dangerously*. Showtime, 2014–2016.

Ehrlich, Pippa, and James Reed, dirs. *My Octopus Teacher*. Netflix, 2020.

Page, Elliot, and Ian Daniel, dirs. *There's Something in the Water*. 2 Weeks Notice, 2019.

Schlosberg, Deia, dir. *The Story of Plastic*. Pale Blue Dot Media, 2020.

Stevens, Fisher, dir. *Before the Flood*. National Geographic, 2016.

Tickell, Joshua, and Rebecca Harrell Tickell, dirs. *Kiss the Ground*. Benenson Productions, 2020.

Podcasts

A Matter of Degrees, https://www.degreespod.com

Mothers of Invention, https://www.mothersofinvention.online

No Place like Home, https://www.noplacelikehomepodcast.com

Refugia Podcast, https://debrarienstra.com/refugia-podcast/

Warm Regards, https://warmregardspodcast.com

Apps

Cornell Lab of Ornithology, *Merlin*, bird identification app, https://merlin.allaboutbirds.org

Glority Global Group, *Picture This*, plant identification app, https://www.picturethisai.com